King Ralph

King Ralph

The Political Life and Success of
Ralph Klein

Don Martin

KEY PORTER BOOKS

National Library of Canada Cataloguing in Publication Data

Martin, Don, 1956-

   King Ralph : the political life and success of Ralph Klein / Don Martin.

Includes index.

ISBN 1-55263-469-8

   1. Klein, Ralph, 1942–. 2. Prime ministers—Alberta—Biography. 3. Alberta—Politics and government—1971–. I. Title.

FC3675.1.K54M37 2002   971.23'03'092   C2002-903552-X

F1078.25.K57M37 2002

The publisher gratefully acknowledges the support of the Canada Council for the Arts and the Ontario Arts Council for its publishing program.

We acknowledge the financial support of the Government of Canada through the Book Publishing Industry Development Program (BPIDP) for our publishing activities.

Key Porter Books Limited
70 The Esplanade
Toronto, Ontario
Canada M5E 1R2

www.keyporter.com

Text design: Peter Maher
Electronic formatting: Jean Lightfoot Peters

Printed and bound in Canada

02 03 04 05 06 07 6 5 4 3 2 1

For my father,

H. GEORGE MARTIN

1921–2002

Contents

Preface

This is not an authorized, sanitized, official biography of Ralph Klein. But it must be clearly understood that a writer cannot complete a book about Klein without, at the very least, Ralph Klein's tacit co-operation. Several have made admirable attempts without his blessing in the past, but Alberta's political realm is just too tight, the premier's circle of insiders too loyal, and his family and friends too private for any writer to crawl inside the subject's skin without having Klein's consent to unfetter their contributions. My calls to any of his closest friends or advisors for an interview were routinely delayed, anywhere from an hour to a day, until the Kleins could first be contacted for permission to speak with me.

I knew this would happen. I had briefly tackled this project in the late 1990s and a thick impenetrable cone of silence had descended from above. Whenever I approached any of the key people involved in the Klein story, I was immediately brushed off because they had received word this was not an approved project. Sorry, they'd say, no interview. Even a background chat was out of the question. An intrepid journalist might have persisted, but it had all the makings of a thick head banging against a brick wall, so I opted to save myself the migraine and wait it out.

On the evening of October 15, 2000, the twentieth anniversary of

Klein's first election victory, I was invited to attend a party at the Palliser Hotel of perhaps two dozen people who were involved in Ralph Klein's first mayoralty campaign. I felt very out of place, having been the most skeptical journalist on the city hall beat when the rival television reporter started his longshot bid for office. In any event, just as the Kleins were exchanging looks that suggested the slightly tipsy premier was primed enough to leave the party, something possessed me to take a different tact and I asked Colleen Klein about co-operating with the project of writing this book. She looked at me with those dark probing eyes that make you feel as if your soul is under an X-ray beam. "You could make a lot of money on this book," she said. I delivered the facts of life in publishing, that a first-time author writing a premier's biography was definitely not a get-rich-quick proposition. Fine, she said, in that case, the Kleins would co-operate if I donated half the after-tax profits, less expenses, to a charity of mutual agreement. They would have no control over content, I warned, no subject would be off-limits, and there would be no advance reading of the manuscript. Deal, she said, and then left to deliver word of her decision to Ralph Klein and long-time aide Rod Love, neither of whom appeared enthralled by the news.

In the year that followed, both Kleins co-operated with extensive interviews. They clearly didn't like talking about some subjects, but they didn't throw up roadblocks either. They lived up to their end of the bargain. I'll live up to mine. So about a third of the author's share of this book purchase will find its way to a charity. (Sorry, though, no tax receipt to book buyers.)

But back to Rod Love: For the better part of fifteen years, he amassed what he called The Book File. During Klein's mayoralty, when Love was his executive assistant, the file spilled out across his office floor in accordion boxes and ended up cluttering his garage with stacks of cardboard boxes. And it kept growing as Klein and Love moved to provincial politics. The file wasn't a complete paper trail through Klein's terms as mayor, environment minister and premier, but there was enough offbeat, confidential material to provide valuable insight into the unorthodox thinking and ideological flexibility of Love's only boss. To Love, who granted me lengthy interviews and unlimited access to files I would've killed for during my stint as city hall columnist in the late 1980s, my thanks.

All material in this project is derived from those files, interviews, personal recollection and clippings from the Calgary *Herald*, the Edmonton *Journal* and *Alberta Report* magazine. The Frank Dabbs biography *Klein: A Maverick Life* and Mark Lisac's *The Klein Revolution* were useful for filling in gaps from early in his reporting career and during his term as environment minister when I was off the Klein beat. The Calgary *Herald*, my employer of twenty-four years, assisted with generous access to its news and photo archives. Particular thanks are owed to editor Peter Menzies and deputy editor Gerry Nott for giving me the time and encouragement to profile this provincial icon. My gratitude to Peter Atwood of Key Porter Books for taking my disjointed initial effort and providing the constructive criticism it needed to dovetail into a better book.

Like any writer struggling to deliver a manuscript while holding down a full-time job, my family suffered the most. My long-suffering wife Annette provided fresh eyes for the final draft to keep it from being infected with what Klein would call Dome disease, the insider syndrome that afflicts writers too-long exposed to the Alberta Legislature beat. My three wonderful daughters, Erin, Katrina and Andrea, never complained through the many nights and weekends when their father was disconnected from family obligations, rummaging through Alberta memories and clipping files.

I am also indebted to Klein's communications co-ordinator Marisa Etmanski, who provided access to the vast collection of hard-to-find clippings in the premier's office. Kevin Bosch, the Alberta Liberal party researcher who doggedly pursued Klein through his Multi-Corp nightmare, assisted by dredging his party archives for new material. Thanks to the International Hotel's Sammy Wong for providing a place in Calgary where the premier could be interviewed free of non-stop interruptions. And to the rest of the Klein inner circle, who cooperated but refused to be publicly acknowledged, many thanks and worry not: Your secrets are safe with me.

—Don Martin

One

Night of a Thousand Beers

MARTINI'S BAR AND GRILL SITS under a green awning in an unpretentious retail strip on the northwest boundary of the grounds surrounding Alberta's legislature. It is Ralph Klein's idea of the perfect pub, with a working class atmosphere and plenty of cigarette smoke that spreads its blue haze over the few tables set aside in the obligatory non-smoking section. Beer label signs serve as the dominant art form on its pale green walls. The chairs are solid wood, but some armrests have been worn down to the rough by thousands of glass-tipping elbows. Happy hour languishes for six hours starting at 1:00 p.m. on weekdays, offering cheap draft and daily drink specials to a clientele of government workers waiting out the rush hour. Video lottery terminals, a heinous distraction in most Alberta bars, are not welcome here. If you feel compelled to engage in some activity beyond drinking, there's always the scratched-up pool table sandwiched in front of the bar near the washrooms. Food is available from the adjoining grill, but you'll have to ask for a menu and there's always the nagging sense it's an inconvenience for the servers when there's serious drinking to be done. Patrons are invited to scoop wicker baskets full of popcorn from the self-serve popper. It's smart business. The popcorn is extra salty, the better to create a thirst.

If the right bartender sees a regular straggling up 109th Street after a hard day of capital punishment, she'll have his favorite brand of beer, ice cold with condensation pooling on the coaster, waiting at his regular table. A tab will be automatically opened with his name on the top. It takes only a few visits for a new politician or reassigned journalist to become a Cheers-like regular here—a place where everybody knows your name.

Martini's is a patch of neutral ground between Alberta MLAs of all parties and the reporters who cover them. While inside the premises, it is considered poor form for politicians to berate journalists for negative coverage, and conversations between scribe and source are deemed off-the-record unless otherwise stipulated. You come to drink, to schmooze, to observe—and to learn. It is the Edmonton counterpart to Ralph Klein's beloved St. Louis Hotel in Calgary. In that basement tavern, the former reporter for CFCN Television devoted long liquid hours priming his city hall sources with enough lubrication to spill their secrets. He didn't patronize the Looey very often as Calgary mayor from 1980 to 1989, preferring to let the stories of his legendary drinking bouts ferment into tavern mythology on their own.

In 1989, as a rookie minister in Premier Don Getty's cabinet, Klein was a lonely guy in a capital city where he was merely a former mayor of Edmonton's bitter civic rival. He was tormented almost daily with deep regret at having accepted the offer to run for a Conservative dynasty approaching its twentieth year in power. He held the junior environment portfolio in a government Edmontonians were turning against with such vengeance that they had denied Getty his re-election in a supposedly safe seat in 1989. This forced a snap by-election in the rock-solid Tory rural district of Stettler, an hour's drive southeast of Edmonton.

Klein recalls being cussed at, yelled at and spat upon during his first campaign in Edmonton, a very difficult adjustment for the former mayor so adored in his hometown that he had landed ninety per cent of the popular vote in his final mayoralty victory. As environment minister, Klein preferred being anywhere other than the capital and ordered his staff to find places to visit outside the city on almost any pretext. When duty compelled him to stay in the modest apartment he shared with his executive assistant Rod Love, however, Klein would divide his drinking time between two local bars—Bud's and Martini's. His companion of choice was usually Vermilion MLA Stephen West, a hawkish right-winger who would later become a key player in Klein's privatization agenda.

West was an unholy terror in the late 1980s. Regulars recall how he'd throw a drink in someone's face on the flimsiest of pretexts. It could be their clothes, their long hair or just a look he didn't like. As a veterinarian, he was legally allowed to carry a gun in his car in the event he stumbled across a wounded animal in need of a mercy killing. In at least one instance, with last call approaching, West threatened to fetch the rifle and use it on the hapless victim of his rage. He took a public vow of temperance in 1991 after being appointed solicitor general, a sensitive job incompatible with his rowdy after-hours conduct, but he would often joke he'd start drinking again if Klein needed a noisy public diversion from contentious policy issues. By contrast, regulars of the day recall Klein quietly observing his pal's antics with a bemused smile on his face. He was, they say, a happy drunk who wouldn't harm a fly, but could sure pound back the booze.

Ralph Klein stopped patronizing Martini's after he became premier. He didn't want a boozer image to interfere with the difficult task ahead. Besides, too often journalists were there to monitor the number of rum and Diet Cokes entering his bloodstream, and they'd wink knowingly the next morning when the premier's schedule was thrown into disarray by a sudden bout of the "flu." So Klein opted for more discreet hospitality alternatives with small groups of friends or colleagues in private rooms, far from the media's prying eyes.

But in the late spring of 1994, Ralph Klein's government was in the mood for one hell of a party, and he didn't much care how many eyes were watching. In the old days, government leaders would motivate a summer adjournment by throwing open the legislature windows to let the wind carry in the musty smell of surrounding fields being tilled for planting. No one needed a whiff of spring to induce the recess this year. This sitting would go down as the most gruelling in the province's history.

The 1994 sitting of the legislature was, in essence, the entire Klein revolution condensed into four hectic months. Three-year targets for cutting spending by twenty per cent were rolled out as the blueprint for a balanced budget in four years. Education taxes were seized from local school boards for redistribution by the province to smaller districts that had no corporate tax base. At the same time, more than 140 school boards, some with no schools to govern, only students bussed elsewhere outside the district, were amalgamated into sixty larger districts. Some two hundred hospital boards were replaced by seventeen regional health authorities for more effective administration. Seniors benefits were cut or put to a means test. Kindergarten was deemed to be extraneous learning and its government funding was cut in half. The privatization of government services steamrolled on. Liquor retailing and automotive registries were turned over to entrepreneurs amid rumbles that prisons would be put out for private tender next.

All told, the legislature had endured twenty-one thousand minutes of debate when House Leader Stockwell Day decided there was the risk of an uprising from within his own bone-weary ranks and opted to recess the session until fall. At 4:15 p.m. on June 1, 1994, the lieutenant governor gave royal assent to a handful of bills and Day pulled the plug. Journalists lining the press gallery above dumped boxes of Hansards and press releases onto the fleeing politicians below. With a final Conservative caucus meeting scheduled for the next morning, few MLAs would be flying out to their constituencies. And when Alberta MLAs were stranded in Edmonton and in the mood to celebrate, Martini's was their destination of choice. A thirsty invasion headed for the green awning. The Night of a Thousand Beers was set to begin.

After a few hours all the seats were occupied by media, MLAs and legislature staff. By the time Ralph Klein arrived after a dinner engagement, he was the most sober person in the place. He took a seat in a booth to watch, with unfettered amazement, the antics of those with a five-hour head start. A right-wing Edmonton columnist was necking with a drunk Liberal researcher in one corner. An attractive female Tory MLA was cuddling on a reporter's lap in another. Klein shook his head as *Edmonton Journal* reporter Joan Crockatt and I regaled him with the story of a fight a few hours earlier between bitter Tory backbencher Jon Havelock and Klein's chief of staff, Rod Love. The pair had exchanged punches and thrown a glass at the wall, leaving shards of beer bottle surrounding the popcorn popper. "This could be a night to remember," Klein mused as he ordered a catch-up cocktail.

The speed of consumption actually picked up as the night wore on. Klein's Tories were ecstatic. They were celebrating their first year in office as a party of renegade revolutionaries, and they were more convinced than ever that they sat on the side of the angels, a sentiment backed by the Conservatives' surging popularity in the polls. The prospect of a summer-long breather from implementing cuts and arguing on committees was an intoxicating tonic. When the bartender announced last call at 2:00 a.m. and urged patrons to clear their hefty tabs, a groan went up among the troops, many contemplating the coming pain of their morning-after caucus meeting.

Klein and his security guard, Lloyd McDonald, had moved to a bar stool to join *Edmonton Journal* reporter Ashley Geddes and me. He gently complained we'd been too hard on his deficit elimination plans. Still, he mused, it was too bad the night was over. He'd had a lot of fun. I lamented Alberta's archaic drinking laws and the early last call, reminding Klein that bar hours were extended until 4:00 a.m. when he presided over Calgary during the 1988 Winter Olympics. It had worked so well then, why not now? Geddes pressed the point, noting that the power to set the drinking hours rested with Klein's own solicitor general, the once notorious Steve West. With West in a sober slumber, Geddes noted gleefully, didn't that make Klein the acting solicitor general?

It was neither cowboy politics nor an arrogant abuse of power that made him do it. Klein is aware of his enormous influence, but he uses it sparingly, with great reluctance and only under extreme provocation. No doubt it was the many drinks, mixed with a flashback to boyhood mischievousness, that made the premier reach for a napkin, scrawl down a few words and hand it to Rose, the bartender on duty. "I hereby author-ize Martini's to remain open until 5 a.m." it read. "Signed, Ralph Klein, premier." It was as good as gold for Rose. She smiled, tucked the napkin under the bar just in case the liquor board inspectors came calling, dropped the blinds and declared the premises a private party until dawn. This was met with cheers from Tories and Liberals alike.

If Ralph Klein stretched, his hair would brush the five-foot-eight-inch mark on a tape measure. His love of rich, exotic food, corn dogs and his former passion for red wine have, at times, ballooned his weight to well above 220 pounds. Since he became premier, he reserves, nay *demands*, a ninety-minute break in his schedule for a daily run on the legislature treadmill, and his weight now hovers around 190. He's surprisingly fit, but doesn't show it; his genes have cursed him with a fat-magnet around his midriff and a dangling pair of chins that friends say have been hanging around since the 1960s, when they howled at the sight of young Ralph wearing a chin vibrating device in a local gym. He only wears a medium shirt size, but in gratitude for his many fundraising activities, he is con-stantly given large and extra-large golf attire, unintended insults immediately tossed off to burly staff or his security guards.

One pupil of his grey-green eyes is, almost imperceptibly, smaller than the other, the result of a collision between his cornea and a squash ball dur-ing a game with his son, Brad. Despite this, his eyes are the clearest reflection of his emotional state. When he's bored, they glaze over, shift-ing lethargically in their sockets and disappearing behind long, weary blinks. When he's interested in the topic of conversation, they fire up, zeroing in on the listener or speaker with an almost unnerving, luminous intensity. When he's angry, they open wide as he lowers his head into a glare of furious indignation, his displeasure emphasized by the tomahawk chop of his index finger, stabbing the air at the object of his fury. When he's drunk, those expressive eyes are, or at least were, prone to an abrupt flow of shameless tears.

Klein's dark brown hair turned grey in tandem with the budget cuts of the mid-nineties, but the grey hair is only thinning slightly at the crown and he'll let it grow over his collar periodically. His nose is the most prominent feature of his face, spliced straight off his father Phil's proboscial genealogy. With slightly oversized ears to match, it's a face cartoonists adore.

He wears little jewelry—just a watch and one ring, a giant gold square with diamonds embedded in it. It was given to Klein during his reporting days by the grateful subject of one of his stories, a clerk at the Calgary Housing Authority who was convicted of defrauding the agency of five thousand dollars. Sentenced to one year in jail, she reported to the authorities to begin her sentence, but no record of her conviction could be found. She was sent home, but kept showing up, suitcase in hand, trying to begin her sentence. It was the sort of human interest story Klein relished, and he gleefully chronicled her experience until the documentation showed up several months later and she was placed in custody. When she was freed after four months, the grateful woman had a family brooch reconfigured into a diamond ring and gave it to Klein. "The ring is a reminder of what the justice system can do to a person," Klein once said, twirling it with his other hand. When it was stolen from a gymnasium locker in 1996, he turned to the media, appealing for help and offering a reward to get it back, citing its extreme sentimental value. In a country where millions of heirlooms disappear into the hands of heartless thieves, Klein had the luck to fall victim to the one with a conscience—or at very least an opportunistic parent. It was returned and the juvenile delinquent's mother claimed the reward.

Klein is not a flashy dresser; the most expensive suit he owns is still the one he bought on Canadian Airlines' tab on his third day in Tokyo in 1996 after his luggage went astray. He didn't intend to exploit the largesse of the airline, lest it be perceived as a conflict of interest for the premier who had loaned the ailing operation fifty million dollars during its 1993 cash crunch. With a formal meeting only hours away and the suitcase given up for lost, however, something other than a rank sweatshirt and casual slacks to wear was urgently needed. With no time for alterations, it had to come straight off the rack, and the only suit that would fit a body that, while of average height in that country, wasn't quite of everyday Japanese girth, was a spiffy, top-of-the-line, blue Armani knockoff that he wears to this day. When he gave up his $5,000 per year clothing allowance, which came with the premier's job in 1993, to lead the cost-cutting trend by example, his tastes shifted back to his old standards. His last suit came from Tip Top Tailors.

As Calgary's mayor from 1980 until 1989, Ralph Klein was labeled by detractors as "His Warship," a slap to his bulging girth, or "Hizzoner," pronounced with a slur, a derisory reference to his hard-drinking reputation. When he became Alberta's premier on December 5, 1992, a more respectful handle arose: Elvis. The King.

Among his staff in the 1990s, the moniker is used with a color code. A blue Elvis is a grumpy Ralph, miffed at his overloaded schedule, or staring balefully at a pile of mundane paperwork on a perfect summer day when the golf course beckons. When a black Elvis arrives for work, it is a premier whose night-before antics have put him in such a stormy, sleep-deprived state that sensitive meetings must be rebooked, media scrums cancelled and his schedule cleared to ensure that Elvis will have left the building early.

Most of the time, though, Klein is just content to follow the orders of his appointment assistants—assistants who are so swamped by meeting requests that they're nicknamed Dr. No for their standard response to the many groups seeking the premier's time. There is a reason for the high demand for his time, and it goes far beyond the business of merely bending a powerful ear. Curiosity motivates many requests from visiting politicians, dignitaries and businessmen. They know it doesn't add up: a high school dropout with a couch potato physique and a legendary liver-bruising thirst (which didn't take a sobering turn until late 2001) could not possibly have triumphed in two political realms (municipal and provincial) in difficult economic times, winning three elections at each level by ever-increasing margins and still remain an ordinary guy in attitude, outlook and image. They know it can't be done. If Ralph Klein is real, they want to see it for themselves.

The first time I met Ralph Klein was under circumstances that hardly suggested he would one day be worthy of a biography. After sleeping off a bender in the Calgary detention centre in 1978, he was released into the hands of a city alderman who had brought me along for moral support. When Klein emerged from the cell, his eyes were the colour of sugar beets, his breath would have turned a locomotive in its tracks and his mood was dark and ominous.

As a journalist, Klein was my most unorthodox competitor. When he became a mayoralty candidate a year after we met, I wrote him off as a longshot. When he became mayor, I suspected he'd be a one-term wonder. After that, I stopped underestimating him. Whatever the reason, whatever the explanation, whatever the attraction, Alberta voters have embraced Klein in whatever he's done. When circumstances far beyond Alberta give the economy a boost, they credit Klein for the improvement. When it falters, they blame factors far away for the downturn. When he does things right, they sing his praises. When he makes mistakes, they forgive him. When he says he drinks to excess, but vows to stop, they applaud him louder than ever. The more they know him warts and all, the more they vote for him in numbers that astonish the world.

Even Juan Antonio Samaranch, a Francisco Franco fascist and former International Olympic Committee president, was fascinated by Klein's never-faltering popularity. At a private meeting to discuss last-minute hiccups in the 1988 Winter Games planning, somebody wondered what a Calgary mayor was doing at the lofty IOC executive table. Samaranch turned to his friend, the politician he'd entrusted to sell the games to Calgarians. "Tell my staff," he said to Klein, "how many votes you got in 1980." To which a blushing Klein replied, "Forty-eight per cent."

"Tell my staff how much of the vote you got in 1983," Samaranch continued.

"Eighty-eight per cent," Klein told him.

"In 1986?" he persisted.

"Ninety-three per cent," Klein answered.

"See," whooped Samaranch, "not even in Russia do they get such numbers!"

The Spanish aristocrat would have been even more impressed by Klein's numbers at the provincial level six years later, when his mayoralty track record was duplicated in a fashion that makes capturing lightning in a bottle seem infinitely easier. An administration hovering near death, with a twenty per cent public approval rating in the waning months of Don Getty's reign, reversed its romp toward oblivion under Klein's leadership to win fifty-one of the eighty-three legislature seats in 1993 and sixty-three seats in 1997 before his greatest triumph in 2001 with seventy-four seats. The rival Liberal and New Democratic parties were left squabbling for attention as a single-digit opposition. Klein was in control of every seat outside of Edmonton except one, that being the Lethbridge fiefdom held by future Liberal leader Ken Nicol.

Alberta's a difficult province to govern with its gaping voids between the hard-right rural sentiment and moderate urban constituency. Surviving and thriving there has earned Klein respect across Canada. He governs as a fiscal conservative with social liberal sympathies. His approval ratings routinely soar above seventy per cent and have never, as of this writing, dipped below fifty per cent. It's a popularity that crosses all lines—rural, urban, young, old, rich, poor. He is without a mentor, without a mould, without precedent in Canadian politics.

With the sky lightening to the east, enough was finally enough at Martini's Bar and Grill. The Night of a Thousand Beers was rapidly losing its hyperbole. As a few dozen survivors headed for the door, muttering about their morning meetings, I reached behind the bar to retrieve the order-in-council napkin, which had priceless souvenir written all over it. A giant fist closed over my hand. "Nice try," smirked McDonald, the security guard. "I'll take that."

A handful of us hopped into the premier's car for a ride to a nearby all-night restaurant where Szechwan cuisine was offered with the traditional nightcap—whisky served in Chinese teapots. When the sun came up, we finally headed home, most of us trying to decide whether to bother going to bed or just go straight to work. Later that morning, indoor sunglasses were the fashion accessory of the day on ministers and media alike. Over at Klein's office, staff were in crisis mode, revamping his schedule. Somehow the premier had come down with the flu overnight.

Two

In the Beginning

FIFTY-SIX YEARS AFTER Ralph Philip Klein was carried out of the maternity wing of the Calgary General Hospital wrapped in his mother's arms, his Conservative government ordered 1,733 kilograms of dynamite strapped to the building's 100-year-old innards and blew it to kingdom come as a cost-saving measure. The twenty-second implosion was triggered by 5,908 blasting caps at 9:03 a.m. on a sunny October 4 in 1998, before ten thousand morbidly fascinated Calgarians. It created a pale brown cloud of dust and debris so huge that environmental monitoring equipment could not accurately track it as light winds carried the plume eastward over the city.

The Calgary General baby who had grown up to become premier caught the replay on television that evening. He didn't enjoy it a bit. It wasn't sentimentality tugging at his heartstrings. He instinctively knew the spectacular detonation, which had turned the city's only downtown hospital into rubble, was an indelible image that would haunt his plans to tear down and rebuild health care in revolutionary style. He was absolutely right.

But we're getting ahead of ourselves. It was Ralph Klein's grandfather, Andrew, who brought the Klein name to Alberta in 1907. He was a short, thin man, only five-foot-six, with a chronic cough. A self-taught chef, he had fled his German homeland rather than endure compulsory military service. He then lived in France, Switzerland and Austria, mastering four languages, before landing a job at a London hotel. Working alongside him was a teenage brunette named Kate Drury. Chemistry developed in the short-order kitchen and the pair soon talked of a long-term future together in marriage.

But Andrew Klein was not the sort to be a chef for his whole life. He had a powerful travel bug and America seemed just the ticket to satisfy his wanderlust. In 1906, he kissed Kate goodbye and boarded a steamer bound for the Ellis Island docks under the outstretched arm of a twenty-year-old Statue of Liberty. He liked New York, but his congested lungs couldn't cope with the pollution of America's budding metropolis. Word eventually rippled through the immigrant communities about a remote corner of the Canadian prairie where land was being given away free to new arrivals, courtesy of Prime Minister Wilfrid Laurier. It was only two years old, but the province of Alberta, and a tiny speck on the home-steading map called Rocky Mountain House, caught Andrew Klein's eye. Joining an immigration rush of Europeans, Russians, Scandinavians and Americans that would more than double the young province's population to 375,000 in less than five years, Klein boarded a west-bound train for Calgary and made it as far north as Red Deer before the tracks stopped and the vast grasslands began.

He invested a hefty slice of his savings in a pair of oxen, christened them Joe and Gus for conversation purposes, and aimed the wagon at the mountain peaks on the western horizon where his promised land lay. The lousiest winter in Prairie history was just thawing as he arrived. They called it the Winter of Blue Snow. In mid-October, 1906, blizzard after blizzard had raked across the cow pastures around Red Deer, gradually sweeping thousands of emaciated cattle carcasses into the coulees where they lay buried until the snow melted in May, just when Klein was riding by, wondering what on earth he'd got himself into. It took him a week to cover the hundred roadless miles to Rocky Mountain House, a small set-tlement that had served as a Hudson's Bay Company trading outpost until it was abandoned in 1875. The local coal industry was experiencing difficult times. Disgruntled workers, fed up with the killer conditions in the cold, dark shafts, were joining the United Mine Workers of America and had shut down the industry with a short, violent strike.

However, neither lousy weather nor uncertain economic times deterred Andrew Klein from his Alberta adventure. He staked his claim, fired off a telegram to London inviting his future bride to join him on the frontier and set to work building her the log cabin where she would spend the rest of her life. A few months later, Kate, a Londoner who had never set foot beyond southern England, stepped off a train in Calgary, a cow-town proudly heralding the arrival of its first two buses that very month. She rushed directly to a local church and bravely vowed, for better or worse, to be Andrew's wife in this strange, new, wild world. The next day, they struck out on horseback for their new homestead.

Clearing land in the heavily wooded region tickled the entrepreneur-ial instincts of Andrew Klein, and it was not very long before the thirty-three-year-old decided it was time to cook up another career. He invested what remained of his savings in a saw wheel to start what, in those days, passed for a sawmill. A lumber shortage was created when the entire 1906 winter cut was lost. A massive flood on the North Saskatchewan River propelled the logs over the Edmonton booms, sending them all the way to Battleford, Saskatchewan. Demand from settlers was high and Klein's enterprise grew quickly. One of his bigger clients was CN Rail, who contracted him to supply material for several dramatic wooden tres-tle bridges between Rocky Mountain House and the coal mines of Nordegg, eighty kilometres to the west, on the eastern slopes of the Rockies. Nine decades later, historians tried to prevent the giant struc-tures on the long-abandoned line from being destroyed. They noted, with sad irony, that it was the government of Andrew Klein's grandson, Ralph, which set them ablaze.

With the help of midwives, Kate Klein delivered four children in their modest log house—three daughters before a son, Philip, was born in 1917. Seven years later when she died, Phil's only recollection of his mother was his father lifting him up to peer inside her coffin. He's never been able to recall the face, just the satin-lined coffin. His mother is a lost memory, but his father lived for another thirty years and never remarried. A man struggling to raise four young children was not considered a prize bridal catch.

Andrew Klein was a severe parent and deeply religious. He left his children on their own six days of the week, while he worked at keeping his business going, before resting to worship on the seventh. When discipline was required, it was delivered hard and fast with the swish of a willow stick. The children grew up with a healthy streak of independence and a healthy fear of God. Nobody was pampered but, then again, nobody went hungry.

Phil Klein was a strong boy, an important asset in the aftermath of the First World War for the only kid of German ancestry in his elementary school. Called "Klink Klein" by his classmates, and a favorite target for bullies, Phil defended himself in the traditional schoolboy fashion of the day, with his fists. "I was fighting pret' near every day for a while there," Philip recalls with a cackle. "I could whomp some pretty good-sized kids too. But I'd get a lickin' from the teacher for doing it and a lickin' from my dad when I got home."

In the fall of 1931, at age fourteen, Phil ran away. He wasn't escaping the tough life at home or daily trauma at school. It was just that the coal trains left the town every day going somewhere else and, blessed with his father's itchy feet, he wanted to see where those tracks ended. He borrowed fifty cents from one of his sisters and sneaked aboard a coal car heading east. He had no particular destination in mind. That would be decided day by day. At Red Deer, he crawled into a straw pile to sleep and discovered the two quarters had disappeared through a hole in his pants. Flat broke, he continued as far as the cattle pens of Mirror, Alberta, where he slept in the roundhouse at the end of the line.

For weeks, he drifted aimlessly, scrounging for food, until he finally landed work in a service station in the tiny town of Swalwell. Before too long, he signed on at a logging camp for the winter. The following spring, he took a farm job, harrowing fields behind a team of horses. It was brutal work, walking behind plodding horses from dawn to dusk, trying to turn dust into wheat-sustaining soil. The team hit a nasty rock one day and the horses spooked, threw their reins, and raced toward the horizon, never to return. It was an unforgivable loss for a Dust Bowl farm caught in the tightening noose of the Great Depression. The farmer fired him on the spot, ending his third career in six months. Phil Klein was fifteen years old.

After a brief respite at the family cabin, Phil and a buddy hit the rails again, this time with a more exotic destination in mind. South America, they decided, had a nice ring to it. Better weather, easier jobs, cuter girls. When the boys pulled into Regina on July 1, 1935, though, their arrival coincided with a future history lesson unfolding. Thousands of desperate men, organized by Communist sympathizers, had struck out for Ottawa. From as far west as Vancouver, they were on their way to confront the prime minister about the intolerable conditions in federal relief camps. Prime Minister R. B. Bennett had different ideas for the mass protest, and on the very afternoon the two lads jumped off the train, he ordered the RCMP to break up the "On-to-Ottawa trek" using any means at their disposal.

The confrontation in downtown Regina was violent. Police fired tear gas into an angry mob numbering in the thousands, shots were fired and a police officer was beaten to death while the horror-stricken pair of seventeen-year-olds cowered in a baseball park. "I learned very early on what tear gas was," Phil recalls. "The canisters would land and I found out if you got there in time, you could throw them back. If not, they went off in your face."

The pair fled to Winnipeg, more determined than ever to escape the northern hemisphere, but at the Ontario border police were checking every coal car and removing any drifters, including young Phil and his buddy. Their South American dream died amid a year-long series of odd jobs of the sort that keep wandering souls from starving in lousy economic times. For pocket money, Phil Klein decided to put his schoolyard skills to work and entered the boxing ring. It paid five bucks a bout. He had big, strong hands for a kid, but slow feet. After a handful of contests, he had scored no victories but had endured many a bloody-nosed battering, and quit boxing for good. "It was a little too hard on the face."

After two years on the rails, the boy who ran away from home returned to Alberta as a man and took a job helping his brother-in-law on a farm just outside Calgary. On a trip back to Rocky Mountain House one holiday weekend, he went to a local dance where a pretty teenager from Calgary caught his eye. Florence Harper was no shrinking violet. She smoked, drank, cussed and loved to dance. The pair spent their first evening together doing all four. Phil was attracted to her unique spunk, colorful tongue and no-nonsense attitude, uncommon in a teenage woman in those days. Before they parted that night, he pocketed her phone number and, after taking a job in Calgary's Dominion Bridge factory a few months later, he dialed it.

With the Second World War breaking out in Europe, Phil enlisted in the army. It was a short stint. Three days after signing up, he failed his medical exam because the army doctor claimed he had a goiter condition. For a man of Phil Klein's fine health, brute strength and proud stamina, this was an intolerable insult. He went to a Calgary clinic for a second opinion and was given a clean bill of health, which he took back to the recruiting office. The army doctor threw it in the garbage. It wasn't hard to connect the dots. "He was an old Brit who'd been our family doctor in Rocky Mountain House and knew my father had lived in Germany," Phil says. "I've no doubt he lowered the boom on me because of my German heritage."

A few months later, laborer Phil Klein and waitress Florence Harper were wed in her parents' basement, where they also made their home. As a young couple of modest means, they led a simple life in the working class community of Tuxedo Park. On weekends, they went to house parties where the host would provide a modest meal, but everyone brought their own booze. If the mood was right everyone danced to big band music. Two years into their marriage, with few signs of the trouble ahead, they decided to start a family. On November 1, 1942, a chubby bundle of baby boy arrived at the Calgary General Hospital. They named him after Florence's brother, with the newborn's father getting the middle-name honours. Their first son was Ralph Philip Klein.

The parents' relationship quickly soured, however. The free spirit of Ralph's father and the dynamic rebel that was his hard-drinking mother became a volatile mix with a child in the home. The couple began to fight in the cramped confines of her parents' basement. The couple had another child, Lynn, born in 1944, but his birth did nothing to reverse the steady deterioration of their marriage.

Ralph Klein's first memory is of retrieving his mother's cigarette butts as a six-year-old and lighting them with the furnace pilot light. When his father caught him, he was forced to smoke a cigar as punishment. He puked his guts out and smoking lost its allure—for a while.

Divorce was a rare last resort in those days, but it was an absolute certainty for Ralph's parents. Just after his sixth birthday, the couple finally split up in a loud and angry chorus of irreconcilable differences. The strain of long work hours and the challenge of raising two young boys in the small, four-room house were too much for a high-strung couple with little money. Phil stayed in a downtown Calgary bachelor pad for a year, then trekked north to work as a foreman on the crew that was building the Edmonton International Airport. For the next twenty years he'd move from job to job, from Fort McMurray to northern Quebec, building dams, roads or railways. In the last years of his marriage, Phil had taken up wrestling under the name of Killer Klein—it was easier on the face than boxing. He won a few bouts, and still goes to watch wrestling matches as often as possible. Florence stayed in Calgary after the divorce and worked as a waitress. She dated a few customers and eventually married one of them, a CN train engineer named Lorne MacBeth.

Following his parents' divorce, Ralph went to live with his grandparents, the Harpers, and stayed there for most of his early youth. His mother's new husband moved around Alberta chasing engineer jobs and his father roamed from one construction project to the next. His grandmother, Christine, had a firm but gentle hand and kept their humble house spotless, despite the unholy terrors she was charged with raising. Her husband, Hollins, was a labourer on the railway who earned pocket money selling honeycomb from beehives in the clover fields adjacent to their house. He also recycled copper and lead that his grandson and his friends would find. Klein's buddies now admit with a sly wink that most of the metal may have been "found" on local construction sites. Harper was a deeply religious member of the local United Church, and Ralph Klein remembers his grandfather as a "Mr. Magoo sort, going down the road in his little car, singing hymns and driving right through stop lights and signs."

Friends say that young Ralph seemed unfazed by the acrimony of his splintered family. His grandparents' Tuxedo Park home was on the northern edge of the city, with the open prairie under a big blue sky on his doorstep. He spent days roaming nearby Nose Hill with his friends, playing cowboys and Indians, winning marble competitions and fishing the odd sucker out of tiny, winding Nose Creek.

In daring moments, they'd bunch together tufts of grass and light small fires. One windy Sunday afternoon, after returning home from church, eight-year-old Ralph and his buddy, Ron Shaben, discovered a small cave on a nearby hillside that offered ideal shelter for lighting a fire. The two struggled to light a pile of grass amid the gusty conditions, until Klein reached into his pocket, pulled out some pieces of paper and offered them as fuel to fire up the effort. It worked well—so well that flames roared over the lip of the cave and hitched a ride on a gust of wind. They erupted into a roaring grassfire that seared the hillside black as it raced toward houses on the city's north end. Watching in horror from a safe vantage point further up on the hill, a terrified Ralph sobbed uncontrollably as fire trucks knocked down fences in hot pursuit of the blaze. He had checked his pocket and discovered that the paper he'd used was his Sunday School homework. This, he decided, was God's revenge for using a scripture lesson as fire starter.

Ralph Klein wasn't the leader of the so-called Tuxedo Park gang that formed in his neighborhood in the years leading up to his tenth birthday. There really wasn't any one leader whom his boyhood friends can recall. Judging by some of Ralph's actions, he wasn't the brightest crayon in the box, either. When one of the older boys wanted to test a new pellet gun, he drew a bullseye on a piece of cardboard and asked Ralph to hold it up for target practice. Klein complied, and held the target directly in front of his face. The first pellet passed through the cardboard and embedded itself in young Klein's mouth. He screamed for hours, they say. Another time the gang renovated an old chicken coop into a clubhouse, using wood and canvas lifted from a nearby lumber yard. They didn't hang around it much, but used the gaps beneath the floor as a hiding spot for Flat 50s (metal tins of fifty cigarettes). It burned to the ground not long after it was built, and the boys rushed to the rescue after the fire truck pulled away. To their great relief, their cigarette stash had survived.

As he grew into adolescence, Klein built strong friendships within the working class confines of Tuxedo Park, friendships that last to this day. He can recite from memory the home phone numbers of his first friends and effortlessly rhyme off their old addresses. His aunt still lives in the same house on 1st Street N.E. that she occupied as young Ralph's occasional guardian. His closest friends, the Shaben twins, the Williams brothers and Tom Minhinnet, get together every year or so to rehash old memories, or to think up some new ones.

Klein would see his father whenever his dad drifted into town during down times between construction projects, perhaps a couple of times a year. They weren't close, but enjoyed each other's company. Relations between Phil Klein and his former in-laws were far from amicable, however. His occasional between-job visits were not encouraged. Once, when Phil arrived unexpectedly to see his pre-teen son, Hollins Harper slammed the door on his former son-in-law. "They wouldn't let me see him so I got a bit obnoxious and of course, old Holly Harper, he got a bit obnoxious and I guess he took a swing at me and I kinda pushed him and he kinda went through a wall, accidentally of course," grins Phil. "They got an injunction against me to stay away from the house. That put a dent in my access to Ralph."

Ralph Klein never excelled academically. Truth be told, he never really tried at school. His marks were average to slightly below. Sports didn't interest him as much as the lure of the great outdoors. He was shorter than most kids his age and prone to baby-fat chubbiness. That combination made him a slow runner and easy prey for a school bully named Jimmy

David. He regularly endured severe beatings from the tall, burly pre-teen. Four decades later, in what must surely rank as every bully victim's ultimate fantasy, David re-entered Mayor Ralph Klein's life. A blue collar worker for the city, he had just been handed a pink slip during a round of layoffs in the mid-1980s. He fought the firing, and when officials approached the mayor to verify David's claim to having a guardian in high places, Klein asked for his name, then curled his lip into a twisted grin as he delivered sweet revenge: "Fire the prick."

For summer evening entertainment, Klein and his penniless buds would sneak into the Sunset Drive-In and hang out at the snack bar to catch the audio track, drink coffee creams and eat mustard and ketchup packets as snacks. The drive-in operator usually tolerated his unauthorized guests with a wry grin. If he was in a bad mood though, they'd have to watch from the base of the screen, where they would stare up at three-storey faces and try to imagine what was being said. For pocket money, Klein took a job at age nine in the city's west end Bowness Park selling popcorn for ten cents an hour and all the product he could eat, followed by a stint as water-boy for the Calgary Junior Broncs football team.

Later that year, Ralph was retrieved by his mother for what he describes as five depressing years away from his tight group of friends roaming the Alberta towns where his engineer stepfather could find work. He was enrolled in four schools during those five daunting years, alternating his name between Klein and MacBeth to suit the temperament of the times. It was the witch-hunting era of Joseph McCarthy and where it was risky to be saddled with the Germanic name, he went by MacBeth. The little-known fact that he was registered in some schools as Ralph MacBeth is a source of amusement to his close friends. One of the premier's least favorite politicians is former Alberta Conservative cabinet minister Nancy MacBeth, who contested Klein for the party leadership in 1992. She resurfaced in the 2001 provincial election as the Liberal party's leader, and then became the Leader of the Opposition to Klein's government.

Klein struggled academically during the difficult transitions between schools. He failed grade five, which left him the oldest in his class and further complicated the search for lasting friendships. His mother and stepfather had become heavy drinkers and MacBeth had a hair-trigger temper that did not mix well with alcohol. When drunk, he ranted and raged against his family and beat anyone he could find under almost any pretext. "He was a nice man when he was sober," Klein recalls, "but very abusive when he'd been drinking. It was not just me. He physically abused everyone—my mother, my stepbrothers and me. He left my little brother alone, though."

Ralph Klein's mother finally surrendered her oldest boy to his grandparents' care at age fourteen in 1956. His grandfather had retired from his last job, as janitor at the local flour mill, and could help care for his grandson, who had begun to show signs of having inherited the rebellious, adventuresome genes of his parents. Klein was mighty relieved to be back in his hometown neighborhood. His grandparents represented stability, order and life with his closest friends. It didn't last long. He went to live with his father in Edmonton only a year later. He tried boxing and performed badly, his father says. Klein didn't like to hurt people and just wouldn't go for the knockout. When he returned from Edmonton after eighteen months, friends recall a changed youth. He was quieter, prone to seriousness and thoroughly hooked on nicotine.

If there was a missing element in Ralph Klein's upbringing, it was politics. Family dinners did not dwell on the topic. There was no huddling around the radio to hear speeches or discussions of the day's events at city hall. The closest Klein got to dreaming about politics was lusting after the cute daughters of Mayor Don Mackay, Tuxedo Park's second most famous politician, who lived a few blocks up the street. One friend spins a tale that Klein was first inspired to seek the mayoralty after he was offered a ride in Mackay's Cadillac as a pre-teen and instantly believed the chain of office came with a lavish lifestyle. Klein calls it a pleasant fiction. He does recall, with considerable relish, how a frustrated school guidance counsellor, despairing at his lack of enthusiasm for completing homework assignments, suggested he quit school and get a job at city hall—ditch digging was his drift. Political office was beyond anyone's wildest imagination, including Ralph Klein's.

Limping out of grade ten at Crescent Heights High School with passing grades, Klein convinced an uncle to support his entry into the Royal Canadian Air Force. Just six weeks after his seventeenth birthday, the earliest age one could enlist with adult approval, his uncle Bob took a pair of shears to his nephew's head. He sculpted the required buzz cut, then drove his nephew to the recruiting office to sign on for a five-year stint. Klein shipped out for basic training at St. Jean, Quebec, and spent the next eighteen months shuttling between the bases at Borden, Aylmer and Portage-la-Prairie, serving as a safety equipment technician.

It didn't take long for the teenager to realize he'd made a terrible, terrible mistake. He was no rail-riding drifter like his dad, no free-wheeling spirit like his mom. Any enjoyment he could have derived from the discipline and orderly life in the RCAF were overwhelmed by an incapacitating attack of acute homesickness. "I became terribly depressed, to the point where I had to be hospitalized," Klein recalls. "I wanted to go back to school. I wanted to be with my friends. I had severe emotional problems. I needed to get out." He applied for an early discharge and appeared before a panel of senior officers to plead his case. It is not easy for a soldier to secure a release just a third of the way through an enlisting commitment, then or now. A convincing argument had to be made that Klein was mentally unfit to perform his military duties. The sad state of his despair was obvious; it was no act. He was given an honorable discharge and headed home to Calgary in a rusty 1957 Volkswagen Beetle with hardly a penny to his name. In the passenger seat, his first serious girlfriend, eighteen-year-old Hilda May Hepner, was along for the ride.

On his return, Klein's immediate priority was to complete high school. However, the rules of the day prevented him from simply rejoining the classroom he'd abruptly departed two years earlier. As a deemed air force veteran, he was given free tuition and sixty dollars a month for vocational training at the Calgary Business College. At the college, he was no longer the apathetic student he had been at Crescent Heights school. He excelled in subjects such as accounting and commercial law, and two years later, he graduated with honors. The school's administrators were so impressed by his performance they offered him a shot at teaching. He jumped at the chance. Events in his personal life had taken an unexpected turn that made finding a paycheque a matter of extreme urgency. In the spring of 1961, restaurant hostess Hilda Hepner told her eighteen-year-old student boyfriend he was about to become a father.

Abortion was out of the question in the early 1960s. As a result, Ralph found himself being pushed in one unexpected, unappetizing direction: the altar. "My grandparents had some pretty old-fashioned notions about what to do if you got a girl in trouble. There was a terrible stigma to having a baby out of wedlock, so at eighteen, I was married with a kid on the way." The two married on April 29, 1961, and their son Bradley, the first of two children, was born seven months later.

Klein enrolled in a "quick and dirty course" on teaching and began to lecture business fundamentals to students his own age. It was material he'd only learned a year earlier himself. He excelled at the task, and logged extra hours when struggling students requested help deciphering the fundamentals of basic business practices. A year later, he was promoted to principal, a glorified teaching job with a few management headaches thrown in. A new personality was emerging in Klein, one with deep compassion and greater self-confidence. The new job was a big boost to his self-esteem but it came with one small problem—the paycheque. It was tough to cover the costs of being a new father with a mortgage on only $230 a month.

As he scanned the career ads one day in 1963, Klein spotted a position as southern Alberta public relations director for the Canadian Red Cross. He lacked most of the job requirements, but he did possess a born-to-schmooze personality. "I didn't know what public relations was all about. I thought it was being nice to the public," Klein admits now. He polished up a resume that already looked impressive, coming from a twenty-one-year-old business college principal, and fired it off, supremely confident that the job was his. His friends expressed doubt that his resume would survive the initial cut. "You slide further on bullshit than on gravel," Klein told them. A week later, he had the job.

The hundred-dollar-a-month raise was a godsend, and Ralph Klein tackled his new career with gusto. The social aspects of the new job were particularly appealing to him. It was a tough assignment to sell story ideas on Red Cross swimming programs and blood donor clinics, but hanging out with contacts on somebody else's bar tab was Klein's idea of paradise. He quickly adapted to the culture of journalism, as it was in the early 1960s. They were a tight-knit bunch of heavy smokers and hard drinkers, who would hang around the press club and carouse with sources or rub their buddy's nose in their latest scoop. It was not investigative journalism at its finest and it didn't take Klein long to figure out the media manipulation skills he would later perfect as a politician. He learned it was possible to massage the message by cultivating personal relations with the reporters and columnists of the city. He'd stroke the egos of publishers in the oft-ignored smaller rural newspaper markets and deliver clean news copy and broadcast-ready public service messages to places looking for quick filler to stuff between the ads. Most importantly, he learned reporters were much more inclined to swallow a story idea if it came with a few beers to wash it down.

Word of his communications skills began to get around in Calgary's network of flaks and hacks; Klein was considered honest, trustworthy and imaginative. His home life, however, had started to deteriorate despite the arrival of Angela, his first daughter, in 1965. He tried a separation from Hilda and returned, split again and came back. The late-night carousing with his growing network of business and media contacts had begun to take its toll. He had become a regular in many downtown bars, and had developed a particular affinity for a seedy, east end basement tavern with twenty-five-cent draft and fried chicken and potato wedges as its culinary signature. The St. Louis Hotel tavern later became the place where Klein spent countless hours with friends, milked his contacts and partied as mayor. Klein eventually replaced chicken-and-chips as the establishment's most famous feature.

With the Red Cross office run by remote control from the Toronto headquarters, Klein eventually wearied of playing in the little leagues, and, in 1967, he jumped at a communications job with the United Way of Calgary. This was a premier position in his industry, and Klein excelled at generating interest in the charity's annual campaign. He worked the media hard. He organized high-hoopla news conferences and hosted boozy promotional events to link the reporters, but even more importantly, the editors, with the fundraising beneficiaries. He had a knack for spotting the offbeat human interest angle or quirky news value in the charities linked to the umbrella fundraising agency. He found that he was short on the writing skills he needed for press releases, radio copy and television productions, so he lobbied a *Calgary Herald* editor named Merv Anderson to let him take a newspaper writing course the paper offered for student reporters. While there, he took fictitious scenarios and scripted them as stories alongside future Calgary media heavyweights including *Herald* city editor Jim Knowler and city hall columnist Stephanie Keer. The plan was to learn the secrets of crafting an effective news release, but Klein immediately discovered that writing the news itself held considerably more appeal than selling it. A few months later, in the fall of 1968, Klein quit public relations for another dramatic career change. He had decided to become a reporter.

Joe Hutton, a CFCN radio station manager, is the man credited with taking a gamble on this unproven talent. There was no star treatment awaiting Klein upon leaving his lofty perch as the sultan of schmooze among Calgary's fundraisers, and he was put to work rewriting police releases and farm reports and jazzing up weather stories in mundane newscasts. Two weeks after his induction into the media world, however, Hutton walked in on Klein plucking away in two-fingered style at a typewriter on his desk. Hutton told him to get into the booth. The regular news reader was sick and his rookie reporter was going to announce the hourly news. He had five minutes to get ready.

A trembling Klein stepped into the soundproof cubicle and put on the thick, padded headphones. A finger pointed at him from the control room signalled he was live on southern Alberta's most-listened-to radio signal. His mouth opened. Five seconds passed, then ten. Not a word filled the airwaves, only a rasping gurgle as the gasping rookie lost his nerve in a sudden attack of hyperventilation. Hutton charged into the booth, yanked the script out of Klein's clammy hands and read the newscast himself. He took pity and gave Klein another chance the next night. The distinctive voice of

Ralph Klein was finally heard, fifty thousand watts strong, reading crop conditions.

For two years, Klein worked the radio game. He gathered credibility and gained seniority amid the high staff turnover, and at the same time, he developed an offbeat network of contacts. An impressed Hutton finally decided to give the energetic twenty-eight-year-old with a double chin and mop of curly hair—a great face for radio, they said—a shot at the spotlight. CFCN Television boasted the broadest reach and highest ratings south of Red Deer. Its team of reporters were young, aggressive, and as the ratings leaders, influential. Klein was allowed to make the move to television, but he would have to start at the bottom. CFCN needed a weather man with the ability to write numbers backwards on a glass weather map, and Ralph Klein became that man. It wasn't until another two years had passed that Klein was eventually assigned to cover Calgary's city council. It was the council he would chair eight years later as its 37th mayor.

Back on the home front, Ralph Klein's marriage was finished. Hilda was raising the children mostly on her own while Klein worked long hours on night and evening shifts. The pair had their share of fun times, but they fought like alley cats. "It was a very rocky, sometimes violent marriage, I have to admit that," Klein says now. "We used to fight back and forth and throw stuff at each other and hit each other."

By this time, as well, Klein had spotted a pretty, young cashier in one of his favorite bars. One Saturday night in 1971, Colleen Hamilton had succumbed to a girlfriend's pressure to stop by Calgary's Westgate Hotel for a few drinks. The emotional scars of her abusive first marriage still fresh, Colleen was in no mood to meet a man of any calibre, particularly of the tipsy, chubby, married variety who hovered over her table, wondering if he could buy her a drink. Surprised by her curt rejection, the television reporter backed up and attempted another route to impressing the petite, striking brunette with the dark brown eyes and the low, soft purr of a voice. Sucking in his gut and stretching as tall as he could, Klein played the celebrity card. "Don't you know who I am?" he asked.

She didn't. And once enlightened about his on-air credentials, she wasn't particularly impressed. The answer was still the same: Get lost, chump. It took a second night of gentle persistence for his loquacious charm to land a date. "She thought I was an absolute asshole," Klein recalls fondly. "I met her again and asked if she'd go to a football game with me. She did, and by half time we'd gone through a pint of rum." Strangely, perhaps, their first date remains among Klein's fondest memories of their thirty-year relationship.

Utterly smitten with Colleen, Klein filed for a divorce from Hilda. The divorce was granted on March 29, 1972, and his adultery was cited as grounds for the end of the stormy eleven-year marriage. The divorced couple still see each other periodically, whenever Hilda needs her famous former spouse to help out with a worthy cause in her hometown of Airdrie. Three months later, twenty-nine-year-old Ralph stood in the basement of his future step-mother's humble Calgary home and took Colleen Hamilton as his second wife, adding her two children, eleven-year-old Christine and seven-year-old Lisa to his family.

They were married by Reverend Bob Simpson, who later became an alderman on the Calgary city council. The couple honeymooned in Bragg Creek, a quaint village a half-hour's drive west of Calgary. Their first meal as husband and wife was at the town's famed steak pit, where you could save a few bucks by cooking your own entree over an open fire. Being such a special occasion, they ordered their steaks brought to their table, cooked by the chef.

Today, despite being a sought-after couple surrounded by celebrity and influence, the Kleins rarely go out. The last stage show Colleen can recall attending with her husband was *Evita*. The last movie was *E. T.*—in its original release. Gambling is a weakness for both Kleins. Colleen plays the video lottery terminals while her husband often hits the card table in private casino gaming rooms, the better not to be spotted by journalists. He wagers hundreds, not thousands, of dollars some nights and claims to win often, now that he's not drinking. Klein ruefully acknowledges losing up to seven thousand dollars and having been up ten thousand dollars over the course of a wagering year. During his reporter and mayoralty heydays, Klein was a racetrack regular. He admitted to a borderline gambling addiction but the cure, he said, was to buy a racing horse and watch the industry from the inside.

The Kleins' home is their private sanctuary, where the whirlwind of outside influences is buffered to the mere wisp of a disturbance—at least until Greenpeace stormed the roof in the spring of 2002, erecting solar panels to protest Klein's opposition to the Kyoto Accord. The few friends who have been in their Calgary home for dinner parties know better than to bring political commentary inside the front door.

Ralph and Colleen live in the same three-bedroom bungalow on Calgary's Lacombe Way they bought in 1980, when she still worked as a cashier at the local grocery store and he commanded a $25,000 television reporter's salary. It is only their second house since they married in 1972, and it will be their last if Colleen has her way. The purchase still hadn't closed when Klein stunned the Calgary establishment by claiming the keys to the city hall's mayoralty suite. After his upset victory, their banker, who suspected Klein's new job would end as a fiery, one-term train wreck, wondered aloud if living on a single political salary didn't put his mortgage loan at risk. The couple burned the mortgage in 2000.

Klein calls it a "mish-mash" of a residence. A former Danish occupant added plenty of dark woodwork and the subsequent residents, a Chinese family, attached a room at the back. The underground irrigation system was one of Klein's first accidental discoveries. He sheered off the sprinkler heads with a lawnmower, thereafter surrendering the task of lawnmowing to his wife. Colleen and Ralph have changed very little in their home, beyond a hot tub they installed in the back yard to unwind in after days apart in their hectic parallel worlds. The tub achieved a certain notoriety in 1997, after a slightly unsteady premier emerged from its bubbling waters and, as he reached for a towel, somersaulted over a patio table in a thunderous crash that drowned out the sound of four ribs cracking. For weeks, Klein thought he had a bad bruise. Only halfway through an Edmonton party fundraiser, unable to cope with the pain any longer, despite an injection of painkillers from a doctor in the crowd, did he apologize for his abbreviated speech and dash for the hospital. He stayed there for four days, suffering the added physical discomfort of being a patient while he presided over the stiffest cuts to hospital budgets in the country.

Klein used to list his home phone number as a way to keep in touch with the public. He answered it too. It doesn't ring anymore, feeding silently to voice mail or a fax machine. Colleen always viewed it as an unwanted, unwelcome invasion of her privacy, an outsider's peephole into their family life. In 1994, at the peak of her husband's government cuts, she picked up the phone and listened to a man who said Klein had reduced welfare benefits so dramatically that he had no money left to feed his children. Colleen woke up half the social services department that night, demanding someone deal with a hard luck story that turned out to be bogus. Obscenities have flowed over that telephone line too, from people upset by the Klein revolution. At times, usually after a generous sampling of wine, Klein would become so agitated by the calls, he'd pick up the phone and call his antagonists back to defend himself personally. When dozens of salty calls besieged their home after the Calgary General Hospital's 1998 demolition, some picked up by their visiting grandchildren, the Kleins disconnected the line. Public business would stay at the office, they decided, and their house would be a private retreat.

I have yet to meet an MLA or city council member who has been invited over for a social visit, and it goes without saying that journalists are under an absolute visitation ban. The one time I was inside was to use the washroom briefly, while en route to my Calgary home after a long, liquid night with the reigning mayor. Nothing struck me as extraordinary: basic bungalow, three bedrooms, dark woodwork, flag on a pole out front, major freeway a few hundred yards to the north. It was severely ordinary.

Ralph Klein picked up an additional real estate investment in 1998 when he became one of seven partners in the two-million-dollar Eagle Pointe Lodge, an isolated resort forty-eight kilometres north of Prince Rupert on B.C.'s Whale Island, just off the northwestern tip of the B.C. coastline. It is accessible only by float plane and charges $1,895 (U.S.) for five days of fishing sockeye and coho salmon out of Canadian and Alaskan waters. It has not been a shrewd investment for the premier, who only gets up to the lodge about once a year to check out his ten per cent stake. The partners have been forced, at times, to ante up a little extra to cover operating losses. "It's smart business for Ralph, though. As an owner, he didn't have to clear his bar tab," cracked one of the staff when Klein completed the purchase. Perhaps wisely, his chief of staff, Peter Elzinga, sold out his share in 2001 to kickstart a ranching operation back in Alberta.

Colleen Klein is the first to admit that her husband was an absentee father and that he still doesn't see much of the grandkids. It is, in fact, an almost inexplicable side of Klein. A cuddly politician, capable of bonding instantly with people he's never met, he almost never mentions his family in public, except for his wife. He never cites them as a demand on his time or an obligation missed. His children and grandchildren never appear in public for political events—or at least never receive recognition for being there. "Raising the children was my responsibility. He was simply away too much to be of much help," Colleen Klein sighs. The couple each have two children from their first marriages and one of their own, Teresa. At the time of this writing, those offspring have delivered ten grandchildren and two great-grandchildren.

Being Alberta's first lady has handed Colleen Klein a lonely life. If her husband is not on duty at a political function, he's at a golf club, a fishing resort or, until his vow of temperance in December 2001, somewhere with a drink in his hand. She's a widow on all counts. Colleen doesn't enjoy fishing. She's too much of a perfectionist to begin the long, humbling process of learning golf, bewildered at her husband's devotion to what she calls the "incomprehensible chasing of the little white ball." She's never been a big drinker, preferring to keep her wits about her—and a clear eye on her husband for telltale signs of overstrain on his liver.

It is not, however, a fairytale marriage. There have been nasty fights, nights when she has sent her husband packing from the residence, and long periods apart when he takes to the road on work and she stays back with her extended family. On several occasions she has learned of life-altering decisions—the movement to draft Klein for the Alberta Liberals in 1987 and his midnight visit to a homeless shelter in 2001, to name a couple—from the morning newspaper and has not been amused. "We've had ups and downs and yelling and so on," Klein acknowledges. "It's been tough on

Colleen. She gave up her job and cashed in her pension to support my first mayoralty bid. Now she's a volunteer and works harder than when she got paid."

It is the little things in their private life that Colleen recalls with knee-slapping glee. She once treated Jessy, her pet Lhasa Apso, to a roll of meaty dog food. A couple of hours later, she found Ralph Klein poised to chow down on a plate of cheese and crackers and hefty slices of the dog's dinner. When she attacked an infestation of mice using Irish Spring soap shavings as a rodent repellent, a phone call interrupted her. She returned just in time to watch her husband pop what he thought were chunks of mint chocolate into his mouth.

As premier, the demands on Klein to be in Alberta's capital have forced the couple to purchase a condominium in Edmonton, a city Klein regarded with considerable disdain when he was mayor of its rival. "You sort of have to think that when Louis Riel was fighting for this territory, he didn't have Edmonton in mind," he once mused. His divided political loyalties have forced him to publicly embrace Calgary's rival as an equal Alberta jewel. Even so, the couple stay overnight in Edmonton as infrequently as possible. It's just not home.

Three

Ralph the Reporter

R ALPH KLEIN'S POLITICAL HEART has never completely lost
its journalistic pulse. The reporter's dictum to listen more than
talk is still the essence of his politics; formidable communications
know-how is still the key to his success. He nostalgically tells and retells
stories of the eleven years he spent as a senior television reporter on the
city's hottest newscast scouting Calgary's back alleys and city hall corri-
dors for offbeat stories. He'll tell you, even if it takes a few drinks to pry
loose the acknowledgment, that the job of crusading journalist was the
best gig he ever had.

As a reporter, Ralph Klein refused to follow the basic script laid out for a
1970s Calgary television journalist: read news release; cover news conference; seek reaction from talking head; deliver signoff against scenic
backdrop; file two minutes of tape; hit the bar. After his brief weatherman
stint, during which he overcame his fear of the camera's unblinking eye,
Klein began to cover soft news. He generated the same feel-good, human
interest stories he had promoted from the other side as the cheerleader for
the United Way campaign. As his confidence grew, he tackled news features
and took delight in ones that tweaked the establishment's nose. The most
memorable, perhaps, was when he checked a homeless man into the upscale

Palliser Hotel because the stay included a tee time at the posh Calgary Golf and Country Club. The plan was to catch on film the many appalled reactions of upper crust Calgarians. It worked like a charm. The feature had ordinary office workers giggling around the water cooler for days.

When he discovered that the media were barred from a glittery, oil patch fundraising dinner for Alberta premier Peter Lougheed in the late 1970s, a peeved Klein took his camera a few blocks down the street to interview homeless Calgarians eating at a soup kitchen. He spliced their hard luck stories into coverage of the exclusive three-hundred-dollar-a-plate affair. Complaining Calgary Tories burned up the lines to the CFCN executives within minutes of it airing.

Klein's favorite stories were the ones that gave him the chance to vent his thinly disguised contempt for the privilege of the silver-spooned establishment. His disdain of official protocol persists to this day. He abhors stuffy titles designed to artificially elevate someone's status. Klein recalls quite clearly standing to question Lougheed in 1971 at his first news conference as premier. Throughout the preceding campaign, Lougheed had been on a cozy first-name basis with reporters, but when Klein addressed him as "Peter," an aide immediately hushed him up, informing Klein that from now on, the proper salutation was "Premier." It made a lasting impression on Klein. To this day, he asks to be addressed as "Ralph" and, when his signature requires political formality, he signs it with flourish: "Premier Ralph."

In the mid-1970s, Ralph Klein was inexorably drawn to the city hall beat where he quickly fell in love with the news scoop. His desk was at the centre of an open press room that would fill barely half the space of his premier's office now. Surrounded by a dozen journalistic rivals and monitored by a parade of aldermen and bureaucrats on their way to and from council chambers, Klein's privacy was in short supply. Mind you, his typewriter was never occupied before noon on those rare days when it was occupied at all. When Klein did show up, he rarely wasted time chatting up the competition. He was there to retrieve messages, pound out a script with a frantic, two-fingered punching of the keys on his black Underwood and get back to the street. "There are no stories in the newsroom," he'd say if anyone sarcastically welcomed him back to city hall.

Klein rarely bothered with news conferences and usually dispensed with covering city council's official reaction. He abhorred the pre-mixed pablum his profession was expected to dish out as civic affairs coverage. He covered the beat from corner tables in local bars, where trays of draft beer opened up his sources. He hung out with the oddest cross-section of contacts any Calgary journalist ever had: city planners like Wilf Morgan, who later became his mayoralty assistant; development lobbyists like Bruce Green, who became a key member of Klein's municipal kitchen cabinet; the secretaries he eventually hired; the union leaders he relied on to keep his mayoralty years free of strikes; a big-name accountant named Jack Halpin, who became a key fundraiser; Bob Scott, a charismatic lawyer who provided strategic advice during his years as mayor and was later named a judge by Klein. It was at the loveable Looey, as is affectionately known, where Klein made friendships and connections that last to this day.

To his competition in the media, Klein was at his most dangerous when he'd show up in the press room wearing the smirk of a cat with a canary struggling in its esophagus—a gotcha look that suggested he could barely contain a giddy howl of triumph at his latest exclusive. "Watch it and weep," he'd advise. Sure enough, the next nightly newscast would lead off with his mug grinning into the camera, reporting on the latest skyscraping development project, highway expansion or proposed property tax increase. God, we hated him at times.

Klein was not above rummaging through garbage or eavesdropping to find a story. Occasionally, he could be found standing silently outside the city commissioner's boardroom, his ears glued to a crack in the door with a finger to his lips. In a rare display of camaraderie early in my posting on the city hall beat at the *Calgary Herald*, Klein showed me a removable access door. It led to the mechanical corridor that runs behind the council chambers, and from there, private meetings could be surreptitiously monitored. Peering through a crack, I found myself looking at the back of Mayor Ross Alger's head as he discussed a controversial land development. It was a dusty conduit, dusty enough to make me sneeze, and I let out the kind of raspy honk that results from pinching your nostrils to try to keep the noise in. Alger's head swivelled around to stare baffled at the coat of arms on the wall behind him. Klein's furious glare said it all. I would never get back inside the corridor unless it was over his dead body.

If he didn't have the story, Klein would make damn sure no one else did, and to hell with professional ethics. In the mid-1970s, a television reporter for the CBC was fascinated by alleged business connections between incumbent mayor Rod Sykes and the people backing a new Calgary convention center. The reporter was convinced it was a tangled web deserving of a judicial inquiry. Klein didn't care much for the story. It had too many meetings and not enough visually stimulating material for television, he recalls. Rummaging through garbage cans just ahead of the cleaning lady one evening, however, Klein found copies of discarded CBC scripts that hinted at a major convention center controversy in the works. Piecing it together with snatches of conversation overheard the next day, Klein figured out that the CBC, then his main television rival, was co-operating with a local radio station on a major conflict of interest connection to the development.

Klein knew he didn't have enough factual material to put the story on air himself, but he had a better idea. Charging into the mayor's office, he warned Mayor Sykes that media were linking forces to expose an alleged conflict of interest on the convention center development. With Klein seated on his couch, an incensed Sykes called the Canadian Radio and Television Commission to complain about unethical journalists ganging up to tarnish his halo. Klein went to air with the mayor's attack against an alleged media "conspiracy," which, in a stroke of evil journalistic genius, gave him a big story and simultaneously killed the competition's scoop. The next day Klein found his typewriter in pieces with a note on his desk crediting "The Conspiracy" for the vandalism. He had it repaired and now keeps it on display under glass in his legislature office, using it in nostalgic moments to pound out letters to old friends.

A different chapter in the same convention center story gave Klein his first brush with the law as a reporter. A judicial inquiry had been convened to explore the controversial connections between the Four Seasons Hotel convention center and various businesses in the city. A disgruntled member of the inquiry began to tape the in-camera hearings and offered the recordings to Klein. Unfortunately, the tape recordings proved to be indecipherable, but Klein was not so easily deterred from a good story. He simply went to air with news of the secret taping, waving the cassettes in his hand.

Klein and CFCN were promptly charged under a new Criminal Code statute that prohibited anyone from revealing the existence of an illegally recorded communication, an offence punishable with five years in the slammer. The television station was searched, and Klein was fingerprinted and "mugged." He then found himself sitting in a prisoner's box throughout a long preliminary hearing. The judge evenually dismissed the charge as bogus. As the judge noted at the trial, a person merely informing another person about Klein's story might also have violated the same law if it were interpreted broadly enough. As a direct result of the Klein case, the Criminal Code of Canada was amended to delete the offence.

Despite his unorthodox conduct, Klein's work as a reporter did demonstrate a conscience. When he was tipped off by police sources of an upcoming drug bust against the mayor's son, Klein warned Sykes that his son was being set up and the mayor took steps to scare off the sting. Sykes also recalls that Klein once called his wife to offer her assurances that her husband wasn't involved in any hanky-panky. His television station had been tailing the mayor after hours—just in case.

To break up the monotony of covering civic affairs, Klein would periodically dive into documentaries. He won a provincal broadcasting award for investigating a new cancer treatment for the dying. He researched and produced another acclaimed feature about a former Grim Reaper biker who had emerged as a promising artist while serving a life sentence for murder. What Calgary author Frank Dabbs describes in *Ralph Klein: A Maverick Life* as Klein's "epiphany," however, is a three-week sojourn Klein made on the dirt-poor and dusty Siksika First Nation reserve, an hour's drive east of Calgary, near the town of Gleichen. The documentary he produced was in a simple bear-witness style, and its effects on Klein, emotionally and spiritually, linger to this day.

The one-hundredth anniversary of the signing of Treaty 7 was in 1977, and in July of that year, civic celebrations featured a visit to Calgary by Prince Charles. CFCN's news director, Thompson MacDonald, was disgusted by what was, in his view, a royal publicity stunt using natives as a photo-op. He was also appalled at the tight media controls imposed by the event organizers. At the time, CFCN was under pressure from the CRTC to increase its coverage of native affairs. MacDonald seized upon the idea of revisiting Treaty 7 from the natives' point of view. He wanted not a sanitized white man's view, but raw insight into the life experienced by the descendants of those who had surrendered vast tracts of territory under the treaty. It would take a special kind of reporter to penetrate the insular world of native people, especially since the media, in the 1970s, devoted no resources or manpower to covering aboriginal issues. It was the perfect assignment for a people person like his star reporter, Ralph Klein.

Klein's only exposure to native people before he set out for the Siksika reserve in May, 1977, was in the east-end bars of Calgary. He arrived in Gleichen to discover a people living in appalling conditions, their culture imperilled by poverty and booze, their children kept in residential schools. For three weeks, Klein toured the reserve. He gradually earned the confidence of the people he met, as well as their trust that he would listen with an open mind. His powerful thirst was a bonus.

Klein took his television camera into grocery stores to confront proprietors about their huge stockpiles of vanilla extract, which they sold at inflated prices to desperate alcoholics. He challenged Gleichen bar owners on their practice of allowing natives to drink themselves into a stupor before they kicked them out into the snow, where some died of exposure as they stumbled home in the cold. He learned to eat their food, speak bits of their language, embrace their spirituality and absorb their history. "When you look back, it's quite something to realize that in 1977, it had only been ten years since natives had been granted the right to vote, sell their own livestock, buy liquor and leave the reserve to take up residence elsewhere," Klein says. "When they were put into these schools, their hair was cut short, and one of the crimes was to speak their language or sing a song in their native tongue."

Klein was horrified by "payday," the weekly ritual students in the local residential school endured before they were sent back to the reserve on Sunday. "The nuns would chalk up all their misdeeds, and before they were sent home, they got a whack on the ass," Klein says. His half-hour documentary was heavily promoted and aired in June 1977. It received glowing reviews inside the station and impressed those Calgarians who bothered to watch, but Klein says that wasn't important. The audience he aimed to please was clustered around black and white television sets back on a dusty reserve, watching a white man's rare sympathetic portrayal of their plight. When the show aired, a trust was confirmed: they christened him White Writer and called him a friend.

Afterwards, Klein received calls from the reserve that tipped him off to new scandals, or merely to inquire when he might next be coming out their way for a brewski or three. He became close friends with Adrian Stimson, now a Siksika band administrator. In the spring of 1978, Stimson invited Klein to cover the start of a relay run from the reserve to Ottawa that was designed to highlight the band's plight. Klein grabbed a cameraman and set out for the reserve on Friday morning, before the event's start the next day. He never suspected he was also heading for a night in jail. As was his custom on such trips, Klein was in the Gleichen bar that afternoon with a table of his native friends, when he noticed a young woman taking pictures of the group. He'd had enough drinks by then to find this very disturbing, so he confronted her. She was a weekly newspaper reporter from a nearby town and she said she found the sight of Klein, by then a regional news personality, seated with native leaders to be something worth photographing. Klein gruffly ordered her to stop. She refused. Klein dispatched Jimmy Jackman, his shooter, to get their television camera. "You want to take pictures, I'll take pictures," Klein told her, aiming the camera with its intense sun-gun light into the shocked woman's wide-open eyes. "She went nuts and pretty soon everything was in an uproar and the bartender called the cops," Klein recalls with a grin.

A couple of hours later, Klein and Jackman found themselves alone in a cell, charged with disturbing the peace. "It got a lot more interesting and exciting as time went on, because the welfare cheques had arrived that afternoon. By midnight the place was packed with forty or fifty people," Klein says. "They were all Blackfoot, except for us and two other guys in there for impaired driving. We were shouting 'Remember Wounded Knee,' having a howling match with our Indian friends. It was great fun." The two white warriors were found guilty and and sentenced to time in custody.

Klein's relationship with native people and culture has grown and evolved since the White Writer entered politics. Klein finds their spiritual belief in the living earth and the Creator more inspiring than the strict by-the-Bible upbringing he received in his grandfather's United Church. Klein still visits sweat lodges to prepare himself mentally for provincial elections, he carries an eagle feather in his briefcase and he hangs braids of sweetgrass in his offices. Shortly after being elected mayor in 1980, Chief Jack Big Eye made Klein an honorary Blackfoot chief, gave him the name Oots-squi-peeks, or "Blue Bird," and bestowed a chief's headdress on the young politician.

In the weeks following his 2001 election victory, Premier Ralph Klein worked feverishly in his Calgary and Edmonton offices on a special project. Not on a new approach to governing for a booming province on the verge of becoming debt-free. Not on revolutionary policy or revamped budgets to guide a surge in spending under his massive majority. Klein was writing a biography, of sorts, that is the best indication yet that his third term as premier will be his last. It was a project to bring his life full circle, back to his first love—journalism.

Immersed in a pile of textbooks—among others, George Bain's 1994 journalism analysis *Gotcha!*, *The Canadian Guide to Managing the Media*, and, ironically, *How to Win an Election*—Klein was writing a directed field study for a Mount Royal College communications course with the title: "How does one run a successful election campaign?" The subject: His own massive majority re-election.

Klein waved off offers from his stable of spin doctors to assist with the the research and writing. He sought to tailor established academic theory and historical analysis in order to explain his 2001 election victory, and paid particular attention to the role of the media in delivering or obstructing his message. After weeks of work, he proudly submitted a twenty-eight-page study to his instructor. It concluded: "In an election campaign, the only way to measure its success is by the outcome. And 74 out of 83 seats is a fairly impressive result." The paper's overall analysis is reasonably sophisticated, but the instructor complained that Klein's bibliography lacked depth and noted that the party leader hadn't identified enough precedents to back up his observations. As a result, the premier who wrote the book on political domination and media management in Canada was given a C grade for his inside analysis of his own election campaign. Feeling a bit like Winston Churchill earning a passing grade on a Second World War military thesis, Klein promptly transferred to a correspondence course at Athabasca University for the degree in communications he aims to earn before the end of his mandate. Then, he muses, perhaps he can put his media criticisms and theories into practice and teach budding scribes the truth about modern-day media.

Ralph Klein's reporting background has given him an acute sensitivity to press coverage. He often challenges reporters to do their homework, as if he were teacher and they mere students of the craft. On the night of his first mayoralty election victory, his mother Florence told reporters that her son was too thin-skinned to survive in politics. Her pessimistic forecast was clearly wrong, but media criticism, particularly cheap shots, nag at Klein far longer than they should, and he can't usually let them pass without comment.

When Klein senses reporters are making too much of small controversies in provincial politics, he diagnoses an outbreak of what he calls "Dome Disease," the condition of being holed up under the Alberta legislature's dome instead of out listening to the concerns of The People. For offending reporters, he readily prescribes a week of hunting after stories at least ten blocks away from the seat of government. In speeches where he critiques the media, he laments the replacement of journalism's traditional five Ws—who, what, where, when, why—with the five Cs—conflict, controversy, chaos, confrontation and crisis. He warns his MLAs not to expect the twenty-first-century media to cover the story, but to merely report the reaction to the story, or the reaction to the reaction. While he rarely complains to reporters directly, on a morning when the media write up the news following an agenda at odds with his own, Klein's staff can expect a verbal blast from the peeved premier.

Klein's 2001 election victory saw his bitter Liberal enemy, Nancy MacBeth, vanquished from her own Edmonton seat, and only nine of Alberta's eighty-three seats in opposition hands. At the euphoric private party celebrating that victory, the last thing expected from the re-elected premier was a media slagging. That, however, was exactly what a tipsy Ralph Klein delivered.

After making a hasty escape from some partyers intent on debating my coverage of the Klein campaign, I approached the premier in the Red Carpet Steak House, a modest hideaway in his Calgary Elbow constituency, to offer congratulation. After a most perfunctory greeting, Klein tore into me about the media having missed all the important issues of the campaign. He was particularly incensed at the press's infatuation with the Stockwell Day caper. Red Deer lawyer Lorne Goddard had won an $800,000 settlement in a defamation suit he launched against Day that stemmed from an incident which occurred during Day's tenure as Alberta's treasurer. "Nobody gives a shit about Stockwell Day's legal woes," Klein fumed. "Come to my office and read the stack of letters on my desk. That's where you'll find out what concerns people. It's about parks. It's about electrical power. It's about quality of life. You guys have lost touch."

His wife Colleen detected my incredulous reaction. "Don't worry," she whispered with an understanding smile and a pat on my arm, "I'm taking him home soon." It was more than just Klein's intoxication speaking, though. The incident was a glimpse into his sincere frustration with a press that fails to reflect public priorities. In his own mind, he is still an ex-officio member of the fifth estate, and when it comes to what's on people's minds, Klein is convinced he knows best.

For better or worse, Klein still respects most journalists for telling it straight, even if their version of events does not square with his own. When the premier tried to persuade me to run for his party in the 1997 election, I asked him why he would want a loose-cannon columnist inside his gagged-and-bound Tory caucus. After all, this was a caucus where unwavering loyalty to the leader and dutiful adherence to the party line are requisite behavior. "It's because you're a journalist and journalists tell the truth. We don't have enough of that in politics," he said.

When I snorted that Prime Minister Sheila Copps would have to sweep every seat in Alberta for the federal Liberals before I'd consider a run for public office, he frowned slightly, looked at Rod Love and shrugged: "I tried." We were well into the sauce, but only then did it occur to me this was a serious offer. The only journalist in his caucus wanted company.

In my view, the Blackfoot experience was not Ralph Klein's true epiphany as a journalist. That came a year later, when a grandiose redevelopment scheme called the Calgary Civic Centre was proposed. It was set to swallow three blocks of downtown land surrounding city hall. Klein always held sympathies for historical preservation, but his feelings bubbled to the surface in 1977 when retired mayor Rod Sykes happened to spot a camera crew recording, for want of a better description, bums and creeps in an alley behind city hall. At the time, Ross Alger's new administration was looking to redevelop the area, and Sykes correctly deduced that the filming was for a television commercial to highlight the area's seedy reputation. Sykes immediately called Klein, who jumped in the CFCN van and rushed down. With the television camera rolling, he burst in to catch actors being made up to look like beggars and panhandlers for an ad agency's redevelopment commercial. It was a great story—and the start of a crusade.

The underhanded secrecy of the powerful politicians and bureaucrats who sought to tear down Calgary's past offended Klein's sentimental attachment to the area. This was particularly true as some of the businesses set to swallow the wrecking ball were his favorite watering holes. After he spotted an elaborate model of the new Civic Centre in the mayor's office, showcasing the giant structure surrounded by reflecting pools where the hotels, pawn shops, used furniture stores and pubs then stood, Klein turned to advocacy journalism. His final documentary as a reporter was called Dreams, Schemes and Sandstone Dust—a biased title if there ever was one, and one fitting for a documentary as one-sided as this. He interviewed bar regulars, permanent hotel tenants and small businessmen. He glorifyed the area's ragged and rundown attractions as treasures worth preserving, and embellished them into Calgary's answer to Vancouver's Gastown. Not one Civic Centre proponent was interviewed in the production.

The day after it aired, Klein was mocked by the entire press gallery for daring to call it objective journalism. Due in part to Klein's preservation push, however, a grassroots organization sprang up and gathered enough signatures on petitions to force a plebiscite on the development. The voters shelved the project later that year. Ironically, an only slightly less grandiose version, featuring a blue wedge of offices fronted by the fountains and arches of Olympic Plaza, was officially unveiled four years later by Calgary's next mayor—former television reporter Ralph Klein.

Four

The Beautiful People

R ALPH KLEIN'S ENTRY INTO the 1980 Calgary mayoralty race is the stuff of folklore in the city now. He had planned to run for alderman, but with the mayoralty contest whittled down to two bland establishment candidates—the incumbent Ross Alger and a former alderman named Peter Petrasuk—Klein decided the race for the top could use a maverick. On August 18, 1980, just fifty-eight days before the vote, his resolve was fortified by his usual gaggle of drinking buddies in the St. Louis tavern. He left the tavern, took a taxi home, woke up Colleen and giddily shared his grand plan to take over city hall. In typically pragmatic style, Colleen advised her tipsy husband to sleep it off before making any bold declarations. Two days later, after some sober second thought, Klein walked into his television station's 10:00 a.m. story meeting. He arrived about fifteen minutes late, as was his custom, and announced to the room of reporters and editors downing their morning caffeine, trying to dream up stories while most of the city was on vacation, that he had a newscast-leading exclusive for their consideration. He was going to mount a challenge to become the next mayor of Calgary, and he was going to win. A snicker went up around the table.

News director Thompson MacDonald, who went on to feature promi-nently in Klein's political career, dismissed it as a joke. He had endured regular pitches from Klein for newsroom management jobs, but rejected his applications on the ground that "a guy whose wife had to be called to get him out of the bath in the morning did not have great leadership abilities." He told Klein to hit the road and find something newsworthy to cover at city hall.

Offended, Klein called up the *Calgary Herald* to sell senior civic reporter Robert Bragg on the newsworthiness of his candidacy. The *Herald*'s editors were torn on what to do next: should they treat it as news or dismiss it as the ranting of a journalist known for flights of well-lubricated fancy? But the call, coming as it did in mid-morning, suggested this wasn't a last-call lark. Besides, the paper was suffering through the late summer news doldrums, so they slapped ten paragraphs on the front page and hoped the candidate wouldn't sober up and abandon his plans a few hours later. "I've lived here all my life and it just seems to me a lot of people are paying very little attention to the quality of life in this city," Klein was quoted in the story that ran in the *Herald*. "There's not enough attention to the heritage of the city and the community spirit has been lost."

The notion of thirty-seven-year-old Ralph Klein as a credible force in the 1980 election campaign took time to take root. The incumbent, Ross Alger, a chartered accountant with deep connections in the Calgary Chamber of Commerce, had a clean name and a $150,000 warchest, the largest in the city's history. His chief rival, Peter Petrasuk, was a slick lawyer with a large ethnic voter base and a hefty bankroll behind his challenge. There just didn't seem room for a third serious contender in the very short campaign.

Klein's father Phil shook his head in disbelief when he heard the plan, but cut a cheque for a thousand dollars and donated his rickety motorhome to his son's bid. He was convinced it was a waste of money and gas. Klein "borrowed" a television camera from CFCN, stood on a hillside overlooking the city and shot his entire television campaign in a single take on one roll of film. Two of the first volunteers to sign on to his campaign—oilman Rich Jones and his spouse Norma Sieppert—had heard about a Spokane, Washington, television anchorman named Ron Bair who had won the city's mayoralty on a $7,200 shoestring budget. They arranged for Klein to fly down to Spokane for a meeting. Bair advised Klein to stress communication and steer clear of specific promises, suggesting that he pledge only to listen to the voters and to do what he could to help.

It was magic to Klein's ears, as it confirmed his initial instincts that people will accept unpopular decisions if they believe their input has been considered and valued. "Even if I can't solve your problems, at least I'll give you a forum and I'll listen," he told a mayoralty debate a few weeks later. "Honest communication is the key." Those words could easily have been delivered twenty years later during his third campaign as premier, and nobody would have thought them out of character for Klein.

Three weeks into the election race, with six weeks to go until voting day, Ralph Klein called together his campaign team of about a dozen people, and announced that he was quitting the race. His campaign manager, former alderman Nomi Whalen, had bowed out, his warchest was down to pocket change and the odds of beating his powerful rivals appeared insurmountable. The campaign team refused to accept his decision. They offered to take turns running the campaign, starting with Rich Jones. They printed up a couple of thousand black and white pamphlets proclaiming "It's Time for Klein" and delivered them in blue-collar quadrants of the city where an anti-establishment candidate would have the greatest appeal. Money was so tight that they printed only enough to cover every third door, urging homeowners to share the material with their neighbors.

Despite the high-flying economy and a seemingly competent civic government, something about the underdog candidate was starting to strike a chord with Calgarians. Klein sensed he was closing in on second place, an instinct that was confirmed when Petrasuk visited Klein in his campaign office and urged him to withdraw from the race. Klein threw him out, and warned the former alderman that he was going to "whump his ass." On his way back to city hall, Petrasuk stumbled and fell into a construction trench for Calgary's future Light Rail Transit line. To Klein's eyes, it was a good omen. Even so, he wasn't thinking about winning. He was just hoping for a respectable defeat so that he could return to his old city hall sources as more than just a candidate who had lost his nomination deposit. Then, one month before the election, destiny dialed his campaign office. Klein, busy counting out his trickle of donations one dollar bill at a time, picked up the call.

When Rod Love joined the Klein team he was a twenty-seven-year-old University of Calgary political science undergraduate hustling three hundred dollars' worth of tax-free tips per weekend as the head waiter at a trendy eatery called Pardon My Garden. He was a hot property in Calgary's booming hospitality scene. Whenever Mayor Ross Alger's office staff needed five-star care in a four-star restaurant for large groups of dignitaries, they called on Love to be their server. As he hovered near their tables, Love listened in on the conversations, gleaning the political intrigue and intricacies that weren't in his university textbooks.

When talk turned to re-election strategy in early 1980, Love decided to reveal his political ambitions in a big way. He contacted the mayor's campaign office and offered his services as the strategic brain for their operation. The Alger team laughed at the notion of putting their favorite waiter in charge of a $150,000 campaign for an incumbent whom they believed was on a re-election cakewalk. Perhaps stuffing envelopes, they suggested, or phoning volunteers or putting up lawn signs. Fine, then, Love shrugged, none of the above. He went down the road to make the same offer to the next mayoralty candidate on the list. Petrasuk was generally viewed as a contender, if the incumbent stumbled. His reaction to Love's offer was more or less the same as Alger's. Here's a pile of literature, there's a pile of envelopes, stuff one inside the other and affix the correct postage.

There was only one other, rather unappetizing name on the candidate list. Love dialed the third campaign office phone number and a voice, husky from late nights filled with too many cigarettes, answered on the first ring: "Ralph Klein Headquarters." Love asked to speak to the campaign co-ordinator.

"Nobody here but me," the voice said.

"And you are?" Love asked.

"Ralph Klein speaking," came the answer.

A few hours later, on a break from waiting tables at a nearby restaurant, a bespectacled face with a tangled growth of bushy muttonchops and a brown Afro walked through the front door. "Hi, my name's Rod," the stranger said, holding out his hand for a shake.

Nobody knew it yet, but Ralph Klein had just won the 1980 civic election.

Rod Love's political initiation dates back to 1967. As a fourteen-year-old kid, he breezed through the lobby of the Royal York Hotel with his dad during the Progressive Conservative convention in Toronto, when the party elected Robert Stanfield leader. The hoopla was huge, the excitement high, the party action frantic. Young Roderick was enraptured by the sights and sounds of politics in a frenzy. He bought the hottest-selling political narrative of the day, *The Distemper of Our Times* by Peter C. Newman, and couldn't stop turning the pages as he read about the back-stabbing intrigues of the Diefenbaker and Pearson era. "A light came on. It was like I'd written it myself," Love recalls. "I knew exactly what was going on strategically, tactically and from a communications standpoint." After high school, he enrolled in political science at the University of Alberta and delivered selective excellence—top marks in politics and literature, failing grades in biology and chemistry. Before finishing his degree, he moved to Calgary with his family and enrolled at the University of Calgary to similarly unbalanced academic results. When he was away from the books and the restaurant tables, Love was fleshing out his fledgling political resume. He volunteered on any campaign he could find, be it a contested aldermanic seat, a race for a federal riding or the 1979 Joe Clark prime ministerial campaign. Nothing he'd seen or read, however, would prepare him for the undisciplined, unorthodox 1980 Ralph Klein campaign.

The day they met, Klein, as usual, was late for a meeting to plead for better office space with Calgary developer Jack Singer. As a result, Love's first job was to pilot the motorhome while the candidate changed into his best Tip Top Tailors suit. As they drove through the construction zone that was downtown Calgary in those days, Love remembers turning around to ask his new political master for directions. He immediately drove off the road. Klein was standing at the back of the swaying motorhome with a cigarette in one hand, a rum and Coke in the other, a grin on his face and not a stitch of clothes on his body. What, Love wondered to himself, had he got himself into?

With Love added to the campaign's inner circle, order was brought to chaos. He had just finished a university course in public opinion polling, taught by Roger Gibbons, and he decided this was a golden opportunity to put classroom theory into practice. He wrote up a questionnaire, then rounded up half a dozen volunteers to put the questions to a random group of Calgarians. The results, while unscientific, put Klein in second place, far behind Alger. What caught Love's eye, though, was that forty per cent of the voters polled were undecided. This didn't add up. A reputable mayor with blue-chip backing should not be facing so many parked votes four weeks before an election. Calgarians were a backlash looking for a place to happen.

Love went to Klein and told him that the time for yuk-yuk gladhanding and happy-hour campaigning was over. Aggression and discipline were essential if the longshot had any hope of winning the election. If this was a social experiment, he wasn't interested. If Klein was serious about being mayor, Love said, he wanted a key role to finish the job. Two nights later, not having heard a word from Klein, Love figured he'd overplayed his hand and was off the team. Then the phone rang. It was Klein. "I'd like you to take over the campaign."

Petrasuk was surrounded by legal problems that would ultimately see him thrown in jail for embezzling trust funds from, among others, his own mother. A confident Alger was sleepwalking his way to a second term. Klein went aggressive. He painted city hall as a cold, uncaring institution that failed to keep Calgarians informed. He recited the Municipal Government Act ad nauseum, noting that the legislation did not require the mayor to manage city hall, but merely to serve as the representative of the people, who shall "communicate from time to time the finances and well-being of the municipality." It was a boring message, but that was the whole point. The campaign aimed to project Klein as knowledgeable about civic affairs, yet unlikely to radically alter the status quo. He was a guy who would represent the voters to the best of his ability, keep them in the loop on public business and not turn city hall into his own private pub. It wasn't flashy, but it was reasonable.

In an all-candidates' debate soon after, the two lead rivals directed all their fire at each other, and ignored the political neophyte who was getting the loudest applause. Klein cornered me afterwards. "I know you don't believe me, Don, but I'm going to come in second," he boasted. "Just watch me."

Two weeks before the election, Klein ordered the two phone lines into his campaign office expanded to ten—and that still wasn't enough to handle all the calls. Rich Jones remembers people lining up in shopping malls to pocket the same Klein election buttons he couldn't have given away two weeks earlier. Campaign office volunteer Bruce Planche received a call from his father, Hugh, a senior member of the Peter Lougheed cabinet. The provincial government had tacked a few questions onto its regular province-wide polling, including one about the Calgary mayoralty race. Hugh Planche hinted to his son about the results: "Better tell your boy to get a new suit," he said.

Still, there was one thing missing. Klein needed a respectable name to give his bid a final credibility boost. Former mayor Rod Sykes received a phone call from the Klein campaign a week before the vote, asking for his endorsement. He refused, insisting that he would maintain his neutrality, but, he said, if he was asked the right question, he'd be willing to say Klein had a good chance of winning the election. Ten minutes later, Klein's home station of CFCN was on the phone, requesting an interview. Sykes became the first to say what many Calgarians sensed—the longshot candidate had become the overnight favorite.

On October 15, 1980, *Calgary Herald* reporters on the afternoon shift hit the phones to get the heads-up on voter results. They were utterly astonished by what they heard. Six out of every ten voters had marked their ballots for a television reporter who hadn't made a campaign promise and who didn't have a single minute of hands-on political experience. An hour after the polls closed, Ralph Klein was proclaimed the city's thirty-third mayor. In an election with 142,000 ballots cast, he beat an incumbent who was twenty-three years his senior by fifteen thousand votes. He had spent $30,000, was $12,000 in debt and as the dark horse, hadn't even planned a victory party. That soon changed, and he invaded the Jade Garden Restaurant with forty family members and campaign workers.

Klein called it a victory by the "beautiful" people. They were actually a ragtag assortment of barflies and misfits, mostly volunteers he had befriended on reporting assignments. There were the young, the inexperienced, the apolitical, and then there was Mitch. On election night, Mitch had sat in a corner of Klein's rustic campaign office as the results poured in, glumly holding a beer in his hand. No one had expected a longshot like Klein to need real security, so when a drifter with a big knife showed up a few weeks before the vote and offered to be the candidate's bodyguard, they shrugged and put him to work stuffing envelopes. When Klein won, Mitch was in his glory. He rushed forward from where he sat, unbuckled his knife and declared himself ready to take a bullet for Calgary's new mayor as the chief of security. He was quickly hustled into a corner by the police, who relieved him of his knife for a few hours. When Klein's campaign team last heard from Mitch, he was living in southern Ontario with a view of the St. Lawrence River through a window with iron bars. He's not expected back any time soon. He was in Kingston Penitentiary serving life for murder—beautiful.

Five

The Chief Magistrate

On OCTOBER 27, 1980, city brass recoiled at the sight of a pesky thirty-seven-year-old journalist being sworn in as their political master. There was a chubby stranger in their clubby midst. Ralph Klein settled into the black, high-backed mayor's seat for the first time—a chair less than a metre from the crack in the wall behind which he had eavesdropped only a few months earlier. He wrestled for a little while with the computer system designed to track the voting and speaking order during council meetings with electronic precision. "I give up," he shrugged a few minutes into the meeting, and opted instead to recognize the speakers himself, a right he wisely reserved for the next three terms. "I give him a year," one alderman smirked to reporters while Klein consulted with commissioners on a fine point of procedure. To some minds, even that dim prospect seemed wildly optimistic.

Ralph Klein had become the head of a city that was at the peak of its biggest economic boom, but which also faced some of its biggest problems. Calgary was growing at the frantic rate of five per cent annually. More new office space was built in Calgary in 1980 than in New York City and Chicago combined, and business rents were the highest on the continent. The city's unofficial bird, the construction crane, squatted over numerous concrete nests, as new towers of reflective glass began to dwarf the landmark Calgary Tower. At one particularly industrious period, twenty cranes were silently pivoted over city streets, reshaping the skyline into a modern metropolis, one bucket of concrete at a time. It was a city on the move in a hurry—even the escalators ran faster in downtown Calgary, author Peter C. Newman noted in *The Canadian Establishment*. It was a heady time for Calgary residents. They boldly predicted their city would be a lovely place to live, once it was uncrated. It would be a city whose growth was self-sustaining and beyond the fickle fate of an energy industry downturn, a city that could still afford the sneer of its legendary oil wars bumper sticker from a few years earlier—Let Those Eastern Bastards Freeze in the Dark.

Two weeks after Klein's election victory, federal energy minister Marc Lalonde rose in the House of Commons to announce the National Energy Program. It imposed a wellhead tax on oil production and a stiff rise in refinery taxes; it unleashed incentives favoring domestic interests in a foreign-owned oilpatch, encouraged exploration on the frontiers and established Petro-Canada as a Crown corporation. For a generation of Albertans to follow, NEP became the acronym for western alienation, and a symbol of the greedy federal bogeyman seeking to cash in on Alberta's resource wealth. It is a Liberal legacy that bedevils Prime Minister Jean Chretien to this day.

Lalonde's announcement sent a shiver through the Alberta oilpatch. A tax on profits was just business. A federal tax on raw production, unheard of for any other natural resource, was specific to the province's main industry, and Albertans took it personally. Nevertheless, an analysis of the NEP that a city hall economist wrote for Klein a week after Lalonde's announcement was far from gloomy. "In a world economy that is energy short and desirous of a stable supply of energy, Alberta's long-term prosperity in the next decade is almost assured," the economist boldly prophesied. "The city can expect a one- or two-year reduction in the rate of growth in demand for services followed by a catch-up period in the mid-1980s."

To Klein's thinking, this wasn't necessarily bad news. Urban expansion was outpacing the city's ability to pave the commuter routes from the expanding suburbs into downtown. The rapid transit system was incomplete and the city's water treatment facilities were strained to the limit. A demolition derby of development was ripping apart Calgary's architectural heritage in a race to build the biggest, tallest or best office complex in town. Amidst all this, an economic breather sounded mighty welcome in early 1981.

In the end, the less-than-gloomy forecast proved to be wildly optimistic. Hundreds of drillbits were yanked out of the western sedimentary basin and a flotilla of oil rigs rolled south to the friendlier, lower-tax environment of the United States. However, the spillover from the NEP, and the world oil price freefall of 1983, took time to poison Calgary's economic well. In the interlude, Klein was having a wonderful time. The election victory had more than doubled his reporter's salary to $55,000. The air in his wood-panelled suite was filled with a blue haze from his chain-smoking staff of political neophytes. He'd hired his hard-drinking buddy Wilf Morgan to be his planning assistant; he'd lured attractive Lori MacDonald from her post as an aldermanic office receptionist to be his personal secretary; he'd hired crusty, east-end activist Rose Kalababba to monitor social issues; and he'd placed campaign aide Bruce Planche in the job of special assistant, all of them operating under the watchful eye of the former waiter turned executive assistant Rod Love.

One of Klein's first acts as mayor was to deliver on a promise to roll out the complete list of campaign donors, along with the precise degree of their generosity. For Klein's campaign, a modest $29,878 had been collected, a fraction of the warchest assembled by incumbent Ross Alger, and most of it didn't roll in until after Klein's victory. The average donation was $221, mostly from friends, family and small businessmen. Calgary's corporate elite was noticeably under-represented on his disclosure list, and Klein rebuffed several attempts from major developers who wanted to cover their bases by slipping some post-election cash into his hands. Klein figured that he had enough. If the job was done right, he surmised, campaign money would never again be a problem.

The priority Klein has placed on communications throughout his political career was evident from the minute he stepped forward to seek office in 1980. His only campaign pledge was to communicate the business of the city to the voter, and that meant working hard on media relations. Love recalls his first meeting with Klein in the mayor's office. "He looked me in the eye and said, 'Never fuck the media. We need them and they need us and we're going to treat them like pros.' My ability to survive and stay in the good books with my boss was figuring out how the media worked, what motivated them and what they wanted. I knew if I got called in and had to tell him, 'The media are ganging up on you,' I was finished."

Less than two months later, Love began the tradition of long, boozy get-togethers with the mayor and the media at Christmas. Later in Klein's mayoralty, he introduced select reporters to DPOs, or "Document Perusal Opportunities," during which journalists were left alone in an office with sensitive documents—usually relating to the 1988 Winter Olympic Games—while Love briefly attended to some other civic business. Klein's goal was to get to know journalists on a personal basis so they would find it more difficult to stab him in the back. Love puts it more colorfully: "If they hear an outrageous rumor about someone they don't know, they put it in the Probably Box. But when they hear an outrageous rumor about somebody they've gotten to know on a social basis, they put it in You're Fucking Crazy Box."

When Love and his boss weren't busy communicating with the media or leaking information, they were living according to Klein's office motto: work hard, play hard. Love's hubris and sense of humor caused trouble at first. He brazenly stormed into the city commissioner's offices a few months after the 1980 election and declared that he was on a surprise inspection. The incident resulted in a curt warning from the city brass to the mayor that it had better not happen again—and it never did. In his second year, Love invited members of the media to help him blow the mayoralty office surplus on a one-night Christmas party in San Francisco. Some scribes were quickly on the phone, calling in for official comment, before they discovered the joke. The second page of Love's media release regretfully announced that an Air Canada strike had forced the event to be replaced by a couple of beers at a local Chinese restaurant. In 1982, when Klein was injured in a car accident while the deputy mayor was out of town, reporters asked Love who was in charge at city hall. In what he calls his "Al Haig moment," Love declared himself in control. The rest of city council was incredulous.

Klein had a wide mischievous streak too. After Friday afternoon drinks one day, he asked bureaucrats to study the feasibility of "Squirrel Crossing" signs along the heavily treed streets of Mount Royal, where squashed rodents were becoming a regular eyesore. A month later, reports and sign designs were submitted to the appalled mayor's office for approval. "You can't joke," chief commissioner George Cornish scolded him after the prank was revealed. "You're the mayor now."

Despite the pranks, Klein fearlessly challenged the civic power grid. Top bureaucrat Denis Cole, the city's chief commissioner, was in the habit of sitting at the head of the commissioners' boardroom table. During the dinner break from his first city council meeting, Klein ordered Cole out of the chair, a sign that Klein was nobody's pushover and wasn't afraid to make enemies. Cole opted for early retirement a few months later and was replaced by Cornish, a lifelong civic bureaucrat who had started as an engineer in the streetlight department, and worked his way to the top.

After negotiating a peace treaty with the commissioners, and specifically with their new chief, Klein acted quickly on his pledge to be a hands-off mayor. Klein claimed the right to craft and sell the civic vision. The bureaucracy would manage the rest and he wouldn't interfere. Every day, a red folder would appear on his desk from Cornish with items requiring Klein's urgent attention. It was rarely thick, usually a couple of memos and a few executive summaries, but even that was too much information most of the time, says Love. "He'd call me in and say, 'I don't give a shit about this,' so from then on fifteen pages would come in and he'd get a one-page summary." Knowing intricate details was a waste of Klein's valuable memory space; he had total recall for the the names of the city's movers and shakers, and has a legendary memory for the names of average voters he's met, no matter how intoxicated the encounter.

Klein relished the excitement his mayoralty generated in Calgary, and rarely turned down an invitation to attend an event, however insignificant it seemed. If it came with a morning-after headache, as most of them did, well, that was the price of being a social communicator. "The mayor is running late" became a standard refrain in his office.

While to outside eyes it all seemed a very novel and novice operation, Klein was savvy enough to begin preparing for his re-election immediately after his upset victory. Rod Sykes warned Klein that several rivals were already hatching plans to challenge him three years down the road. He pointed to a couple of aldermen who had the potential to become dangerous if the mayor didn't learn the ropes quickly. "Brian Lee has already started mapping out his strategy for 1983 and it involves going after Ralph as soon as the honeymoon is over," Love warned office staff in a memo just a month after the 1980 election. "It is vitally important therefore that we do everything we can to learn about budget debates, agendas, committees, etc. because this is where we are weak."

Brian Lee was an energetic, second-term boy wonder whose career path was on a fast track for the mayor's office until Klein's victory derailed his path to coronation. It had been widely expected that Ross Alger would leave after two terms, and that during those terms Lee would receive preferential treatment as the heir apparent. With Klein's arrival in the big chair, Lee began scheming against the rookie mayor. "He disliked me and was conniving all the time because he wanted my job. He would do anything behind my back to undermine what I was trying to do," Klein says, his voice still dripping with disdain twenty years later. "I had it out with him in the office and I said, 'If that's the way you want to play ball, nobody knows better than me how to play it.'"

Making Brian Lee look bad became a political passion for the mayor's staff. A thick folder on Lee's every utterance and council stand was created, and Klein took great pains to personally undermine any of Lee's initiatives. "That's politics, and if someone is after your ass, then you've got to be defensive," he says with a grin. Revenge was sweet when Lee finally abandoned his quest for the mayoralty and, in 1982, successfully ran as a Conservative for the Alberta Legislature. Even then, Klein was relentless in his vengeance. He quietly moved his then-formidable campaign machine behind a Liberal named Sheldon Chumir to bring about Lee's defeat in 1986, after just one term in provincial politics. Ironically, the Tory seat that Klein helped swing remained Calgary's lone Liberal seat for fifteen years until a determined effort by the Conservatives under Premier Ralph Klein claimed it back in 2001.

The new mayor, however, had much more powerful enemies than Lee to worry about in his first term. Chief among them were the Olympic bid committee that sought to bring the 1988 Winter Games to Calgary and its head, Calgary businessman Frank King. In November 1980, less than a month after the election, King led a delegation to Europe in order to bolster Calgary's candidacy. When Klein arrived with the delegation at the hotel, he found the suite reserved for the bid city's mayor was already occupied by the rival he had defeated months earlier. Ross Alger was graceful enough to vacate the suite.

Klein also took an instant dislike to International Olympic Committee vice-president Dick Pound. "Dick and I never saw eye to eye," Klein says of his relationship with the Canadian IOC member. At a reception for IOC president Juan Antonio Samaranch in his Westmount home in Montreal, Pound objected to involving the IOC president in a ceremony with Blackfoot dancers. Not sure how the aloof Spanish aristocrat would respond to being decorated with war paint amid native singing and dancing at an upcoming reception in Montreal, Pound vetoed Klein's suggestion and was supported by local and provincial officials. Klein refused to back down, however, and insisted his Blackfoot friends be allowed to make Samaranch an honorary chief. No dancers, no mayor, Klein warned, and refused to attend unless his demand was accommodated. A few weeks later, the dancers found themselves in a five-star Montreal hotel performing an elaborate swearing-in ceremony.

To the Olympic officials' surprise, Samaranch was captivated by the ceremony and thrilled to receive a chief's headdress. As a result, throughout Olympic preparations in the years that followed, Klein continued to add pieces of Blackfoot attire to Samaranch's wardrobe, so that, shortly before the Games began, he had a complete Blackfoot chief's outfit. The morning after the controversial ceremony, when Rod Love went to pay the city's bill at the hotel, he discovered that the Blackfoot dancers had rewarded themselves by dining out lavishly on gourmet food and washing it down with fine wine. Love smiled to himself and diverted the tab to the Alberta government's hospitality suite.

During the next nine months, Klein became increasingly worried Calgarians would not be strongly represented in the Games' planning. He grew nervous about the private-club aura emanating from members of the Calgary Olympic organizing committee (OCO'88), who were the ones working with senior levels of government. On the eve of the historic vote that would give the Games to Calgary, Klein decided to play a trump card. He wrote a confidential letter to OCO'88 chairman Frank King, hinting that he would withhold the host city's required signature if he wasn't guaranteed membership on the powerful executive board. "The Games are awarded to a city," he wrote, "and the reason they are awarded to the city is because the mayor is perceived as being the closest to the people and the Games are always meant to be the games of the people." In response, Klein received reluctant and unspecified assurances of city representation on the committee. But King, in his 1991 self-published autobiography It's How You Play the Game, says the mayor backed down after King threatened to quit as chair and hand back the organizing effort to city hall. Whichever version is correct, it was the beginning of an acrimonious personal relationship. Klein fancied himself the public's ombudsman, who was gatecrashing an exclusive club that didn't have the power to throw him out. For the journalist in him, it was a dream assignment.

On September 30, 1981, Calgary beat out hopefuls in Cortina, Italy, and Falun, Sweden, to host the 1988 Winter Olympic Games. As the victory was announced, key players in the front row, who would soon splinter into bitter Olympic committee and government factions, leapt to their feet in a single spontaneous yelp of joy. Klein suddenly had a new political objective in his sights: to win three consecutive terms as mayor in order to see the Games through to their completion.

Ralph Klein was shrewd enough to know that an anti-establishment candidate could win the mayor's seat once, but that repeat victories would require support from the business community. Within his first year, he shed his rebel colors and began courting the oilpatch establishment. "I would like to thank the people here who voted for me in the recent civic election," the blue-jeans mayor, who some called Calvin, told a Chamber of Commerce luncheon in 1981. "I understand they're all working in the kitchen." The audience laughed with him, not at him. It was a beginning of sorts.

In the sixteen months or so between the NEP's introduction and the energy industry's full reverse thrust, developers still ruled Klein's kingdom. In 1981, the two-billion-dollar building bonanza in Calgary accounted for two-thirds of all commercial construction in Canada, and a quarter of all housing in the country. The opposition Klein had shown to developers for "tearing down the city's heritage" did little to slow the swing of the wrecking ball under his mayoralty. Throughout 1981 and into 1982, planning commission meetings featured line-ups of intricate models for massive new commercial and retail developments, some fronted by longtime Klein buddies such as Al Bell, Bruce Green, Brian Scott and future senator Ron Ghitter.

In his first year, there were problems on multiple fronts that tested his rookie skills as a consensus builder. A light rail transit line (the acronym LRT was quickly redefined "Little Ralphie's Train") into the northwest quadrant of Calgary was a key part of the city's Olympic preparations, but it was being stymied by furious inner-city opposition to the route. Klein lowered the political temperature in inner city communities by creating a task force allowing them vent their concerns while he pushed another leg of the transit system unopposed into the northeast. It was the first example of a strategy he uses to this day: listen first, act later. The final northwest transit decision wasn't derailed from the original plan, but Klein could legitimately claim to have consulted the community. Klein also needed to negotiate city support for a performing arts center. The Saddledome had to be completed for the newly arrived Calgary Flames, and there was a $3.5-billion capital works program on the drawing boards.

During his first term, Klein also revealed himself as a softie when it came to letting go of staff who, for any number of reasons, were not working out. The fact is, Klein is chronically incapable of firing people, no matter how deserving they may be of a forced exit. He puts displays of personal loyalty above all other considerations in assessing the value of his staff. When Klein's personal secretary failed to meet Rod Love's demanding performance specifications, the new mayor couldn't bear to deliver the pink slip himself. On the morning she was axed, Klein fled the office and circled city hall in his car for an hour, phoning Love for updates every few minutes, even as the terms of her departure and severance were being negotiated. Klein couldn't bring himself to fire first-term mayoralty assistant Bruce Planche, either, and left that task to Love. Being loath to deal with staff dismissals to the point of incapacitation would prove to be a major leadership weakness throughout Klein's various political incarnations. Staff with proven loyalties would be retained far longer than required, and MLAs who supported his leadership from the start were ultimately elevated to cabinet portfolios that, in some cases, greatly exceeded their abilities.

It wasn't all trials by political fire for the rookie mayor. When an opening appeared on his schedule, Klein would disguise himself and head down to the Bow River to throw a fishing line into its fast-flowing waters. If reporters became curious about the mayor's whereabouts, his staff were told to invent an important meeting. If an important meeting was actually called, they were told to fabricate a personal emergency. If a personal emergency actually surfaced, he'd be the fisherman hiding under a floppy hat and sunglasses near the Bow River weir. But, his staff was warned, it damn well better be a major emergency.

Back at city hall, Klein defied the skeptics who predicted he'd be found sleeping off a bender in a ditch after late-night city council meetings. As the mayor of the fastest-growing city in Canada, he'd given up the mayoral car and was often seen chatting up commuters on the downtown transit line or walking the streets by himself. Periodically he even showed up with VIPs at the St. Louis tavern for a greasy meal of chicken and chips.

This unpretentious style was beginning to endear him to Calgarians, who were increasingly comfortable with his instincts and his communications style. He did have some early hiccups, though. When striking plumbers confronted Klein at city hall, the mayor snatched a picket sign, threw it to the ground and ordered them to "get the fuck off" his property. When a television reporter stuck a microphone in his face, Klein snarled into the camera, "And fuck you too." After events like these, a quick apology was cobbled together and issued and, while he rarely disappointed the media with a "no comment" brush-off, such outbursts were becoming the exception. His mayoral reign was maturing, and becoming increasingly uneventful. Then came the evening of January 6, 1982.

Someone let Ralph Klein out at night without a leash.

Six

Bums and Creeps

L ATE ON THE MORNING of January 7, 1982, Ralph Klein was on his way to work when the car phone rang. Rod Love was on the line. "So how'd it go last night?" Love asked, trying to sound casual.

"Great," gushed Klein, "a good crowd, no problems." There was a pause.

"Uh, you didn't mention anything about 'bums' or 'creeps' by any chance, did you?" Love asked, silently hoping for a denial. There was another pause.

"Well, I might have mentioned something along those lines," Klein answered.

"We've got to talk," Love said. "How far away are you?"

Klein hung up the phone ten minutes from city hall and in his mind began replaying the speech he gave the previous night to the Calgary Newcomers' Club. He tried to figure out what had his top aide so rattled. On Love's desk sat the early edition of the *Calgary Herald*. "Stay Away, Bums Told," screamed the headline. In the accompanying story, Klein describes himself as "a bit of a redneck," and was quoted attacking "a lot of creeps" who arrive in the boomtown without jobs or skills. He had promised to use "cowboy techniques" if they resorted to crime for a living. "Even if we have to put them all in jail, on top of one another, we have to do it." He didn't specifically use the word "eastern," but he did note, erroneously, that there were more Quebecers in Calgary jails than native Indians, a fact he later admitted had been told to him by a cop well into his cups at a Christmas party.

On top of Love's newspaper, a mountain of phone messages was taking shape. They had started arriving from St. John's, Newfoundland, and worked their way westward by time zone until the barrage had reached Victoria. Newspapers, radio talk shows, national television networks— they all wanted the redneck mayor on the line right away to talk about eastern creeps and bums.

The actual notes handed to the mayor when he left his office to address the Calgary Newcomers' Club were in point-form: welcome the new arrivals to the city, salute their expertise and thank them for their contribution to Calgary's culture. So innocuous was the text and so benign the crowd that, for the first time on a nocturnal outing, Klein was not accompanied by an assistant. "We do not need unskilled, uneducated people with little or no money to tide them over, no guaranteed employment, no guaranteed accommodation," the notes read. "These are the people who add to our welfare rolls, unemployment lines and crime rate. Calgary has little to offer the unskilled and they turn to welfare, etc." Neither the word "creep" nor "bum" appears in the notes.

"I had a marvellous time that evening," Klein recalls. "It was all women whose husbands had transferred to Calgary. The economic signs were starting to turn a little sour and the police chief had said something about transients robbing our banks. I was asked where they came from and I said, 'Look at the geography and you'll find eighty per cent of the population lies east of here, so it's proportional to geography.' I got a standing ovation." What Klein failed to notice was *Calgary Herald* writer Bob Bettson in the back row, frantically taking notes and dashing out the door before the applause died down.

The story hit Canada like a bomb. It cracked the line-up of newscasts from coast to coast. Newspapers, including the *New York Times*, were blanketed with analysis and commentary split along Canada's east-west axis, and subdivided further between skilled and unskilled workers. Calls jammed every telephone line into Klein's office and, a few days later, letters arrived from across the country. Snowbirds even wrote in from the sunshine states. "I would remind you that we in Halifax are on the verge of economic prosperity and I suggest that our natural resources will still be plentiful when yours are gone. I would then suggest you keep your bowlegged, dumb calf-ropers in Calgary where they belong," fumed Ken Robinson of Halifax, in a typical response.

The mayors of Sault Ste. Marie, Quebec City, Montreal, North York and Toronto weighed in with their concerns and comments. "The true test of how great a city is can be measured by the degree of compassion it shows its less fortunate citizens," sniffed Toronto's mayor, Art Eggleton. Klein has "made an ass of himself," observed Newfoundland MP John Crosbie. "Klein is a bum and, with less than two years as mayor, he's unskilled and wouldn't make it even as an alderman or school trustee here," fumed North York's Mel Lastman. Lastman wrote to Klein suggesting, "[You] issue a one-sentence apology for your remarks and all of us can get back to dealing with more important affairs." Klein responded curtly: "I totally concur with your suggestion that all of us get back to dealing with more important affairs."

The controversy, however, wouldn't go away. Klein issued a clarification and sent it to every newspaper east of Manitoba, but he was only mildly repentant. "If I sound like a bit of a redneck on this issue, it is because I am not going to be too upset if the police do a little ass-kicking to give the bad actors in this town the message that they're not welcome here."

Finally, Rod Love delivered what, to this day, he claims was the best advice he ever gave his boss—confront the hostile forces directly by taking a tour of eastern Canada. "I went and proposed it to him and he thought about it for three seconds and said, 'Go for it'," Love says. "I was taking media calls for seventeen hours a day and I'd explain it to them and they'd say, 'You should come down here and tell that story 'cause it's interesting.' So that's when I went to Ralph and said, 'Look, we've beat this thing to a draw, but it's not going away. We've got to look 'em in the eye'." A trip to the Golden Horseshoe, Montreal and Quebec City was cobbled together, complete with appearances on all the major talk shows and "Front Page Challenge." Klein held his ground in every speech, and condemnation by eastern Canadians gave way to their grudging admiration for a personable mayor who delivered the straight goods in the face of furious opposition.

Love calls it Klein's defining moment. "Until January 1982, we had been kind of mediocre. We didn't do what people thought we would do, which was party, fall in gutters and basically not be able to run the city and be laughingstocks. On the other hand, we sure as hell didn't set the city on fire. The jury was out until bums and creeps. That changed the character of the mayor to the people. He would say what was on his mind, which people found refreshing. He tapped into a mood that was in the city and what was happening in the city, which showed he had his finger on the pulse. And when he didn't back down, and in fact went down to Central Canada and said, 'Shut up and listen to me,' it made people say, 'He's a fighter'."

Even the Calgary establishment rode to Klein's rescue. "I thought your speech was bang on. You are doing a fine job and said it how it is. Keep it up," gushed Tom Walsh, lead partner of the prominent law firm of Walsh Young. From Toronto, the icon of Canadian broadcasting, Gordon Sinclair, fired off a note of encouragement to the rookie mayor. "Don't let 'em get you, Ralph. What's it all going to matter three years from now? As a blurter, you should read some of my mail, if I'd ever saved it."

Klein did save his letters from the incident. They numbered at least two hundred, and were later submitted to the University of Calgary for analysis as an intergovernmental snapshot of the bums and creeps moment. "It does suggest that he is taken seriously as a participant in Canada's public life," concluded the analysis, which found two-thirds of the letters gave Klein the thumbs-up for being dynamic, competent and honest. "The east–west issue really exists and is deeply rooted. People are afraid of the unemployed, but see hope in youth. Ralph Klein came out of the barrel in high regard here in the west and, although he fared less well in eastern eyes, he survived."

As the bums and creeps backlash dissipated during the summer of 1982, Ralph Klein found himself in the disquieting predicament of no longer leading a city of rampant urban growth where construction cranes dominated the skyline. The impact of the NEP took more than a year to wear down the city's energy-supported foundations, but there was little doubt about Calgary's eventual downward spiral as world oil prices collapsed. When they did collapse, panic seized the city.

Executive floors were emptied by waves of pink slips, creating the eerie spectre of "see-through" office towers. Entire city blocks became economic disaster areas of abandoned office projects, where only concrete pillars sprouting sprigs of rusty iron pile remained, tombstones of a boom gone bust seemingly overnight. A few buildings stood unfinished for the entire decade.

Geologists, who only a year earlier were earning lucrative royalties on their gushing oil and gas well discoveries, suddenly struggled to secure taxi licenses or restaurant jobs. Even the restaurant business was wilting. Pardon My Garden, the trendy restaurant where Rod Love had worked as head waiter in 1980, closed its doors. Housing foreclosure statistics competed with oil company woes for space on the business pages. Dollar dealers—who would buy a house from desperate-to-sell homeowners for a dollar down, assume the mortgage and pocket rent until the banks foreclosed on the property—roamed the upper-class subdivisions looking for firesale acquisitions. A new bumper sticker appeared in Calgary, reflecting the sober mood on the street: "Please Lord, give me another boom and I promise I won't piss it away."

The surging population problem that made Klein notorious as the bums-and-creeps mayor had reversed, and now easterners gleefully laughed as Calgarians took to the highways for economically buoyant Ontario. Alberta's license plate became the bright yellow signature of job-seeking refugees trying to escape the crash of The New West. Every so often, an Albertan would get caught robbing a Toronto bank—and Klein's office would be flooded with letters blaming those creepy Calgary bums for bringing crime to Ontario. Instead of placing newspaper ads to deter eastern job seekers with warnings about a tight housing market, Klein now had to travel east to sell Calgary as a bargain-basement investment opportunity. The billion-dollar Olympic construction effort, which one builder described in 1981 as just another flower in a huge construction bouquet, had suddenly became the only rose in the vase. The city was moving aggressively to deal with its new realities; a horrified Klein cut 421 staff to eliminate an $18-million deficit that would have been illegal under provincial law.

But in his gut, Klein had every native-born Calgarian's understanding about the circle of Alberta life. As a resource-based economy, good times lead to bad times followed by a resurrection, strong revival and, ultimately, another collapse. While Klein often describes the mid-1980s as an Alberta "depression" rivaling the Dirty Thirties, his optimism during those dark times bubbled eternal. "The wheat is still growing in the fields, the oil is still in the ground, the cattle are still getting fat in their pens," he said when confronted by economic pessimism.

Any normal politician would have considered the looming 1983 civic election with alarm, knowing that harsh times create unhappy voters. Not Klein. He had the average Calgarian on his side and he had reinvented himself to satisfy the developers, architects and oilmen who had so enthusiastically aligned themselves with his political rival in 1980. The anti-establishment mayor was no more. "In our efforts to make the commercial core a more human place, we must be careful to avoid the trap of putting sunlight ahead of commerce. Sunlight does not turn the wheels in our factories," he told a business crowd in late 1982. It was music to their ears. As Klein noted, incredulously, in a memo he wrote to his assistants in early 1983: "I was speaking to Stan Waters [a war hero and businessman who became Canada's first elected senator in 1989] the other day and he mentioned that if I was running for mayor again, I would probably receive a lot more support from the Chamber of Commerce this time. I asked him if he would try to keep that to himself. I have a reputation to protect, you know."

Reputation aside, Klein was publicly joining forces with the Chamber of Commerce on a project that became one of his personal legacies at city hall, a concept he took with him to the premier's chair a decade later. The plan was to no longer be content with waiting for good times to return, but to aggressively pursue a revival that would be less dependent on oil and gas.

In 1983, business leader Arthur Smith, who would go on to become one of Klein's top political operatives and advisers, forged an alliance with Klein to create, as a joint project with the Chamber of Commerce, an economic development authority. It would be the first of its kind in municipal government. The traditional method of marketing a city—advertising its charms, distributing some glossy, general information pamphlets and hoping for a relocation nibble—was abandoned. The Calgary economic development authority went outreach. It commissioned a study to determine the types of industry that would thrive in the Calgary area, crunched data on markets, raw material and workforce skills and targeted specific companies for official arm-twisting. The authority pitched presidents or chief executive officers of firms it deemed ripe for relocation in their home offices—a pitch that was hard to ignore with the now-famous bums-and-creeps mayor sitting across the boardroom table. The authority went on to become a long-term success, but more significantly for Klein, voters saw it as a tangible sign that their mayor was more than a colorful personality with good people skills. By working with business to conceive an original idea of lasting importance to the city's economy, Klein had a serious concept to call his own. He was more than a hung-over ribbon-cutter now.

When friends gathered in the Trade Winds Hotel to plot Klein's 1983 re-election bid, their strategic plan reflected an unmistakable cockiness, despite the economic gloom. "We must avoid a Madison Avenue kind of campaign," they concluded. In their planning guide, they adopted the election theme of "Re-elect Ralph Klein. A Good Mayor" because "it makes no grandiose claims about spectacular accomplishment, it would be almost impossible for opponents to easily use against us and it probably sums up what most Calgarians would say about the mayor." Noting their candidate's 1980 observation that the mayoralty "is won with hard work and an honest commitment to people, not with money," the campaign team fretted about the possibility of too much financial support pouring in. "Any perception we are throwing money around would be contrary and fatal to the success of the mayor as just Ralph," they wrote. The $30,000 collected in 1980 could be justifiably inflated to a maximum of $47,000 without optical discomfort, they decided. Six months later, despite a $1,000 cap on individual contributions, the team added up the numbers and found themselves swamped by donations which totalled $83,500.

Klein chose not to campaign on having engineered a turnaround in the economy, nor on promises of a miracle cure after his re-election. He opted, instead, to project the happy face of civic confidence against the criticisms of his chief rival, a crusty city council member named Sue Higgins, who relished being called The Alderbroad. She attacked Klein's loose hand on the purse strings, warned of the city's increasing debt load and vowed to restore fiscal integrity to city hall. "Let the other candidates dwell on the doom and the gloom and the negative," Klein sniffed. When she failed to get even a quarter of his vote, Higgins called the election attempt her worst political blunder and conceded defeat to the Ralphinator. "I was astounded by Klein's complete non-interest in accounting at city hall and I thought you simply couldn't operate like that," she recalled later. "But guess what? I found out that you can operate just fine and the public thinks it's great."

In October of 1983, Klein was re-elected mayor, taking 88 of every 100 votes cast and setting a new record for electoral popularity in Calgary.

Seven

The Olympic Mayor

W HEN RALPH KLEIN TALKS ABOUT elections, he can barely remember the 1983 vote. His clearest recollection, and his most precious memory, is still his 1980 underdog triumph. The second victory, however, marked Klein's vindication as a serious politician, and it ensured that his calls to any executive suite in the city would immediately be returned. In a way, it had been too easy.

He began to feel helpless as the economy tanked with little prospect of a short-term recovery. His drinking increased dramatically, and he missed entire days of work without notifying the office. His weight soared under the strain of a heavy social schedule. He felt restless. He needed a new challenge, and soon after his re-election he thought he'd found one on the menu of his favorite Chinese restaurant. Chatting up the restaurant owners, Klein discovered that all Chinatown duck meat was imported from outside the province. He found a farm that seemed perfect for raising ducks to supply the restaurants with fresh meat, and even hatched a scheme to raise eels as a side-dish operation. Klein and an investment partner drew up a serious offer to purchase the farm before Klein, worried about a conflict of interest, abandoned the idea. Still in pursuit of political alternatives, he decided to open a pub featuring an all-Alberta menu of beef and beer products. Rod Love scoured the city to find a location for what was to be called Ralph's Alberta Bar. Nothing came of the idea, and as time went on, Klein lost interest, but he kept the incorporation certificate alive until a few weeks after his decision to run for premier in 1991.

As Klein cast about for new directions, the Liberals, under the leadership of John Turner, invited him to run in the 1984 federal election. Rod Love was dead set against the idea. "The deep and abiding mistrust of the Liberals in Alberta may be too much for even someone of your status to overcome," Love warned in a memo. Even a riding victory could be a defeat if the wrong party won the election, he cautioned. A Conservative majority would keep Klein on the opposition benches for a full term. A Liberal majority could also be a disaster. "Once in power, the Liberals have historically shown a tendency to shun new blood," Love noted, an observation that has held true to this day. Besides, he pointed out, if a minority government results for either party, they would soon dump their leader, regroup and "write a blank cheque to someone with your credentials. Hold your cards," he urged.

Klein did give the Liberals' offer serious consideration, but his enthusiasm for civic office was revived in February 1984, when he attended the Winter Games in Sarajevo. He watched the festivities, and at the closing ceremonies, he received the Olympic flag that would fly over Calgary in anticipation of February 13, 1988. Klein got a taste of what was coming to his hometown in four years. It was going to be quite the party, and he didn't want to miss it. As he roamed the hospitality suites and first-class venues that would be destroyed in ethnic warfare a decade later, Klein found himself completely at ease with the Olympic aristocracy. He was able to hold his own in conversation with the corporate sponsor executives, the upper class and even the royalty.

As he left an Olympic VIP dinner party during the Games, Klein spotted a dignified man leaning against a pillar outside, having a smoke: "Oh, there you are," Klein said, mistaking the man for his personal driver. "Yes, here I am," nodded King Harald of Norway. "Bring the car around, will you?" the mayor ordered. When his mortified protocol officer corrected his mistake, Klein shrugged, introduced himself, and asked his majesty if he could bum a cigarette. The King grinned and flipped open a pack. Four years later, during the Winter Games in Calgary, King Harald attended a reception at city hall and, spotting Klein at the back of the room during his speech, winked and asked if the mayor would be so kind as to fetch his car. The crowd, baffled by the remark, turned to see Klein and Love doubled over in laughter.

Ralph Klein's delight at being an Olympic city mayor was tempered by hostile relations with the Calgary Olympic organizing committee, of which he was an executive member. Klein detected that Calgarians were feeling disenfranchised as cost overruns on the Saddledome mounted and as a sudden firings and controversial hirings emerged from the OCO'88's secretive deliberations. Klein finally demanded that the meetings be opened to the public. "While OCO'88 is in no way legally compelled to hold open meetings, it is undoubtedly a moral prerequisite to gaining the public trust and confidence, without which the Games will not succeed," Klein fumed in November 1984. The IOC's Dick Pound shot back. "There has not, to my recollection, ever been a suggestion made that full involvement by the public at large is a sensible management tool. My experience, in fact, suggests the opposite." Under pressure from city hall, the committee reluctantly agreed to open its meetings in part, but left most of the important matters to the in-camera portion of their deliberations.

Relations continued to deteriorate when Klein discovered the Olympic logo police. He was utterly appalled by their zealous pursuit of any unauthorized use of the Olympic rings and other symbols, a right reserved for those with the bucks to buy into sponsorship programs. He blew a gasket when a cease-and-desist order was served on Marty's Cafe, a '60s-style coffeehouse in Calgary that featured a placemat billing the tiny cafe as "your unofficial Olympic headquarters" in a corner. As owner Marty Hoffman's legal bills piled up, Klein saw it as a defining act of bad public relations by an increasingly insular organizing committee. "I have absolutely no hesitation in saying that the time has come to spend less time trying to impress the International Olympic Committee and more time trying to impress people like Marty Hoffman, the average Calgarian," Klein told the Chamber of Commerce in September 1985. "If we set out to sell the Olympic movement to Calgarians the way we once sold Calgary to the Olympic movement, then a spirit of volunteerism would sweep the city unlike anything ever seen before. That is our challenge."

In addition to its unpopular crackdown on Olympic words and symbols, OCO'88 was being savaged in the media for dedicating huge blocks of tickets to sponsors and IOC family members. Consulting contracts were handed out under suspicious circumstances and controversial local builder Bill Pratt was hired as president of the organizing committee, despite Klein's objections. Press coverage deteriorated to the point where Juan Antonio Samaranch pressed Klein to establish a communications commission in order to stem the flow of bad blood between the IOC and the media.

In the press relations department, of course, Klein had no equal. He tormented the organizing committee by inviting reporters into his office every month for "Document Perusal Opportunities," where accordion file folders stuffed with confidential board agendas and background information were left open for their perusal. Klein and Love believed the Olympics were public business, and that the public had a right to know the internal machinations of the organizing committee.

Headline after headline about secret OCO'88 business rolled off the presses, fleshed out by entire pages of confidential material. The tarnished Olympic brass were apoplectic and tried madly to trace the leak back to their prime suspect at city hall—Ralph Klein. They assigned each committee member a number that was stamped in the page corners of every document he or she received. This, they hoped, would allow them to trace any leaked documents back to their source. On my DPOs, Klein simply ordered me to fold the numbers back. When Klein heard that OCO'88 was altering budget information slightly in each director's agenda, so they could identify any leak by the specific figure reported, Klein asked me to round out any numbers I used in news reports. Finally, utterly beside themselves, a special hairline mark, designed to appear as a photocopying flaw, was inserted in the mayor's paperwork. Tiring of all the games by this point, Rod Love simply marched across the hall once a month to switch his agenda with Chief Commissioner George Cornish, a fellow OCO'88 member and a strict, by-the-rules mandarin who was the board's least-likely news source. Frank King and company finally gave up the pursuit of their nemesis. "It was a bit like a dog chasing a bus," King wrote in his book. "What were we going to do about it once we caught it?"

Problems with the Games aside, the Calgary economy continued to worsen through 1984 and 1985. When Klein appeared before the Royal Commission on the Economic Union and Development Prospects for Canada to present his ideas for pulling Calgary out of its recessionary slump, there was definitely a New Deal mentality evident in his thinking. He told the commission he was inspired by former Calgary mayor Andrew Davison, who pushed hard to build the Glenmore Dam during the Depression, far ahead of actual need for its electricity-generating capacity. "The city again is going to be in a boom situation where we're going to be faced with the same problem we faced in 1980 and 1981 when there was phenomenal growth," Klein explained. "We should be putting in that infrastructure now when we can get it at forty per cent less and put people to work." Herbert Hoover couldn't have said it any better.

Despite his "Ralph the Knife" image, as premier Klein never worried much about debt as mayor. He inherited $650 million of debt in 1980, and he left city hall $1.6 billion in debt nine years later. Civic debt was like a mortgage on a house, he said—and Calgary was one hell of a house. Klein struggled to put the situation into terms the average voter could understand. The debt worked out to one Bloody Caesar per day per taxpayer for just six years, he said. The public shrugged an understanding shrug and went back to looking for work.

In late 1986, amid the persistent and continuing economic downturn, Klein faced his final civic election. He'd had a few hiccups along the way, as he tried unsuccessfully to secure a world-class casino, supervised a botched bid for a Miss Universe pageant and struggled to save the Stampeders from folding. Still, the only opponents who surfaced on the ballot were publicity seekers who groped ineffectually for ways to attack the bulletproof Klein. The incumbent barely broke a sweat in the 1986 race. Running under the election theme of "Ralph," he claimed ninety-three of every hundred votes cast. Nobody in Calgary's history had recorded a victory anything like it. If he wanted, Klein could have been mayor for life.

"Now what?" Klein asked himself the question as he settled in for a third term. His main reason for running had been to be mayor of the host city for the 1988 Winter Olympic Games. That was still fifteen months away. Klein felt his passion for the job flicker as he contemplated the problems he faced: the on-going controversies of the Olympic organizing committee, the Sunday shopping debate, opposition to the creation of Nose Hill park, telephone wars with the Edmonton-owned phone company that supplied Calgary's residential service and the escalating cost of power generating plants.

Barely two months after Klein's incredible victory, Rod Love decided that he wanted a new challenge once the Games were successfully over. He was probably contemplating picking up the political science degree he never completed or entering law school. First, though, he needed to find out if Klein was looking for a change too. Taking keyboard in hand, Love pounded out a twelve-page analysis of the options available to a mayor without party loyalties or ideological limitation. Klein could, Love wrote, stay at city hall forever—"a Drapeau-like regime could clearly be established and last as long as Klein continued to avoid scandal." Federally, Love didn't like the looks of Klein's chances with Brian Mulroney. He could explore provincial politics. While the Liberals were the "ascendant party," their 1986 electoral performance did not inspire Love's confidence. For either opposition party to win would require "such an alignment of circumstances that, should it occur, we should look to the East for a bright star and three wise men on camels." Another Tory victory was the only logical conclusion.

The Conservative party would undoubtedly welcome Klein as a candidate, and dangle a junior cabinet portfolio in front of him during his first term as bait, Love concluded. Once in cabinet, Klein could ready himself for "a leadership coup-d'etat" and attempt to take over the party. Again, Love advised his boss to wait and let time run its course. No federal or provincial elections were expected for two years. Besides, he pointed out, the fundamental question was still a simple one: "What does Ralph Klein want to do?"

Klein was restless enough in 1986 to talk informally to both the Tories and the Grits in Alberta on the condition nothing would happen until after the Olympics. He green-lighted exploratory work on a draft-Klein movement for the Alberta Liberal leadership convention set for the fall of 1987 or early 1988. Jon Havelock, a city council member who ran as a provincial candidate for Klein in 1993 and became the province's justice minister in 1997, quietly distributed "Ralph 88?" buttons and lobbied behind the scenes to stall the Liberal leadership convention until after the Games. Word of his attempt didn't take long to reach media ears, and a front-page *Calgary Herald* scoop on Klein's organizational plans rolled off the presses in September 1987.

It was a day that could have changed the course of Alberta's political history. If Klein had bothered to check with one pivotal person, he would almost certainly have contested the leadership, likely won it and gone on to an uncertain fate as leader of the Alberta Liberals, an office ultimately claimed by rival Edmonton mayor Laurence Decore. As it was, Colleen Klein learned of her husband's career-altering plans when she retrieved her morning newspaper from the doorstep. Her furious reaction spooked everyone in Klein's orbit, and her veto was non-negotiable. Klein did not seek the Liberal leadership, and from then on, the first person he consulted about any change in political direction was his wife.

Rod Love, worried that Klein's disinclination to pursue higher office was permanent, started toying with the idea of striking out on his own. He sketched out ideas for starting his own newspaper and for opening a bar, before he officially notified his boss that the 1988 Winter Olympics would be his grand political finale. After the February Games, he planned to retire from politics and either finish his degree or enter law school.

Love, however, would not be able to resist taking a stab at becoming what until then he'd only created—a politician. Later in 1988, after the Calgary Olympics ended, he ran for the federal Conservative nomination in Calgary Southeast against established Tory Lee Richardson and a taxi company president named Harry Sohal. (Sohal later became an MLA in Klein's first government.) Despite having strong campaign support from his business contacts, Klein's strong endorsement at the meeting and a showstopper of a speech, Love's bid fizzled into a dismal third-place finish. Law school beckoned.

With his higher political ambitions on ice and the Winter Olympics only a few months away, Klein set out to drum up interest in the Games. He toured Alberta, the rest of Canada and the northwestern United States. Throughout 1987, the Games were still in choppy waters. The ticketing manager was convicted. He had set up a private company to sell prime event tickets to Americans, charged them the Canadian price in U.S. dollars and skimmed off the exchange for himself. While communications had improved, OCO'88 still found itself in damage control mode over the hefty prime ticket allocations to sponsors, IOC members and their families. The seating capacity of the venues was expanded and the IOC's demands for seats were scaled back slightly. Klein, doing his part, had kept the public in the loop through a fountain of leaks from inside the organizing committee. Despite all the controversy, nothing could prevent the city from meeting its destiny. The enthusiasm was unstoppable. More than twenty-two thousand Calgarians stepped forward to volunteer, and thus forced the organizing committee to cut off applications a year before the event.

By opening day on February 13, 1988, the personnel storms had passed, the rivalries were forgotten and an adoring public was enraptured by the main event. "The Olympics should be the best party any of us has ever been to," Klein told Calgarians. "If it's not, we may have missed the point." They didn't need to be told twice. As chinook after chinook rolled over the Rockies and strained the capacity of snowmaking guns and outdoor ice refrigeration plants, the athletes competed—then partied. The visitors watched—then partied. As for Calgarians, well, any city that hosts an annual Stampede where residents spend ten days alternating between intoxication and hangover already knows how to party.

The Calgary Tower, flames flickering on its spire, became the world's tallest Olympic torch and presided over a city on a celebratory binge. Every night the downtown Olympic Plaza, a public square preserved from development five years earlier after fierce lobbying by Klein, became the city's focal point. Thousands gathered there for medal presentation ceremonies under fireworks and laser light shows that flickered across the surrounding skyscrapers.

The Calgary Olympics were the first profitable Winter Olympics ever. While Canada didn't strike gold on the medal podium, a hero reflective of the public mood did come along to steal Calgary's heart—a hapless British ski jumper with thick glasses. Eddie the Eagle soared to last place with a euphoric grin on his face. The Games, as the official documentary aptly named them, were indeed Sixteen Days of Glory, and a refreshing tonic for an economically ravaged city ready to rebound.

The magic—and there was magic in the air—was the civic spirit that infected the city. Ten thousand volunteers had competed fiercely for the chance to shiver on duty in traffic control, ticket-taking or scooping the poop behind chuckwagon horses in the lavish opening ceremonies. They were all given free seats for the closing ceremonies in lieu of payment, another Games first. On the final day, as the Wave repeatedly circled a stadium lit up by fifty thousand Olympic candles, the crowd gave the departing athletes and IOC aristocrats a rousing send-off. The closing ceremonies featured the high-kicking twang of k.d. lang, along with hometown favorite Ian Tyson, singing the unofficial anthem of the host province, "Alberta Bound."

The crowd reserved their loudest cheers for the guy who brought the Games down from its modern Mount Olympus in Lausanne, Switzerland (the permanent home of the IOC), and gave the people of Calgary a sports celebration to call their own. When a pudgy guy wearing a parka, a white Stetson hat and an ear-to-ear grin entered McMahon Stadium, the decibels hit a new high. As Klein exuberantly waved the same Olympic flag he'd collected in Sarajevo four years earlier, now being handed off to Nagano, Japan, he enjoyed what he still calls the highlight of his political life. He knew, for a mere mayor, it would never get better than this.

Seated in her Edmonton home with her son watching the event, the education minister for the Alberta Conservatives was getting a gander at Ralph Klein for the first time. Her name was Nancy Betkowski, and her young son giggled at the sight of the beaming mayor. Little did she know that man would soon enter her life—and destroy her political ambition.

Eight

Lost in the Shuffle

ITTING IN DOWNTOWN Calgary's Cannery Row bar with Rod Love for drinks in November, 1988, a revelation arrived around pint number six. Columns topics were in short supply, so I mentioned my plan to write a list of predictions for the year ahead, an old chestnut for columnists desperately seeking easy filler to span the holidays. "I've got one for you," Love grinned, "Ralph Klein won't be mayor this time next year."

Rod Love has a mischievous streak as long as the ski out at Sunshine, but he never played games concerning his boss's future and he appeared lubricated enough to be telling the truth. Still, it seemed so utterly incomprehensible. Calgary had a mayor for life who had just presided over the biggest event in the city's eighty-three-year history. He was leaving? Now? Impossible. But a desperate columnist will print desperate guesses. "Prediction #1," I wrote a few days later, "Ralph Klein will not seek re-election in next fall's municipal election." My editors said I was nuts.

A week earlier, Ralph Klein had attended a free trade rally on the eve of Prime Minister Brian Mulroney's second majority election victory. There he shared the stage with Alberta premier Don Getty. The two men had become friends a couple of years earlier, after a friend of Getty's had visited Klein to urge the third-term mayor to ratchet down the political rhetoric and work with the rookie Conservative premier. "He's facing some difficulties with the downturn in the economy," David Mitchell told Klein in 1987. "The premier's trying to fulfil the expectations of Albertans, but you're complaining all the time. It would be helpful if you would give him some support and try to get along." Klein gave it a try and was surprised to find a couple of private calls to Getty landed him ten million dollars toward the preservation of Nose Hill Park, as well as money for the northeast LRT line and cash for a new bridge across the Bow River, conditional upon it being named after the transportation minister, Henry Kroeger. "It's amazing if you start to say nice things about government and get to know the individuals involved how their attitude can change," Klein marvels. "It was a lesson well learned."

When Getty asked Klein for a chat after the rally, he figured it was about routine intergovernmental business and, given the sour economic times, it was probably bad news about the upcoming year's municipal grant. The pair adjourned to the premier's hotel suite with their top aides, but Getty asked for a few minutes alone with the mayor. The pitch came straight out of left field: Would Klein run for the provincial Conservatives in the next election?

Klein's private notes from the meeting indicate that the premier saw him as a marquee recruit. Getty, who had been recruited by Peter Lougheed and first elected in 1967, sensed that the Conservative dynasty was on a slide and had detected an alarming weakness in the party's southern Alberta stronghold. He offered just about everything to get Klein aboard the foundering ship. Klein said he would require a cabinet portfolio, an office in Calgary's McDougall Centre and employment for some of his staff. He was shocked when the premier agreed to all his terms and, without being asked, offered to confer upon Klein the title of "southern Alberta lieutenant" in his government. The notes also show that Getty promised "matters can be arranged" to secure Klein an acclamation for the party's nomination in any vacant or opposition riding. Getty suggested either the downtown Calgary riding held by Liberal Sheldon Chumir, or a northeast seat held by New Democrat Bob Hawkesworth, a former alderman. Klein flatly refused to consider running against either, citing old friendships. Getty shrugged, not quite sure what to make of a politician whose personal relationships transcended partisan battle lines, but said he'd leave it with Klein and gave the mayor a Christmas deadline for his decision.

Rushing out of the hotel suite after the forty-minute meeting, a pale Klein didn't speak a word until he was safely back in his city hall office. There he gave a wide-eyed Love the lowdown. "They want me to run and I can pick my post," Klein gasped. This was a no-brainer for the ambitious executive assistant, who saw a fresh opportunity unfolding before his eyes. He immediately urged Klein to leave city politics. Klein was initially receptive to the idea, but as the rum and Cokes flowed, Klein turned nostalgic and said he was happy being mayor. His office was just a twenty-minute drive from home, and everyone from broompushers to presidents called him "Ralph." Love pushed harder, pointing out that Klein's best years at city hall were over. He warned that the mayor's life was "going to become endless refinement of cat control bylaws." It was time to tackle new challenges with long-term potential, Love argued. As the pair staggered to their feet for the cab ride home, Love's persuasion had carried the day. With only Colleen Klein's approval standing in the way, Klein's mind was made up. He was leaving city hall.

Rod Love went to work that night to map out Ralph Klein's future. He wasn't thinking about winning Klein a mere MLA seat; he wanted to land Klein the entire province. He compiled an instant analysis of the various portfolios searching for the *de facto* deputy premier spot which "could lead to other advances on the political scene." He scratched treasurer, agriculture, solicitor general, advanced education and energy off his shopping list due to his candidate's lack of expertise in those areas. "No one gets out of this alive," he warned of Social Services. Career Development was "for people on the way to nowhere," he wrote. Public Works was merely "booorrrrring." Health and Education were "worth considering," but they all paled before the numerous advantages of Economic Development, or the dark horse portfolio of Environment.

When Klein phoned a week later to accept Getty's offer, he insisted that the premier and his wife, Margaret, meet with Colleen and him before the deal was done. It was a condition that impressed Getty. One of Getty's few legacies in Alberta is Family Day, a popular paid holiday on the third Monday of every February. It was proclaimed in 1989 and is often attributed to Getty's desire to reaffirm his family-values reputation after his son was charged with drug trafficking.

After some small talk at the meeting, Klein said he'd decided to accept Getty's offer to run for the Conservatives, and conversation turned to the delicate task of the appropriate reward in cabinet. Getty suggested tourism, a junior portfolio that was quickly abolished once Klein became premier. Klein balked, and countered with either economic development or environment. In those high-spending, big-deficit days, economic development operated a network of opulent foreign trade offices in London, Hong Kong, Tokyo, Seoul, Los Angeles and Beijing, staffed by dozens of patronage appointments. It was indeed a plum worth picking. Environment, by contrast, was a snakepit of a ministry and Getty knew it. Environmental concerns were rising to the top of the polls in the late 1980s, and the premier was facing constant grief from natives and environmental activists who were protesting the Oldman River Dam and the dioxin-discharging pulp mills he had blueprinted for northern Alberta.

Getty seized on the idea of a proven public relations expert with close aboriginal ties taking over the contentious portfolio, and he granted environment to Klein immediately. Klein's notes show that when he raised concerns about how his promised role as southern lieutenant would be received by a caucus full of loyal, lifelong Conservatives, Getty brushed his worries aside. He insisted Klein was better suited to the role in a family-focused government than more obvious contenders like Energy Minister Rick Orman or Treasurer Dick Johnston, both of whom were suffering marital breakdowns at the time. As they wound up their negotiations over a glass of Christmas cheer, Getty told Klein to be ready for an election in March. Klein breathed a sigh of relief, and said he welcomed the fifteen months to get his civic affairs in order and prepare the difficult transition to party politics. No, Getty said, you've only got three months. A public inquiry into the collapse of the Principal Group, a trust company with heavy investments in Alberta's wobbly real estate, which would eventually cost the province $100 million in compensation to investors, was due out in April. Getty had been tipped off that the government would suffer a lot of heat and wanted a snap election before the report's release, even though it was less than three years into his mandate. Klein didn't like the sound of desperation in his new master's voice.

Three weeks later, on a wintry January day, after a frenzy of speculation kickstarted by my desperate predictions, Ralph Klein walked up to a microphone in front of the Downtown Rotary Club at the Palliser Hotel and announced his decision to depart from the mayoralty after eight years of ever-rising popularity. He fought back tears during his speech and had to be taken into a side room to regain his composure before he faced the media. Yes, he confirmed, party politics would be difficult because he was a "loose cannon." He promptly proved that by sharing with reporters Getty's promise to put him in cabinet and appoint him the government's "southern lieutenant." He had inadvertently slit his own throat.

The words exploded in the capital, mushrooming into outrage from veteran MLAs. This mere mayor, a former Liberal, who had not earned his party stripes and did not understand his place in the pecking order, would, they vowed, pay for his insolence.

Ralph Klein decided to seek the party banner in Calgary-Elbow, a constituency that included some of the city's most prestigious and pricey real estate, where incumbent MLA David Russell was retiring. The Tories went to the polls in such a rush, that they didn't have time to redraw the electoral boundaries, as they had planned. When the writ was dropped for the March 20 vote, Klein was left a non-resident of his political turf. Getty did not deliver the promised party acclamation either, forcing Klein to face off against a loyal Conservative named Fran Drummond. "Friends, neighbors and former Liberals," she said, taking a dig at Klein as she opened her nomination pitch to four hundred shivering Calgarians in a high school gym.

Although he swept through the Tory nomination process with ease, Klein was alarmed to learn he would face off against a popular and charismatic Liberal lawyer named Gib Clark. This, he fretted to his campaign team, was not going to be another mayoralty cakewalk—this was going to be a bumpy ride. So it was somewhat prophetic that the launch of Klein's election campaign caused a string of rush-hour accidents on a busy street corner. A dusting of snow had fallen and, standing at an icy intersection waving to commuters, Klein claimed three collisions inside of fifteen minutes. Wide-eyed, he kept gasping, "Oh my God," as distracted motorists banged into each other while television crews, pinching themselves in disbelief, caught it all on video.

On the doorsteps of his upscale riding, voters were not rolling a warm welcome mat out for the former mayor either. He was not of their ilk, and Don Getty wasn't helping matters. The premier was blanketing rural constituencies with pricey promises that he would pave every secondary road and that every homeowner would be guaranteed a private phone line. This was all part of a desperate ploy to shore up farm support and neutralize an effective campaign led by Laurence Decore, the new Liberal leader. A respected lawyer and former Edmonton mayor, Decore gleefully used the parade of promises against his rival. He ridiculed the Conservatives' attempt to bribe voters with their own money by waving his wallet in the air and by dumping a wheelbarrow full of Tory election promises on the ground in camera-friendly stunts. The attacks were resonating with voters, and polls indicated Tory support was soft, shifting and on the verge of collapse.

Klein was feeling a hostility on the doorsteps unlike anything he'd ever felt before as a candidate. This was the first election in which he was not the star attraction and here the campaign was careening off the rails. Late in the campaign, over drinks after a hard day of slogging, Klein confided to his inner circle that he thought he might have run himself out of a job by defecting to provincial politics. On March 20, 1989, however, the unbeatable mayor of Calgary squeaked to victory by an 819-vote margin over Clark. The bad news for Klein: the wave of support for the Liberal and New Democrat opposition had snared his political godfather in its undertow. Don Getty went down to defeat in his own Edmonton riding.

While Getty searched for a safe rural place to force a by-election for his return to the legislature, Ralph Klein's punishment for publicly disclosing the sweetheart terms of his recruitment was meted out. He was given environment ministry, period. No top committee job, no southern lieutenant duties, no office in the government's Calgary headquarters. He was pegged second last in the pecking order of cabinet precedence, and shoehorned into a basement office as far removed as physically possible from the premier's third-floor suites.

On his first trip to the legislature as a cabinet minister, he finally located his modest office only to find secretaries from a previous minister packing up their belongings and crying at the loss of their jobs. He listened to their stories and hired most of them on the spot. A few minutes later, he was approached in the legislature rotunda by another unemployed assistant named Sheryl Burns. She lobbied hard for a job and Klein hired the woman, who would become his powerful executive assistant as premier, without so much as a resume or a reference. He had the good fortune to inherit a deputy minister named Vance MacNichol, a wily veteran of legislature politics. He was hailed by some as the best deputy in the building. Rod Love, meanwhile, had balked at the $45,000 salary paid to most executive assistants, so Klein negotiated a back-door deal by which Love was hired by the department of the environment for $65,000 and then seconded to the minister's office. The staff he kept with him as premier were all in place.

When Klein walked into his first cabinet meeting, Health Minister Nancy Betkowski loudly drew the room's attention to Klein's tardiness and sarcastically offered a quick review of the meeting—a scenario she does not recall now. But Klein was embarrased. "It wasn't a very accepting party," he insists. "I sensed that when I first went to the Conservative party candidate's school and the first cabinet meeting. It was very cliquish."

Within the environment department, Klein was seen as a breath of fresh air. He shocked staff by personally touring administrative offices and by calling managers directly. He quickly regretted leaving the job of Calgary's mayor for a junior cabinet position, though. "I went from a nice office at city hall to the basement suite. They called it the foundation floor, but it was still the bloody basement."

In his first term in provincial politics, Klein was appalled to find that

Getty's government was run by a handful of ministers who sat on the all-powerful agenda and priorities committee, where decisions were arbitrarily made without explanation. "I felt badly as a cabinet minister, so I can't imagine how the private members felt. You find out you're a very, very little fish. This had nothing to do with Don Getty. If you got in to see him, he was very accommodating and understanding, but the way his staff worked and senior cabinet ministers worked and exercised their control over things was something to behold."

Klein found even routine ministerial matters were derailed at the agenda and priorities committee, where Betkowski sat in skeptical judgment of the former card-carrying Liberal mayor from Calgary. "Cabinet had, to some degree, decision-making powers, but usually to rubber stamp the decisions coming out of agenda and priorities," Klein remembers. "The committees of cabinet didn't have any power to make recommendations. They were set up to hear submissions, take a decision from cabinet and see if it could be refined, but the decision was already made."

Soon after his first cabinet meeting, Klein came into contact with a minister who would hand him his first term's greatest personnel crisis. Barrhead MLA Ken Kowalski had gained a reputation in the 1980s as the minister of plaque-unveilings and ribbon-cuttings. He roamed the province to open government projects in his various capacities as public works or transportation minister, or as what was quietly building into the jackpot for a politician who loved the glory of handouts, lotteries minister. By 1989, he was one of the most infamous, colorful and controversial members of Don Getty's cabinet and he threw his considerable weight around on rookie MLAs, including Klein.

The new environment minister first met Kowalski in the legislature's fifth-floor Carillon Room, during a meeting of new Tory caucus members his first week on the job. Klein was handed a polished leather briefcase and told that it was a perk reserved for the ruling Conservatives and that he should flaunt it. "He said we should remember we are the government," Klein recalls. "He said, 'I want to see you carry all your papers in these briefcases so we can demonstrate to the Opposition that we are the government'." It was a heavy-handed, petty, in-your-face style of politics, and

Ralph Klein found it extremely distasteful. Klein's distaste was exacerbated when he later received an invitation to one of Kowalski's legendary golf tournaments in his Barrhead constituency that came with an ominous warning: "It would be in your best interests to attend." It was a not-so-subtle reminder that Kowalski had the power to delay or expedite lottery grants for community projects in an MLA's constituency. Somehow Klein failed to pick up the clues that Kowalski might not be suited to working in a government under his own leadership. Then again, he was not thinking very much about future political ambitions.

For a mayor supported by ninety per cent of civic voters and accustomed to having his views treated as commands, Klein found the many tangled links in the provincial chain of command a heavy burden to bear. He shunned the intense scripting other ministers submitted to and, as a result, didn't always find himself on the same page as the bureaucracy. In the middle of a press conference on the Diashowa pulp mill, Klein stopped in mid-sentence when he realized the news release did not gel with his views. He called a time-out, retreated into his office and rewrote the release on the fly, and emerged, red-faced, a half hour later to correct the mistake.

Klein often found himself out in front of the government on policy as well. He was the first minister to support compensation for investors in the failed Principal Group, when he insisted the government's regulatory failure came with a monetary obligation to investors. "Any reasonably instructed jury would conclude the government had a responsibility," he said, to sharp looks from his fellow ministers.

Socially, he had few friends in provincial politics. He occasionally retreated to legislature-area bars with municipal affairs minister Stephen West and soft-spoken Peter Elzinga, then the economic development minister and almost a decade later Klein's chief of staff. Mostly, he hung out with Rod Love. The pair shared a modest apartment, and through many a late night they commiserated into their cups about the cumbersome, counterproductive power structure that kept even cabinet ministers in the dark. "Those were the loneliest eighteen months of my life," Love recalls of the interminable stretches away from his wife Charlene and their young family in Calgary. His enhanced salary raised a buzz among the other executive assistants, and Love found himself shunned by his legislature colleagues. "I could not get anybody to give us the time of day. Some ministers would scream at us for being late," Love says. "The whip, Stockwell Day, on more than one occasion had to get Ralph out of bed. We couldn't do anything right by them."

"I asked myself if it was a mistake every week," adds Klein. "I hated getting into that God-damned car and driving up the highway. I found Edmonton to be a very unfriendly place at that time." The pair's solution was to find any reasonable excuse to leave the city on government business, which they did with frequent gusto. No party event was too small for Klein to attend as a speaker, no concern too insignificant to rate a personal visit by the minister.

With the environment rated the top concern in public opinion polling, in 1989 Klein ordered an ambitious revamp of the province's environmental legislation. He rolled nine loosely linked bills into one omnibus piece of updated regulation that created new environmental assessment guidelines, tradable emission permits, recycling incentives and stiffer fines for pollution infractions. It wasn't sexy, but it was his. Klein was determined to sell the bill differently than the top-down method perfected under Don Getty's dome. He put into motion an unprecedented, two-year consultation blitz and mailed draft copies of the Environmental Protection Enhancement Act out to all interested parties for more discussion and further amendment. In other areas, he streamlined the Natural Resources Conservation Board, launched an ambitious recycling push and attacked the problem of used tire stockpiling by imposing a tire tax and using the revenue to encourage recycling alternatives.

He had a pragmatic streak when it came to environmental concerns. Faced with growing unrest over the storage and disposal of PCBs, Klein insisted the dangers were overrated, and mused that he'd probably washed his hands in the chemical as a kid. He offered to ride across the country on a barrel of the stuff, provided he could "get a bit of room service" along the way. When natives complained that their fishing stocks were compromised by the discharge from pulp mills, Klein's advice was simple and sarcastic: "Just don't put your fishing line in below the outflow of a pulp mill." He supported water metering before it was politically fashionable. He also showed a new understanding of partisan play, when he defended a plan to raise the swampy water levels of Buffalo Lake, where Don Getty had built a house, even though his own departmental experts questioned the move.

Even as the government rushed to promote and subsidize an economic development agenda, Klein kept trying to sell the environment to his colleagues as a sleeper issue that bore the potential to cause the government problems if it was ignored. Klein had stepped into the environment portfolio just as the Alberta Pacific pulp mill decision was heating up. This $1.3-billion project had triggered howls of protest from environmentalists and from northern natives worried their fish would be contaminated. The boreal forests of northern Alberta had been an untapped resource, until a use was found for aspen, among other things, in the manufacture of chopsticks for the hot Asian export market. In the fall of 1989, Klein ordered public hearings across the province. Then he faced off against his federal counterpart, environment minister Lucien Bouchard, who, in the process, gave him an early taste of the future Quebec premier's separatist sentiments.

When Klein met with Bouchard on November 10, 1989, to discuss federal standards for pulp mill discharge, he was forced instead to listen to a forty-minute rant on Quebec's sorry lot in Confederation. Klein was privately unsympathetic to the hard-luck story, recalling his visit to the Canadian embassy in Paris during his travels prior to the Winter Olympics. Bouchard, then an ambassador, staged one of the most lavish dinners Klein had ever seen, complete with the finest wines served by white-gloved servants. He figured Bouchard didn't seem to mind being a federalist when Canada coughed up a first-class meal ticket.

While Klein had concerns with the rush to build northern pulp mills, he could only delay their inevitable construction and hope to extract concessions on pollution controls. The northern forests were the only economic bright spot for a province reeling under a low-priced oil glut, so cancelling the megaprojects was out of the question. At the Al-Pac go-ahead announcement, Klein faced a furious protest. One activist stormed the podium to give the line-up of ministers and Al-Pac officials a middle-fingered salute. When he got to Klein, the testy environment minister flipped the bird back. At that precise moment, local photographer Mike Griffin clicked his shutter, guaranteeing a front-page picture. Years later, when Klein was premier, a friend of the Conservative party purchased the negatives of the print for a couple of thousand dollars to keep the picture out of circulation.

Throughout Klein's ministerial reign he continued to have trouble with Nancy Betkowski. Whenever their portfolios touched, sparks flew. The greatest friction occurred when his department pushed for the disposal of contaminated soil from old industrial sites. As health minister, Betkowski controlled the landfills where tainted earth would have to be dumped. The two fought repeatedly until a fed-up Klein inked a ministerial order to have the contaminated soil scraped off and landfilled without her approval. The order triggered a jurisdictional brouhaha that required Don Getty's personal intervention, which went in Klein's favor. Again, it's a confrontation Betkowski denies happened. The only contact with Klein she recalls was a note he passed her, asking for a favor for his brother on a health care matter.

It took a while, but during his years at the legislature Klein was slowly making converts among the Tory backbenchers. His willingness to show up for the most obscure MLA's fundraisers made him a rarity among Getty cabinet ministers, who usually considered such mundane tasks demeaning. When his omnibus environment bill was finally ready for debate in 1991, Klein earned begrudging respect. He spent long nights in the legislature and in committees, where he sifted through amendments while the rest of the front bench sat empty. When the bill passed to scant fanfare, Klein was astounded to find that Getty's deputy minister planned to turn the legislation over to the justice department to administer. It was too much for his oft-bruised ego to handle. He stormed into Getty's office and threatened to quit if the bill's implementation didn't stay with his department. Getty wondered what the big deal was all about and said Klein could keep the responsibility.

Klein's feisty reaction reflected the frustration he felt at his waning profile within a government that was itself on a slow, but steady, downward spiral in public approval. Mounting losses in doomed economic diversification projects had tainted the government as fiscally imprudent. Rampant patronage and public fury at MLAs who voted themselves a thirty per cent pay raise had given the government a further reputation for being morally corrupt. Even inside his own government, Getty was perceived as aloof and adrift, with a light work ethic and little heart for the job. Most damningly, on the day when the Principal Group failed, the premier was caught "working out of the office" on a private golf course.

At Calgary city hall, during the launch of Environment Week in 1991, Klein stood off to one side and watched school children swarm then-mayor Al Duerr for autographs. I chatted with Klein for a few moments while he eyed the adulation being heaped upon his successor. I pointed out the irony of the former mayor being a second-string player at the event. "I still think I made the right decision," Klein said, almost wistfully. Later that day, I had lunch with Rod Love and ribbed him about the latest round of patronage appointments coming out of Edmonton. He shrugged into his sizzling beef hot plate. "We've gone through the six stages in coming to grips with our own fate," he said, commenting on the inevitability of the Conservatives losing the next election. "We're at the seventh now—acceptance. And everybody wants a patronage job before it ends." He suggested that I might want to prepare a feature on the Tories' twenty years in power, as that anniversary was coming up in August. "Farewells are usually the best parties," he sighed. Indeed, Peter Lougheed joined Getty and most of his ministers at center stage for the celebration in Calgary in August 1991, where Nancy Betkowski basked in the glow of her designated heir-apparent status. Ironically, Ralph Klein was not invited.

Just eighteen months after becoming environment minister in 1989, Klein's files show he was quietly contemplating a run for the leadership. A discussion paper written by Rod Love outlined the steps the duo would have to climb before Klein could claim the job. The key was changing the party's Constitution to replace a leadership convention with a vote by the entire membership. The process of choosing riding delegates consolidated too much power in the party establishment, which still viewed Klein with suspicion. Klein would need a broad-based popularity contest to win.

Nine

The Premier

IN 1991, THE RALPH KLEIN TEAM saw a glimmer of hope. A Conservative policy convention approved a motion by Calgary lawyer John McCarthy to change the way the party would elect its next leader. Gone was the delegate selection system, replaced by a one-member, one-vote process. Nobody knew it at the time, but McCarthy was inadvertently a stalking horse for Klein. The premier's chair was now a prize that could be claimed by the grassroots. Klein could win it in the back alleys, the wheat fields and the burger joints of Alberta, without wooing constituency presidents or party directors. So the campaign quietly began. No longer was Klein's notorious travel bug driven just by a desire to escape the legislature, now he was test-driving his leadership bid. "On the road, that's where I found out that you could resolve a little problem like a water problem or the flow of a creek bed or a small recycling issue. It might only take $5,000, but people thought it was great and appreciated it. That's where I sensed I could bring the party back," Klein says.

All the constitutional changes in the world wouldn't help Klein's leadership aspirations without one key development, though—Don Getty had to quit. "It can be said that at no time in its nineteen-year history has this government ever been held in lower public esteem," a frustrated Love wrote in his analysis of Klein's prospects. The Tories had abandoned prudent budgeting to prop up economic development projects that were miserable failures, they had spewed patronage appointments all over the globe and they had cozied up to the unpopular federal Tories. The Alberta Conservatives were at their most vulnerable point in their history. "There is little hope the present leadership has the understanding, the desire or the ability to turn the government's fortunes around before the next election," Love lamented.

Actually, Getty's government had started to curtail spending by capping doctors' fees, and by cutting health care and education budgets. Those actions, however, triggered bitter strikes by nurses and teachers. Getty was doing the right thing, but the wrong way. He didn't spread the pain equally, which became Klein's *modus operandi* a year and a half later. While nurses and teachers walked the picket line to protest frozen wages, the province announced deep reductions in royalties for multinational oil companies and MLAs voted themselves a thirty per cent pay hike. Patronage was epidemic; Getty's neighbor, daughter-in-law and barber all landed government jobs.

During the last years of its mandate, in a desperate bid to stabilize Alberta's falling provincial economy, Getty's government built monuments to the folly of economic diversification. The doomed business ventures were propped up with tax subsidies and loan guarantees. A magnesium plant was located in High River, a full day by rail from the raw material. A pulp and paper mill, a heavy oil upgrader and a hazardous waste disposal facility were all built in the remote northwest forests. In an act of costly political desperation, Getty took over Peter Pocklington's ailing Gainer's meatpacking plant. By the fall of 1991, provincial budgets had become the fiscal equivalent of crossed fingers, with inflated revenue projections that were based on estimates viewed through rose-colored glasses. Klein had to swallow his pride and his tongue as he stood in the legislature in March 1991, to insist the government had "a fiscal plan in place and it's a plan that will lead to a balanced budget." It was a lie and he knew it. "The phony budgets being tabled by Dick Johnston were all bullshit," Klein recalled a decade later. "People were mad and the whole agenda was shifting. We were being told to quit spending, get out of the goofy businesses and stick to the basics, but it wasn't getting done."

The crown of the fiscal follies was NovAtel, a partnership between Nova Corp. and government-owned Alberta Government Telephones to produce cellular phones. By early 1992, Nova had bailed out of the partnership, leaving the province searching for a buyer. As the enterprise floundered amid ludicrous marketing and sales incentive schemes, it rang up a loss to taxpayers of a jaw-dropping $680 million. All told, the boondoggles from Getty's reign and the failed ventures he'd inherited from the Lougheed era would cost Alberta taxpayers $2.1 billion. The electorate was not amused.

News of the NovAtel loss was announced just as Rod Love was making a final bid for electoral acceptance. He campaigned as the provincial Conservative candidate in the Calgary-Buffalo by-election in July, 1992, where he hoped to fill the seat left vacant by the death of an almost mythical Liberal MLA named Sheldon Chumir. It was the safest Liberal seat in southern Alberta, but Love was undeterred. He dropped a record seventy thousand dollars on his bid, only to finish a very distant third, with his ego bruised but loyalty to his party affirmed.

The Getty government had hit rock bottom in December 1990, when it registered just twelve per cent in a poll against an imaginary provincial Reform party. Even after Reform vetoed establishing a provincial wing, Getty's numbers were far from reassuring. Just four months before the premier retired in the fall of 1992, the mighty Conservative dynasty struggled back to twenty-seven per cent in the polls. They were tied with the New Democrats and eighteen points behind a majority government-in-waiting, the Alberta Liberals under Laurence Decore. Still, Getty was showing no sign of accommodating Klein's, or anyone else's, leadership aspirations. Getty had been a key player among the premiers at the Charlottetown Accord negotiations, and he was basking in the glow of some rare positive media for his Captain Canada routine. He just didn't look like a guy preparing to step down.

Cabinet documents from the year before Klein took the helm as leader show the Getty government was paralyzed by a lack of focus, consensus and drive. The internal minutes from a Getty cabinet brainstorming session on government reform indicate that the ministers were unable to agree on almost any point, be it cutting the size of cabinet, implementing business plans, tightened spending or taking a harder deficit reduction line.

Midway through the summer of 1992, Love sat with the only boss he'd ever known, in the kitchen of his $123,000, two-bedroom suite in the Marquis Condominiums, a few blocks from the legislature. The wine flowed and the depressed duo's conversation turned bittersweet as they contemplated the demise of their political careers. "If you ever got hold of it, what would you do?" Love asked. Ralph Klein hauled out a napkin and started writing down his priorities—truth in budgeting, a deficit elimination plan that could be completed inside of a single term and more meaningful roles for MLAs. "Good ideas," shrugged Love, as he downed the rest of his glass, "too bad we'll never get to use them." He scooped up the napkin anyway as he headed off to bed.

On September 9, 1992, a routine caucus meeting was suddenly moved to Government House, an historic building perched atop the North Saskatchewan River valley, on the provincial museum grounds. The legislature buzzed with speculation of a cabinet shuffle in the offing. A nervous Love waited in his office, and dreaded the call that would send his minister into strange new territory. When the phone rang, Ted Carruthers, the party president, was on the line. "He's gone," Carruthers said. "Quit fifteen minutes ago."

Despite having been in the Constitutional fight of his life in the ramp-up to the Charlottetown Accord referendum, Don Getty had opted to retire after seven years as Alberta's premier. Love sagged in his seat for a minute. Then he reached into his desk drawer and hauled out a crumpled napkin with a red wine stain in the corner.

The next day, Love assembled a group of trusted friends and advisers to map out a campaign strategy. Among those present were Calgary lawyers Jack Donahue, Bruce Green and Brian Scott, along with political aide Gord Olsen and Klein's brother-in-law, Ted Hamilton. The group was divided to take on membership sales, communications and fundraising duties. It was decided the candidate would focus only on leadership, avoid personal attacks on other candidates and play a statesman-like role.

Notes in his campaign files underlined the need for Klein to distance himself from the Conservative establishment. He would, in the words of one worker, be the "anti-Lougheed." Right from the get-go, Klein's team correctly identified their main rival—Nancy Betkowski. As the meeting broke up, there was talk of when the Klein candidacy should be announced. That's when Donahue leaned over to Love and asked the obvious question: "We're sure he's running, right?" Love laughs at the memory. "It never occurred to anybody he might not be running so I did bullshit them and said, 'Yes, of course. He's running.' I didn't know for sure."

Unknown to Love, when Klein was driving back from the caucus meeting the day before, his car phone rang. On the line was the agriculture minister, Ernie Isley. "We're having a meeting at my place and we're discussing the leadership and we think the only person who can win this thing is you," Isley said. "You've got to be nuts," Klein retorted. Still he made his way over to the apartment and listened noncommitally as Isley and Don Sparrow, the tourism minister, twisted his arm to run. It must have been quite the act, considering that Klein had been lusting at the possibility for a full year.

A private Angus Reid poll taken for the Klein camp the week after Getty's announcement was encouraging. A Tory party under Klein or Nancy Betkowski would surge into a small lead over the Liberals. Among Conservative voters, Klein found himself far in front of Betkowski, with fifty-three per cent to her thirty-eight. Based on those numbers, Klein decided to leap into the fray first. He lined up seven MLAs behind him at the Crossroads Hotel, just off the Trans-Canada Highway in Calgary and confidently announced he was ready to become the next premier. "And folks," he said, "you'll still be able to call me Ralph." Then came the first of many curve balls. "Is Alberta ready for a drunk as a premier?" asked CBC Radio reporter Tom Spear during Klein's announcement. So much for a polite campaign, Klein thought.

Ultimately seven candidates entered the leadership race. Five of them were from the Getty cabinet, but only one posed a serious threat to Klein.

In Edmonton a week later, Nancy Betkowski, the health minister, added her name to the ballot. Only two MLAs—future Klein treasurer Jim Dinning and Calgary backbencher Bonnie Laing—backed her candidacy, but the entire backroom establishment was on her side, including Joe and Steve Lougheed, sons of the former premier, and former prime minister Joe Clark. If Klein was looking for a contrast between the suave Tory establishment and his rumpled, rebel image, he could not have found a starker comparison than with Betkowski.

Born in 1948 as Nancy Elliot, the daughter of a prominent Edmonton doctor, she was raised in material comfort and personal stability. Her family retained one of the few private cottages inside the boundary of Jasper National Park, on Lake Edith. She went to the best schools, studied languages at Laval University and was fluently bilingual. Physically fit, attractive and well-cultured, she enjoyed opera, played the piano at a Grade 9 conservatory level, sang soprano beautifully, skied, mountain-biked, hated smoking, drank very moderately, employed a nanny for her young children and quoted Mahatma Gandhi during her maiden speech in the legislature. She was everything Ralph Klein was not.

Betkowski entered the Lougheed government as a legislature aide, successfully sought election in 1986 and moved straight to the front bench as education minister. In 1988, she moved to health. She did not serve without her share of controversy. She presided over a bitter teachers' strike in 1988, which had to be settled by the labor minister, proposed a quarantine of AIDS victims suspected of dangerous behavior, slashed health insurance coverage for jaw splits, produced a report that eliminated some seniors' benefits at a poorly timed announcement during Seniors' Week and campaigned hard for a Yes vote in the Charlottetown Accord. She had few friends in the caucus, and the MLA she was least friendly with was Ralph Klein. "I always found her to be a very snobbish kind of individual. I always had this sense I wasn't good enough to be there," Klein says.

It was a grudge match waiting to happen. Despite the premier's job being up for grabs, however, the leadership campaign attracted far less interest than one might have expected, perhaps because many Albertans figured it was a race to become the loser in the next election. Klein decided that he needed to show most of his policy cards if he was going to win back disgruntled Conservatives who had watched their party become arrogant, fiscally imprudent and patronage prone. He also needed to distance himself from accusations of being "status quo" in his political thinking. He picked a high school in Leduc, the Edmonton bedroom community where Alberta oil first gushed from the ground in 1947, to deliver a speech that translated the scribbles on Rod Love's napkin into his future government's policies.

He outlined five principles to restore integrity to government—realistic revenue predictions, a four-year promise to eliminate the $2.2-billion deficit, a law prohibiting future deficits, a government retreat into core services and open arms to partnerships with the private sector. "When people ask me which departments should be cut, I think we need to approach the question from the other direction," he told the students, as they squirmed listlessly in their chairs. "We need to ask ourselves: which departments do we keep? It is not necessarily the government's obligation to provide services, but to see that they are provided." It was a speech that, years later, Klein's staff referred to as their blueprint. It sent a quiet signal for thousands of provincial government workers to dust off their resumes, yet it received scant news coverage.

Behind the scenes, Klein's camp was clearly outselling the competition in party memberships. His rivals were increasingly desperate as money supplies tightened. Doug Main, the culture minister, was watching his campaign debt mount, a debt he would ultimately have to pay himself. In a desperate move to disparage Klein, he lashed out during a public forum, warning that Albertans didn't want a "smoking, drinking, paving, glad-handing premier."

Energy Minister Rick Orman was particularly distraught. Bright, articulate and camera-friendly, the Calgary MLA had long been tagged as a serious contender for the leadership, but his campaign failed to catch fire among the grassroots. He had announced a dramatic reduction in royalties to stimulate oil exploration and an economic blueprint for the next decade, but a payoff for his leadership ambitions appeared minuscule.

As the campaign was nearing its end, Orman's camp apparently took a dangerous, desperate step. Two days before the first ballot, at a meet-the-candidate event in Calgary, a woman sporting an Orman campaign button strode to the audience microphone, and in front of fifteen hundred people, asked Klein if his wife, Colleen, had ever been admitted to a battered women's shelter. A flabbergasted Klein let loose a barrage against the "nameless faceless spineless gutless individuals" spreading the lie and called on his wife, seated in the audience, to verify that he'd never laid a finger on her.

Every reporter in the room knew what he was talking about, though. Many had been quietly offered documents purporting to show that Klein was a spousal abuser. A 1978 police report alleged Klein had been involved in a domestic dispute and was taken to the Calgary Detention Centre to sober up. There has never been evidence of anything more than a drunken spat, yet more than a decade later, the rumors persisted. Colleen's denial years later was just as adamant. "You think a Scotch lady like me would let a little fart like that push her around?" she fumed, jerking a thumb at the husband by her side. She found the whisper campaign particularly traumatizing because she was a battered wife in her first marriage.

Klein's suspicion that the Orman campaign was connected to the smear was very bitter, and the vitriolic ramifications were felt for years afterward. Jim Prentice, a lawyer and the former national vice-president of the Progressive Conservative Party of Canada, was Orman's campaign chair. Although there has never been the slightest hint he directed the question—in fact, Prentice says it was a "freelancer" operating without the campaign's knowledge—Love recalls an edict going out from Klein to blackball anyone in the Calgary lawyer's professional orbit from receiving a provincial Queen's Counsel designation. Klein froze Thompson MacDonald, his longtime friend and former television boss, out of his inner circle because of the mere suspicion he knew the question was going to be asked and failed to stop it, a charge he insists is utterly false.

Despite the lack of evidence and Klein's denials, the allegations bothered his campaign team. On a rare evening off, late in the campaign, Klein was summoned to the Calgary Petroleum Club without explanation. With Colleen on his arm, he walked into the room where the entire campaign team was waiting. The chattering stopped and a sea of very serious faces turned toward the Kleins. Stories of Klein's drinking were one thing, but the group wanted to hear it to their face: Had he ever abused his wife? The room fell into a hush as Klein studied their faces carefully. This was not a group to deceive in any way or to leave with the slightest doubt. In the 1960s, as a teenager who had been discharged from the air force, he was forced into a shotgun wedding with his first serious girlfriend. He told them it was a stormy relationship where, in the heat of argument, shoving, pushing, swearing and even punches were thrown by both partners. But, Klein swore, it was a sad and much regretted chapter that he left behind in his first marriage. He'd never laid a finger on Colleen and never would. The room breathed a sigh of relief. It wasn't a pretty picture, but it was an admission they could stomach. The campaign team went back to work on winning.

Freezing rain swept southern and central Alberta on November 28, 1992, as the first ballots were cast. All Don Getty's freshly paved secondary roads were transformed into skating rinks. Farmers knew better than to drive in those conditions, even if it was to cast a vote for Ralph Klein. After all, they said among themselves, he was a sure thing, with or without a few votes from the field. But Klein finished second, falling one vote behind Betkowski, while Orman finished a distant and doomed third. The Klein camp was stunned. They had expected to lead with a wide margin on the first ballot, if not to win outright. It was a rude awakening—and arguably the best thing that could've happened to the candidate's camp.

As the team gathered the next morning, a gloomy silence was broken by long-time MLA Peter Trynchy. "I have just three words to say to this group and then we're going back to work: Premier Nancy Betkowski." Every MLA in Klein's camp pledged to deliver seven hundred votes for Klein on the second ballot. Every one of them did it, too. Betkowski went to work planning her transition team, supremely confident of her momentum, as all but one of her five ousted rivals endorsed her candidacy. Meanwhile, Klein's team blitzed the phones.

Betkowski badly underestimated the threat posed by memberships sold during the week between the first and second ballots. Klein was selling; Betkowski was coasting. "The last week was very demoralizing," recalls Betkowski's campaign manager, Eric Young. "We were going to take the high road and win this thing. They were all very confident, but the response I was getting on the phones was flat. I didn't sense it was over, but I did sense we weren't getting any real growth." Undeterred by pleas from insiders like Young to push harder, officials in the Betkowski camp called on Klein to withdraw in the name of party unity and promised him a key role in the cabinet of Alberta's first woman premier.

Klein not only refused to concede, he challenged Betkowski to another debate. "Come on, Nancy," he baited her, "let's get it on." Betkowski was outraged by the comment, and insisted Klein apologize in writing to her husband. She says the premier-elect promised to do this, but failed to deliver. "She took it as a sexually suggestive thing," Young recalls. "Ralph just wanted a fight and I said to her, 'Go fight him, challenge him on loan guarantees,' but she wouldn't do it. Nancy thought she'd already won." In hindsight, Betkowski acknowledges the mistake. "I didn't do it because this was going to splinter the party if we got at it," she shrugs. "It's the one thing I regret."

Wisely, Klein concentrated his campaign efforts in the rural areas, where he had successfully painted Betkowski's plans to create regional health care authorities as a threat to rural hospitals. Ironically, those hospitals would be just as doomed by his cost-cutting agenda. Media jumped into Betkowski's camp, particularly the *Calgary Herald* where Sheila O'Brien, wife of then-publisher Kevin Peterson, was spearheading the membership sales drive—a fact the Klein camp used, with some justification, as proof of an editorial bias. "It's one of the easiest things I've done," O'Brien gushed in a front-page *Herald* story two days before the final vote. "They [women] can't sign up fast enough."

Alberta was given its twelfth premier on December 5, 1992. There were no ice storms in the forecast that day, and and Klein's camp had turned in thousands of new and motivated memberships. Confidence was extremely high in the Klein camp. So confident was MLA Ken Kowalski that, even before the polls opened that morning, he faxed congratulations to Klein on becoming the new premier. It was a low-risk prophecy.

That night at the Northlands Agricom, a rural landslide put the fifty-year-old Klein far in the lead from the first poll to the last. It was a sixty–forty split, with Klein getting 46,245 votes to Betkowski's 31,722. He had tripled his vote in rural Alberta and doubled it in Calgary, while Betkowski had merely doubled her count in Edmonton with little or no growth elsewhere. Despite the early and overwhelming victory by her opponent, Betkowski remained isolated in her backstage trailer with her husband and with her campaign manager, Susan Green. Loyal backer Jim Dinning knocked on the door and advised her to accept the loss graciously. She closed the door on his face. "She literally shut down and nobody could go near her," Young recalls.

More than an hour after the result was obvious, with media screaming for a concession and a Klein victory speech to meet their press deadlines, Betkowski emerged from her trailer, her eyes red from crying, to concede the race. She did not mention Klein by name or look him in the face. When the premier-elect kissed her on the cheek, she recoiled as though being bitten by a snake and left the stage without looking back.

An analysis of the leadership campaign by David Stewart of the University of Calgary's political science department showed that more than eighty per cent of the new members voted for Klein. All five of the rival candidates failed to deliver any votes with their endorsements of Betkowski. The supposed wave of women buying memberships for the second ballot voting "were overwhelmingly opposed to Betkowski. They were actually more supportive of Klein than were the new male voters," Stewart concluded.

Klein entered the Edmonton banquet hall as an MLA. He walked out the premier of a government sagging under poor public approval, with only fifteen months left before he must face the electorate. He was brimming with confidence, though, as his new security team ushered him out of the victory party and into the premier's freshly washed Crown Victoria, which idled by the curb. "This is for me?" Premier Ralph Klein asked. Indeed it was.

Ten

That Was Then, This Is Ralph

THE WEEK AFTER WINNING the Conservative leadership, Ralph Klein hit the jackpot in a Royal Alexandra Hospital Foundation draw and put the Edmonton hospital's $100,000 top prize in his personal piggy bank. His leadership appeared blessed with good fortune, but if we're going to decipher omens, we must also note that the premier won a high school raffle a year later. The top prize: a pet goat.

Klein's leadership also faced the Alberta Curse, a curse that unerringly reduced the third leader of Alberta's great political dynasties to a mere historical hiccup, and which ensured they survived only long enough to lead their party into an election defeat. The Liberals started it all with Charles Stewart (1917–1921), the United Farmers of Alberta sputtered after R.G. Reid (1934–1935) took their helm and the Social Credit ended its reign with Harry Strom (1968–1971). Following in the footsteps of Peter Lougheed and Don Getty, Klein was up to bat, facing the third out and taking a white-knuckled swing. He had only fifteen months left of the Conservatives' five-year mandate to revamp and reinvent the government so completely that voters would believe Don Getty had been a figment of their imagination. It was not going to be easy.

Behind the scenes, the senior bureaucracy wasn't going to sit idly by and wait for politicians to crash and burn the government. Two days before

Klein's leadership victory, Getty's powerful deputy minister, Barry Mellon, summoned all the deputy ministers to a meeting at Government House to nail down a transition plan. They distilled their thoughts into nine key points that became a blueprint for the Klein revolution in the year to come. They called for a smaller cabinet of just eighteen ministers, a formal accounting of finances within ninety days, a balanced budget within four years, privatization of numerous government services, partnerships with the private sector and a dramatic downsizing of the workforce. Mellon wrote a series of brutally frank assessments of the government's structure and fiscal position. "The government has lost much of its credibility in the way it has managed the province's finances since the 1989 election. The fact the other provincial governments are in the same or worse shape as Alberta is small consolation," he wrote in a confidential memo. "There is no effective on-going control over the balance between revenues and expenditures. The government must bring about some significant and meaningful changes to the way it does business or it will be virtually obliterated at the next election. People want change," he wrote, underlining the words. To shore up the effects of years of eroded credibility, the Conservatives needed to self-flagellate humbly and publicly. "When the government and its members start to practice, as well as preach, restraint, the general public will begin to consider program cuts and even higher taxes."

Mellon's farewell memo went one step beyond merely recommending a pay freeze or reduction. It red-flagged an issue that had already caught the critical eye of a twenty-four-year-old taxfighter namd Jason Kenney, who would have a future on Parliament Hill. "Nowhere in the solar system (except Ottawa) can private or public sector people collect pension benefits like those available to MLAs," Mellon warned. "It is essential that the government take the lead in rectifying this situation prior to the next election." They didn't. Instead, they kicked the ticking time bomb under the carpet and hoped nobody would notice.

Ralph Klein was sworn in as Alberta's twelfth premier on December 14, 1992. He decided to host a party to celebrate and placed newspaper ads inviting the public to attend his swearing in. It was a symbolic act of re-opening the legislature to the people. His bond with Alberta native leaders had followed Klein into provincial politics. In fact, in the critical week between ballots for the party leadership, the Blood First Nation had held a special prayer ceremony for Klein, on the condition he didn't drink alcohol for five days. After Klein's victory, they were first on the invitation list to join the celebration. At his swearing-in ceremony, the rotunda of the legislature echoed to the muffled chant of native singers and the shuffle of dancing feet as Klein grinned self-consciously in the thick of the ritual, wearing a pin-striped suit. When he got down to work, his first order of business, even more pressing than tackling the deficit, was to sponsor legislation returning sacred medicine bundles to First Nations.

The week leading up to the swearing-in was a tough one for a man who detested handing out pink slips, but change in the front benches was critical to his government's survival strategy. He called the ministers in for brief, face-to-face chats. In most cases, he requested their resignations, including those of five of his six leadership rivals. Some went quietly, notably the treasurer, Dick Johnston. "Fine, I'm fired," Johnston said minutes into his first meeting with the new premier. He walked out the door to announce his intention not to seek re-election. Others kicked up a fuss. John Gogo, the advanced education minister, entered the room intending to pitch the premier on his credentials, but ended up complaining to Klein about a speeding ticket he'd received in "your city," Calgary. Klein, who found it hard to believe a minister with his job on the line would dwell on such a petty issue, quietly stroked a line through Gogo's name on his list of cabinet contenders. Later, Klein recalls, Gogo was the most difficult phone call to make, as the senior citizen broke down over the phone, pleading for reconsideration.

Klein appointed Rod Love his new chief of staff on the day of his swearing-in, and Klein's private notes from the transition period reveal Love's fingerprints all over the creation of the new-look cabinet and committee structure. Love's desk became the operations center for the hiring of ministerial executive assistants, communications directors and research staff. He created and chaired a little-known super committee that met first thing on Monday mornings. It had just five members: the premier's deputy minister, representing the public service, the treasurer, a connected member of the caucus, the Conservative party's executive director and Love as the premier's stand-in. Its mandate was to detect and neutralize issues before they crested the horizon and were picked up on public radar. No agendas were set, no minutes kept, but many crises were averted before lunch on Mondays.

Love relished his reputation as a shadowy Darth Vader, who stalked the halls in search of enemies to vanquish. If he was perceived as a force of darkness, that was fine by him if it also meant Klein was seen in a positive light. In reality, though, Love was very much a force for outreach, and brought key people from opposing leadership camps into his confidence. He gave them meaningful responsibilities and used his power sparingly, limiting it to staff who made mistakes. "Everybody's a professional until proven otherwise," Love says. "You could count on the fingers of one hand the number of communications directors that were fired, but I loved the reputation because it made people think twice. The way I looked at it, you've got to be nice to people on the way up, 'cause you'll see the same people on the way down."

When he wasn't fine-tuning the government, Love became the legislature's sultan of spin. He used his persuasive personality to deploy selective facts to a gallery of columnists while he authorized leaks of advance information to deserving scribes.

His impatience with negative or unfair media coverage unleashed legendary temper tantrums. After a particularly devastating series of front-page headlines in the *Calgary Herald* on the eve of the election, on June 15, 1993, Love called me at home to vent. "You'd better buy yourself an Edmonton golf membership because no fucker from the *Herald*'s going to get anywhere near Ralph Klein again," he shouted. I hung up on him and went back to packing for my transfer to the capital as the new legislature columnist. He called back to apologize, but it was far from a unique encounter between journalists and Love's pistol-hot temper, and it only added to his aura as a temperamental evil genius.

Within two weeks of winning the leadership, Ralph Klein had fired seventeen cabinet ministers, but notes taken at the time by both the premier and Rod Love put one name at the top of their must-have list. "Nancy has to be there," an internal memo reads. Having Betkowski prominently seated at the cabinet table was considered essential to healing the rifts of the divisive leadership race. The party's deep wounds needed treatment quickly to prepare for the upcoming election, and even if it was merely cosmetic bandaging, Klein wanted her close by and under careful watch.

Nobody had heard or seen anything of Klein's last ballot rival, however, since she'd walked off the stage minutes after losing the leadership. "She was absolutely convinced the people around Ralph would practice the politics of punishment," recalls former adviser Eric Young. After a week of sending out conciliatory signals, Klein established telephone contact at her Fernie ski condo. Without wasting time on small talk, he asked if she was prepared to play a key part in his cabinet. There was silence for a moment, and then Betkowski delivered her demands. She wanted to be treasurer, minister for women's issues, Edmonton caucus chair and deputy premier. Oh, she added at the last second, she also wanted an apology before agreeing to rejoin the cabinet. Klein was baffled. She could have everything but deputy premier, he said. That had been promised to Ken Kowalski, but what was the apology for? Betkowski, her voice rising, said that her family had been insulted when, during the leadership race, Klein had invited her to "get it on" in a debate. Betkowski insisted it had sexual overtones that required a full public apology. A furious Klein slammed down the phone. Betkowski was out.

Betkowski, now remarried and renamed Nancy MacBeth, has a different recollection of events. She says there was a face-to-face meeting with Klein where she asked him for a personal note of regret for the benefit of her husband, who was upset by the quip. "It was not a public statement, just a little note to my family would be fine. He said he would and I thought, 'Good for him for realizing it was a little bit off', but the note never came." A few weeks later, Betkowski tendered her resignation from the only political party she'd ever known.

What appeared to be a major political setback turned out to be a godsend. Without Betkowski in a senior cabinet capacity, Klein decided to send a signal of reconciliation by bringing in one of her supporters. On day six of the transition period, in through the office door walked his first treasurer.

Jim Dinning was having the worst week of his middle-aged life. As one of only two MLAs to back Betkowski on the first ballot, he was on the political outs. The day before Betkowski's loss, he gloomily turned forty years old. Three days after that, his wife demanded a divorce. So, when an emotionally shattered Dinning walked into the premier's office the next week, he did not go in humbly begging for a job. He figured he was doomed to a life on the back benches and probably wouldn't run again anyway. He decided to take a shot in the dark and he pitched the treasurer's job hard and direct.

On Klein's cabinet line-up chart, Dinning's name was scrawled prominently under the death sentence heading "Toast." Had Betkowski agreed to join the cabinet, Dinning was indeed headed for the last row of the back bench, but Klein was actually listening when Dinning pledged to be the best treasurer the premier could possibly find. Dinning recalls that his opening pitch triggered a laugh from Klein that sounded suspiciously like a derisive snort. However, the pair discussed the challenge of balancing a budget deep in red ink, the need to admit the horror of it all openly and to harness public support for the pain that would be required to restore the province to fiscal health. "We talked for fifteen minutes and I have this image of him after I left, rubbing his hands together and saying, 'Great. I found my sucker'." Three hours later, Klein called to offer him the job.

What Dinning did not realize was that Klein was delighted with his hard sell. He would serve as a high-profile olive branch to the Betkowski camp, and Dinning's keen interest in balancing the budget gave Klein a treasurer who wholeheartedly bought into his fiscal agenda. Dinning hit the books immediately. He fired up focus groups to see how best to sell a balanced budget and he had his bureaucrats program a computer to allow him to play with the numbers. With it, he sliced off bits and pieces of funding from various departments to see how twenty per cent of government funding, $3.2 billion, could be cut. Klein had insisted that core programs be preserved as much as possible. Non-essential services could be hit heavily or scrapped entirely. Dinning spent weeks playing with the numbers. He cut the budgets of transportation, economic development, municipal affairs, tourism and, most aggressively, his own treasury department to see how much health, education and social services spending could be spared the axe.

He ordered a financial review commission to detail in graphic, ugly detail the province's fiscal situation. Klein appointed former TransAlta chairman Marshall Williams as chairman of the commission and his old city hall chief commissioner, George Cornish, as its executive director. Their marching orders were simple: The books are open. Tell us how bad it is, don't hold back, and don't consult with the premier's office until you're done. It was never directly stated, but it was understood that the commission could only help, not hurt, the cause by painting a bleak picture of the Alberta fiscal landscape. When they released their report in April 1993, they didn't pull a single punch. Alberta was threatening to become Mexico North, they warned. With resource revenue plunging, the province was operating under a structural deficit that was getting worse every day. Inflation and population growth were driving spending upward at an unsustainable five per cent per year. Deep cuts were essential. Eliminating the deficit was pivotal. Klein was ecstatic. Such doom and gloom was a key part of his sales strategy: a bad moon was rising. Trouble was on the way and the voter needed to be primed for a bloodletting.

While Dinning and the financial review commission worked on the fiscal agenda, Klein symbolically honored his commitment to open up government in the style he'd perfected as mayor. He opened up his legislature office to one visitors' tour per day. He held a Christmas party in the cabinet room and invited legislature staff to stop by for a beer and a handshake. One incredulous janitor told me Klein was the fourth premier whose trash he'd emptied and he had never even shaken the hand of the other three, much less had a beer on the premier's tab. "I'd like to put up a sign that says: 'Under new management'," Klein said in his first question period. "Let's not dwell on the issues of the past."

When Klein arrived in the premier's office, communications became the top priority in Alberta politics, and he went to work restoring the viperous media relations that had poisoned Getty's reign. Getty's people had drawn an imaginary barrier across the entrance to their suite and dubbed it the Line of Death. To cross it was a breach of security, and violators faced stiff penalties, which could include expulsion from the legislature building. His staff made little effort to connect with reporters, and regarded them as circling vultures best ignored and avoided. Getty rarely scrummed, held news conferences even less frequently and granted few interviews. When caucus meetings were held in historic Government House, Getty ordered media banned from the premises, relegating them to the outdoors even during the most inclement weather.

The contrast with Klein's approach couldn't have been greater. The morning after he claimed the leadership, the new premier arrived to check out his digs and invited hovering media inside for a tour. When one reporter noted he hadn't been inside the premier's office since the Lougheed years, Klein admitted he'd only been inside it once himself, after three years in cabinet. He decreed media no longer had to endure the elements outside Government House, but could wait downstairs for caucus meetings to finish. Later in his first week he further shocked reporters by strolling through their rabbit warren of dirty offices to deliver his own handwritten response to an Opposition accusation. They were little gestures that warmed even the most cynical scribe's heart.

Klein distilled a lot of awkward issues and potential conflicts with his role in the Getty cabinet down to simple, dismissive phrases. "That was then, this is now," would suffice whenever reporters pointed out policies inconsistent with Getty government decisions that had included Klein. "We have a spending problem, not a revenue problem," he'd say, when asked to justify his choice of funding cuts over tax increases. When the public fretted about deep cuts that simultaneously spanned multiple ministries, he'd shrug it off. "You can't cross a canyon in two leaps." When asked why he was cutting core health, education and social services programs—the government's biggest departmental budgets—he'd argue, "You have to hunt where the ducks are." If he was called upon to prop up an ailing industry, he would retort: "We're out of the business of being in business."

Of course, not everything fit nicely within the confines of those catch phrases. In the final weeks of 1992, Canadian Airlines was on the verge of a crash landing unless it received a fiscal airlift from the federal and Alberta governments. Notes from a private meeting with PWA Corporation president Rhys Eaton and Calgary businessman Art Smith, just three days after Klein won the premier's job and only days before Christmas, show them pleading with Klein to authorize a fifty-million-dollar loan guarantee or watch the airline fold at the peak of the travel season. Eaton rolled cash flow sheets out over the premier's desk and warned that the airline had been to the marketplace on the understanding it had a provincial loan guarantee in place. He begged Klein to get a commitment from his treasury to back the deal by Monday. Klein relented. "That was then, this is now" had its limits. It would not be the last exception to the rule.

Just a week after taking office, Klein announced his first cabinet. He gave the promised deputy premier's job to Ken Kowalski, along with such a mixed bag of other responsibilities that it earned him the title Minister of Everything. Klein cut the cabinet to eighteen ministries and loaded it with backbenchers who were ignored during the Getty era: Halvar Jonson for education, Mike Cardinal for social services, Jack Ady for advanced education, Shirley McClellan for health. Stockwell Day, a rural, unknown and unproven MLA who had toiled in obscurity as the government whip under Don Getty, was given labour. When former premier Peter Lougheed called in his congratulations, he offered Klein only one bit of advice: make sure to let MLAs know the route they would have to follow to reach cabinet. Thus, Klein condensed dozens of policy committees into four standing policy committees, each with a backbencher as chair, and he stocked the new Treasury Board and the Agenda and Priorities Committee with private members, all in training for future cabinet gigs. He teamed every minister up with a back-bench "buddy" to keep MLAs in the loop about important decisions.

The internal consensus about when to hold the next election was to wait for at least ten months. It would take time to recover from the low standing in the polls they had inherited. Klein also needed to redraw electoral boundaries, most pressingly in his own constituency, in order to carve out friendlier territory that would ensure his riding became a safe seat.

Skepticism at Klein's ability to win the election lingered, even among those friendly to the new premier. "Betting the entire election on Mr. Klein's personal appeal, in the face of a fractured party and well-prepared Liberal opposition, would appear to be a very risky strategy," warned national lobby firm Government Policy Consultants in a memo the week after Klein's leadership victory. But a few months into 1993, the Klein coalition was starting to gel. The premier invited Betkowski backer Eric Young to organize the party's successful policy convention. Doug Main, who had slagged Klein's smoking and drinking during the election, was punted from cabinet, but he became a Klein fan when the premier spoke at a fundraiser to help reduce his heavy campaign debt. Betkowski campaign manager Susan Green pledged allegiance to the new regime and would eventually run, unsuccessfully, for Klein in the 1997 election. Meanwhile, Betkowski announced her retirement from politics and left the legislature in a pout that even her friends considered unbecoming.

Treasurer Jim Dinning rolled out his first budget in early May of 1993. As much a statement of intent to eliminate the deficit as an actual plan of attack, it was devoid of specific cuts beyond the general goal of a twenty per cent spending chop. The far-ahead Liberals were starting to hear footsteps closing on them from behind, as the Tories' improving poll results gained momentum. Klein was starting to feel he could pull off a miracle in a snap election. He circled June 8, 1993, as his choice for an election date, and put the party on high alert. Then a sleeping time bomb detonated: government pensions hit the headlines in the spring.

The annual release of the budget's public accounts usually attracts little interest, but this year would be a unique exception. The firing of so many cabinet ministers and the imminent retirement of several dozen more MLAs lured media interest to the pension figures at the back of the document. Retiring premier Don Getty was poised to rake in $32,977 per year based on total contributions of $63,000. Nancy Betkowski, at the ripe young age of forty-four, was set to collect a $39,000 pension immediately. Stockwell Day, with only six years of service under his belt, could collect an annual pension of $16,792 were he to retire. The worst case was Al "Boomer" Adair, an original from the 1971 Lougheed government, pocketing over $83,600 per year in pension. What doubly infuriated the public was discovering that ousted cabinet ministers were collecting their ministerial pensions while serving as backbenchers, a practice called double-dipping. The Alberta Taxpayers' Association (ATA) calculated the pensions were forty per cent higher than the average for provincial politicians in Canada, and their figures showed $40 million worth of pension payments would walk out the door of the Alberta legislature in a few months. The ATA, sensing a public relations winner, immediately fired up a petition drive and, with minimal effort, dropped thirty thousand signatures off at the legislature. Future Canadian Alliance MP Jason Kenney, then twenty-four, a director of the ATA, pointed out the taxpayer was paying six dollars for every loonie contributed from the MLAs. Klein was feeling the heat. He mused about doing something, but argued against clawing back pensions retroactively, and waved around a legal opinion that it was an iffy proposition.

The public, however, was not to be denied its anger. Amid all the furor, Kenney's profile was in ascension. He arrived at the legislature for a press scrum one day at the precise moment Klein was heading into the cafeteria for a sandwich. Spotting Kenney surrounded by microphones, Klein stormed forward and accused him of trying to frighten seniors in order to sell ATA memberships. Kenney stood his ground, calmly reciting the incendiary facts and figures while Klein raged on. There is no dispute who lost the oft-televised debate. The next day, a frantic memo from an Edmonton communications official was dispatched to the premier's office in Calgary. "We've had 100 calls in Edmonton by 11 a.m. and Calgary has had 25. They are all mad and demanding pensions be rolled back," a frazzled secretary wrote. "If Premier doesn't roll them back before the election, Decore will because they won't be voting PC." It was still a month before the writ was expected to drop, but Tory hopefuls in active pre-election campaigning began to call in, warning that the doorsteps had turned to ice. "If there is no roll back to 1989, we will be wiped out in Calgary," party loyalist John McCarthy warned Klein in a letter.

The worried premier confided to his advisers that he had no choice but to kill the pension plan and slash the benefits retroactively. He would have to sway the entire caucus and persuade many of them, including the retirees, to make the required personal sacrifice. All eyes were on Klein when he entered a mid-May caucus meeting the week before the election call. In his pocket was a slip of paper Rod Love had passed to him beforehand. "Trust your instincts," it said. Klein's speaking notes, fleshed out by numerous penned additions, reflect his personal anguish about the decision. "I realize the suggestion to revisit retroactively has created a bit of a stir," Klein told the group. "As leader, I'm between a rock and a hard place. Without exception, the candidates have expressed to me that pensions are an issue and in some cases the only issue. Calgary is the battleground in the next election and from all accounts we are in serious trouble in Calgary. We would not win an election if it were held within the next twenty-eight days. I'm not going to send in the troops to fight an issue that is clearly not ours." He opened the floor to suggestions.

It was a classic crossroads scenario—the Lougheed old guard was trying to protect their retirement against a fledgling Klein force that was trying to salvage its future. Fierce disagreements broke out between retiring MLAs defending their pension rights and Tories with re-election on their mind fighting for ways to appease the public. The seeds of a solution came when low-profile MLA Barry McFarland, first elected in 1989, raised his hand and said he'd give up any claim to a pension for the party's future. It forced the hand of the veterans, and they folded.

Hours later, Klein emerged from the meeting to announce the pension plan had been killed. MLAs seeking re-election would have their pension eliminated retroactively to 1989; those leaving would only receive benefits for their service up to 1989. The next day the party placed newspaper ads in the major dailies. "We listened," the ads crowed. "We will be scrapping the MLA Pension Plan. Yours truly, Ralph."

The polls bounced back like a rubber ball off a concrete floor, particularly when some Liberal MLAs complained Klein had gone further than necessary. Feedback from Conservative candidates at the door warmed instantly. If all things remained equal for the rest of the campaign, victory was only a flip of the coin away. "Laurence was doing all the right things," Klein recalls. "He had a fiscal responsibility push and he'd found something in pensions that would rattle the public. The only way to end this was to do something dramatic. Had we just monkeyed with the plan and adjusted the benefits, people would be skeptical. But to eliminate it took the wind out of their sails and knocked them on their ass."

The election was back on, and only a week later than planned.

The one role Rod Love guards above all others is running Klein's campaign itinerary, from the drop of the writ until polling day. Until the 2001 provincial election, no one else had ever piloted a Klein campaign. "The handling and packaging of the leader is the essence of the Ralph Klein phenomenon," Love explains. "Ralph is the campaign, not like the [Gary] Filmon campaign where the Manitoba Conservatives are the campaign. It's the guy here. If anyone meddles with his schedule, it's a firing offence. I know what he can take in terms of pacing." Love always kept the schedule light and flexible enough to accommodate Klein's workouts and morning recoveries from late nights out, and, most importantly, he always overnighted Klein at the starting point for the next day's schedule. "When he wakes up and has to fly, he's irritable, he's tired and if he gets there tired, you get a lousy performance. Even if it's eleven at night in Fort McMurray and you're opening in Red Deer, get him into a bed where he's starting the next day."

Klein christened his eighty-two running mates "Ralph's Team" and dropped the writ on May 18, for a June 15, 1993, election. Almost half of his caucus had opted not to run again and were replaced by fresh Tory candidates. Klein hit the hustings in blue jeans and cowboy boots aboard a small seven-metre motorhome, with only Colleen for company. There were occasional "Run with Ralph" rallies for the cameras, which kick-started a daily fitness program in Alberta that persists to this day, but most of his campaigning consisted of just popping into a Tory candidate's head-

Ralph Klein as a toddler with his mother Florence, father Phil and grandfather in 1993. *(Office of the Premier of Alberta)*

Ralph Klein (front row, second from right) as a safety technician in the Royal Canadian Air Force. He enlisted as a seventeen-year-old and sought an early discharge two years later on the grounds of severe mental depression. *(Office of the Premier of Alberta)*

Reporter Ralph Klein in the early 1970s covering a visit to Calgary by federal minister of finance John Turner. *(Office of the Premier of Alberta)*

Ralph and Colleen Klein soon after their marriage in 1972. *(Office of the Premier of Alberta)*

Ralph Klein wearing one of his native headdresses. He was made an honorary chief of the Siksika Blackfoot Nation in 1981 and christened Blue Bird for his work covering the plight of that tribe as a reporter. He was later given a chief's title with the Blood First Nation. One of his first acts as premier was to return sacred artifacts housed in provincial museums to native communities. *(Calgary Herald)*

Mayor Ralph Klein in 1985. *(Calgary Herald)*

Ralph Klein with International Olympic Committee president Juan Antonio Samaranch dropping the puck to open a Calgary Flames hockey game, during the lead up to the 1988 Winter Olympics. *(Calgary Herald)*

Klein christens the luge track at Canada Olympic Park in Calgary in 1987, taking on Edmonton mayor Laurence Decore in a mock race on the training run. Decore would also leave for provincial politics, win the leadership of the Alberta Liberals, and face Klein's Conservatives in the 1993 provincial election. Failing to win the election, Decore left politics in 1994. He died of cancer in 1999 at age 59. *(Calgary Herald)*

A key part of executive assistant Rod Love's job was to keep the paperwork for Klein's attention confined to summaries of executive summaries. This photo was taken in 1988 during Ralph Klein's eighth and final year as Calgary mayor. *(Calgary Herald)*

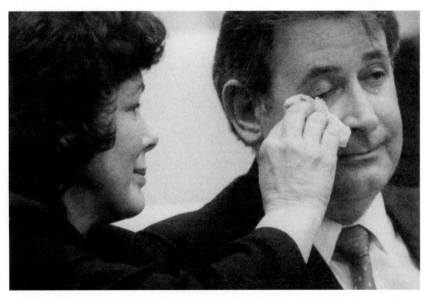

Colleen Klein wipes away a tear after her husband announces in 1989 that he would step down as mayor and seek a provincial seat in the government of Premier Don Getty. *(Calgary Herald)*

Angry protester Randy Lawrence gives the head table the finger at an announcement for the giant Al-Pac pulp mill project in 1990. Only one minister, then environment minister Ralph Klein, flipped the bird back. *(Courtesy of Rod Love)*

Premier-elect Ralph Klein prior to his swearing-in ceremony in December 1992. Watching is Peter Elzinga, the Progressive Conservative party's executive director, who would become his chief of staff in 1998. Standing behind Klein is Ken Kowalski, who would be fired twenty-one months later as deputy premier. *(Calgary Herald)*

Ralph Klein fishing beside the Bow River in Calgary in 1990. As mayor of Calgary, he would take advantage of holes in his schedule to sneak down to the river and cast about for some trout. *(Calgary Herald)*

quarters and letting the local MLA hopeful host a tour of the main street's cafeterias and coffee shops.

Press gallery tagalongs were not encouraged. In fact, Love took pains to make it difficult to track the premier. Travel itineraries were posted only a day or two in advance, and when long distances needed to be covered, the campaign hired a chartered airplane to hop from one small town to the next, leaving the press struggling to catch up on scheduled commercial flights or in rented cars. Rod Love didn't much care if the "big dogs," as he derisively called the city media, howled in protest. He'd rather have his candidate wow the local scribes than worry about the provincial press trying to read another new angle into the same stump speech Klein delivered at every stop.

His theme was soft, gentle, innocent, and he tried to play down the hard work ahead. Billboards were plastered with Klein, his shirtsleeves rolled up and a small smile on his face under the pledge "He Listens. He Cares." It relied on Klein's hugability factor—the notion that he would never hurt anyone unless it was for their own good.

For his part, Decore was ready for just about anything. He called me up hours before the writ was dropped to boast about a Liberal team that was ready to fight and poised to win. He was loaded with policy papers for every conceivable issue and ammunition to blast every step of Tory fiscal ineptitude. On the first day, he unveiled a satellite media truck and produced what he called a "CD Player," which calculated the "Conservative Debt" in stark, rapidly rising numbers. Alarms went off in Klein's camp. If this was day one, they fretted, what gizmos might be coming in the weeks ahead?

In the end, it was a one-trick campaign. The Liberals' state-of-the-art campaign truck, equipped for live transmissions from anywhere in the province where Decore was campaigning, was rejected as political graft by media outlets and was rarely used. The "CD Player" began to look cheesy by the second week. The Liberals obviously hadn't done their homework on Klein, a master in the art of admitting his foibles and winning over voters to get a second chance.

Decore pledged brutal cuts and efficiency audits to balance the books. Klein promised massive cuts to non-essential programs to balance the books. Decore accused the Getty government of fiscal ineptitude and boondoggle architecture. Klein agreed with every word—and promised to do better if given a chance to govern. "We had to out-Decore Decore," Klein recalls. "The Liberals were looking for an issue and they could smell blood." If all this wasn't enough to unnerve the Liberals' confidence, Klein, the self-proclaimed "loose cannon" of the legislature, was about to discovered he had a soulmate in his opponent.

For nine years, through the predictable annual city hall showdowns between pro-life and pro-choice forces over funding for the Calgary Birth Control Association, Klein had walked a non-judgemental line on the abortion issue. It's a decision between a woman, her doctor and her God, he'd recite with verbatim predictability. For reasons never fully explained, only a few weeks into the campaign, Decore responded to a question on abortion by announcing a pro-choice policy position while denouncing private abortion clinics as a "morally repugnant" service he would try to shut down if elected premier. It was quite an accomplishment. He managed to simultaneously alienate both the pro-life and pro-choice sides of the mile-wide divide.

Klein was traveling around Central Alberta when the phone rang in his motorhome that May 20 afternoon. Rod Love, who was traveling with the premier, answered. He listened for a few minutes, then put down the phone. He briefed Klein on his opponent's comments. "I said, 'We just won the campaign or Decore just lost the campaign.' I could tell by the look on Ralph's face he agreed with my assessment. It was very bad."

Klein walked into his next scrum, repeated his standard abortion line and walked away, refusing to condemn Decore's comments. He didn't need to; Liberal women candidates were doing it for him. High-profile MLAs like Bettie Hewes called their leader to demand a retraction, and warned of a deep drop in the women's vote with no compensating increase from the pro-life side. Decore's team had indeed suffered a fatal setback. Before that day, the race was close enough to call with a coin toss, but that night, when Love called the team together for a pep talk, he told them, "All things being equal from this point forward, we win."

Ask Ralph Klein today about his favorite memory from that pivotal

1993 campaign, and what comes instantly to his mind is farting cows—which says a lot about his offbeat sense of humor and irreverent attitude toward political drama. The incident in question occurred during a stop at a cattle auction just outside Wetaskiwin, where hundreds of cows were being sold at firesale prices because of a plunge in demand for beef. The farmers were still fans of the rookie premier and Klein relished shaking hands hardened by work in the fields. He was asked to address the crowd, and, as rows of John Deere baseball hats turned upward to hear him speak, something in the back of his mind clicked. Klein had planned to deliver the standard script, but he recalled a letter Decore had written a few years earlier, urging Alberta's cattle producers to collect the flatulence of their cattle as a methane fuel. The head of the Alberta Cattle Commission had been only too happy to share the bizarre notion with his buddy Ralph to ridicule Decore's city slicker attitude. Klein regaled the crowd with his recollection of Decore's letter. "Laurence would be so very, very pleased to see this," Klein said, as he surveyed the assembled farmers and their cattle. "We've got all the cows together. The only thing Laurence hasn't figured out is how to get them all to fart at the same time." The crowd whooped and Klein knew he'd connected. There wasn't a Liberal vote in the place.

In the end, it came down to trust, believability and likability, and Calgary voters held all the aces. With his stiff, cool courtroom demeanor, it was an uphill battle for the lawyer, Decore, from the drop of the writ. Late in the campaign, with his opponent surging into an insurmountable lead, Decore shrugged heavy shoulders at Klein's ability to divorce himself completely from the government's record. "It's the most perplexing thing that I've ever tried to sort through," he said.

After dinner and drinks on the night of June 15, 1993, Rod Love handed his boss three envelopes, carefully marked for three electoral scenarios. In defeat, Klein would salute the new premier. "When you fish for glory, you catch the darkness too," the concession text read. "We accept our fate, confident in the belief that a future Alberta will look back at our legacy and say: 'They were not always right, but they were never on the side of wrong'." In a second folder was a minority government speech: "This is the first minority government in the 88-year history of Alberta," it noted. "As such there are many unanswered questions this evening. In whatever we do, we will break new ground and set new precedents." Less than two hours after the polls closed, the voter verdict was rendered and Klein ripped open the majority government envelope and strode to the microphone at Calgary's Heritage Park. He'd won fifty-one of the province's eighty-three seats. Half of his new caucus would take their seats in the legislature as high-octane rookies who had run as revolutionaries. The Alberta Curse had been broken. King Ralph had his own throne.

"Welcome," he bellowed to the eager crowd, "to the miracle on the Prairie."

Eleven

Ralph the Knife

THERE'S A PAPER WAITING to be written on how the difference between the budget cuts started by Don Getty and the spending cuts implemented by Ralph Klein was not fiscal recklessness versus restraint, but merely a difference in sales strategy. Getty had already tightened his government's belt considerably, and had sucked in per capita spending by fifteen per cent. Alberta's reign as the nation's most benevolent public service had already ended before Klein claimed power, discovered a deficit crisis and set about hacking and slashing a budget already in reduction mode. While Getty's restraint record would have been tainted, if he had managed to stay in power, by the billions of dollars in subsidies squandered on bogus businesses, what spending cuts he did accomplish were so poorly communicated that, to this day, Getty is reviled in Alberta as a giddy spendthrift.

One of the first things Klein did after being sworn in as Alberta's twelfth premier was anoint himself Minister of Truth. Not in so many words, perhaps, but he did take a scattered, fragmented collection of underutilized flacks reporting to the public works minister and construct a hierarchical organization of advanced communications expertise. They were backed by state-of-the-art technology, and his name was at the apex of the pyramid on its organizational chart. The staff christened it the

"Ministry of Truth"; officially it was called the "Public Affairs Bureau." The front office was tucked away behind the grand stairwell leading to the legislative assembly. There, a deceivingly modest three-person operation quietly controlled more than twenty satellite centers in the surrounding government buildings. Dreamed up by Love and communications director Jim Dau, the bureau was a supposedly non-partisan operation staffed by handpicked communications strategists, but it had one prime directive: to decide what the truth should be, give it positive spin, polish it and make sure the government stuck to the script. It rarely lied to the media, but just as rarely told the entire truth. It delivered positive data in an embellished rush and negative news in a tardy trickle.

A streamlined and scripted communications empire was considered critical to selling the budget cuts. The last things Klein wanted were crossed wires and conflicting messages as the budgetary knives flashed in front of nervous Albertans. Every news release was vetted by the premier's office, and they were rewritten when necessary. The premier's office also implemented a policy of zero tolerance for factual errors in newspapers. They contacted reporters, editors and publishers to demand immediate corrections to prevent the mistake from being repeated.

The Ministry of Truth evolved into a tightly disciplined, highly partisan and powerful tool for the Klein government. It coordinated layoffs and budget reductions so they were not announced piecemeal through twenty-six departments, dribbling out in twenty-six disjointed messages on twenty-six timetables, but dropped on the media all at once, the better to crunch the bad news into a single day of reporting. It also served as an early warning system for the premier's office, as it alerted senior officials to potentially embarrassing inquiries from journalists. Although never acknowledged officially, Ministry of Truth staff were also known to provide the government with such helpful services as clogging the phone lines of talk shows with pro-Tory opinion and blitzing media polls with votes supporting Klein's actions.

The organization gave Klein, who as a crusading reporter would have been mortified by such blatant manipulation, exactly what he needed to shape and control the message. MLAs were subjected to professional media training and were equipped every day with "Talking Points" that supplied suggested answers to hot-button issues. A daily bulletin of media analysis, tidbits and counter-arguments to Opposition attacks was published to arm Tory MLAs for media or constituent phone calls. Clipping services were hired to gather government news from every paper in Alberta, no matter how small, and the content was assessed to determine whether the issue of the moment was rising or fading in public anxiety. Every newscast was recorded and analysed. Staff were connected to the newswires electronically so they could track Canadian Press coverage of their events in real time. All of it fed to the big guy at the top of the pyramid—Ralph Klein.

Klein, the former electronic newshound, ironically is not a television news junkie and doesn't always read the newspapers. When the thick file of clippings and issue analyses landed on his desk, he sometimes gave it a glance—but only if he was bored.

The big challenge, of course, was not so much to analyse the reporting, but to control the messenger. No longer were communications directors simply add-ons to ministerial staff charts. What previously had been an arms-length, quasi-neutral function was replaced with directors who were as close to their ministers and as partisan to their party as executive assistants. Many of them were former journalists. Lumped together, they were a veritable MASH unit of spin doctors, ready to sell the bloodiest cuts as the miracle cure for an ailing Alberta.

Throughout the summer of 1993, the revolution began to take shape in Jim Dinning's treasury. His officials worked frantically to bring expenditures down by twenty per cent while banking on only the worst-case revenue projections. As the numbers added up on paper, education and health were spared their full, brutal share of the cuts, but Dinning could already hear the screams of protest in his sleep. "I remember Ralph saying everybody's got to be touched by this. Everybody's got to feel some pain. Don't single out one group," Dinning says.

The cabinet would be the first to take a hit: ministerial salaries were cut by five per cent. Klein cancelled his own five-thousand-dollar "representative" allowance for clothing and followed it up by ordering all MLAs to surrender five per cent of their gross pay. Combined with the demise of the pension plan, it gave the premier the self-sacrifice ammunition he knew he'd need for the upcoming public union showdown. The budget plans called for all government workers to take a five per cent slash in pay. "I'd returned to the public something like twenty-eight per cent in salary and benefits, but I wasn't about to say I was going to give them twenty-eight per cent less [work]. I was working just as hard," he said.

Despite his lead-by-example sacrifice, Klein was still full of self-doubt about whether he could deliver the promised cuts. "I can honestly say I didn't think that we would have the guts and intestinal fortitude to do it. But we started to feed off one another and once we got into it and made those decisions and saw it unfold, it got easier and easier."

The defining showdown came in the fall of 1993 during pre-budget discussions. Social services officials appeared before the treasury board to warn that, due to rising welfare rolls, they couldn't possibly meet their budget reduction target. Dinning recalls a silence around the table as the officials waited for cabinet to begrudgingly approve the required increase. "Well," he said, "what are you going to do about meeting your commitments?"

The officials exchanged knowing looks. They'd heard this tough talk before and knew just how to deal with easily spooked politicians. "Perhaps we'll have to slash the widows' pension or reduce the Alberta Income for the Severely Handicapped," one official warned, his shoulders sagging at the reluctant horror of it all.

"I looked at my colleagues and nobody said anything for the longest time," Dinning recalls. "I got some nods from around the table, so I said, 'Okay, we accept your recommendations. Now come back a week from now with a communications plan for your minister to announce these reductions'. The bureaucrats in the room went noticeably pale because they knew they'd gone too far," he said. "A week later, they came back and said they'd rethought how they were going to tackle the problem and proposed alternatives."

After the officials trudged out of the room to implement the cuts, Klein burst into laughter and pounded the table. "That's exactly how they did it at city hall," he said. When the budgets tightened around city parks operations, staff would invariably threaten to shut down the outdoor swimming pools on summer long weekends. "When we gave them the go-ahead, the bureaucrats would duck," Klein said. It was a turning point for the Klein Tories. Word spread throughout the bureaucracy from deputy minister to deputy minister: this cabinet is different, this cabinet has balls. Either that or it's nuts.

Ironically, though, the act that defined Ralph's Revolution in its first year was never raised during the leadership race, or floated on the campaign trail; nor had it surface as a concern in public polling. All the same, Klein would still be pointing to it seven years later, on his third election campaign, as proof his government had got out of a business it had no business being in. On September 3, 1993, the media were advised of a 3:00 p.m. news conference they'd better not miss. They entered the press room to find Steve West, the solicitor general, already at the podium, drumming his fingers impatiently while he waited for microphones to be set up. He then stunned the province by announcing the immediate and total privatization of liquor retailing throughout Alberta. He thus threw fifteen hundred government store employees out of their jobs in 210 Alberta Liquor Control Board outlets. Many would be hired back by private operators for a fraction of their eighteen-dollars-an-hour government wage. West boasted it was pure free enterprise. It was, at least as pure as the government would allow, but like everything ideological in Klein's government, there was a wrinkle. Supermarkets would be cut out of the retail business, West decreed, and mom-and-pop operations would get a four-year head start to capture the market.

The government needed to get the ALCB out of business quickly and hoped they could simply hand over the land titles and liquor inventory to private retailers, thus sparing the consumers and the government the headache of waiting for the market to rebuild from scratch. It worked like a charm. The number of outlets doubled in two years and quadrupled by 2002. Hours were extended from the usual 10:00 p.m. closing time until well past midnight, including holidays, and the line-ups that marked long weekend stockpiling became a thing of the past. Initially, Albertans complained about reduced wine selection and grumbled about price increases, but in the average voter's final cost-benefit analysis, convenience won out, and Steve West, the reformed pub crawler, was the toast of the town.

In October 1993, Klein traveled to Korea, Japan and China, with a pit-stop in Hong Kong, where he attended a modest ribbon-cutting for the new office of a little-known Calgary computer company named Multi-Corp Incorporated. Poised for a listing on the Alberta Stock Exchange, the company was developing a translation technology between Chinese and English. It was just another abstract business notion to Klein, who delivered bland encouragement and best wishes to the small group of executives, but his wife, Colleen, showed more than a passing interest in the firm. It might, Colleen thought, be a ground-floor stock investment with a lot of upward potential for the wife of a premier without a pension plan. She resolved to make inquiries upon her return to Calgary. The couple had no inkling how that unscheduled event and a passing mention in a Klein speech several months later would be the catalyst for a conflict-of-interest nightmare that would drag Klein to the brink of resignation.

The first serious blood of Ralph's revolution, however, was shed on the morning of January 18, 1994. The night before, Klein delivered a folksy television chat to Albertans over CTV affiliate stations, including his former employer, CFCN. It was a brace-yourself address, a message that underlined the precariousness of the government's financial picture, pointed out the fat still hanging off the system and insisted that Alberta had a spending problem rather than a revenue problem. It ended with an upbeat promise that short-term pain was going to lead to better days, when the government would be streamlined and more efficient, albeit smaller. The next day, all hell broke loose.

The knife fell everywhere that week. As a columnist, I remember sitting in front of my computer, utterly overwhelmed by the plethora of major daily developments to write about. Ultimately, I was forced by space constraints to give a hundred words of analysis to each of a handful of issues, issues that on their own could have justified a special newspaper series.

The top communications directors in Klein's government—Jim Dau, Gord Rosko, Fay Orr and Gordon Turtle—knew precisely what they were doing. With so many consequences, so many victims and so much potential opposition, we couldn't possibly do justice to all that needed covering in what was clearly a strategic carpetbombing of bad news.

Three-year spending targets were rolled out for each department, which sounded the alarm for workers in virtually every ministry. Health would henceforth be administered by seventeen government-appointed regional health authorities, which would have to make do with seventeen per cent less, thus ensuring widespread hospital closures. Social services was ordered to chop thirty thousand employable welfare recipients off the rolls by forcing them into job training or workfare programs. If they didn't like it, they could move to Ontario where benefits were sixty per cent higher—and Alberta would even throw in a free bus ticket to get them there (one way, naturally). Tuition fee caps were lifted, and fee hikes ensured a fourteen per cent chop to university and college spending. Seniors programs became income tested, dental and vision coverage for the elderly was reduced and lodge rents were raised. Transfers to municipalities were cut by forty-seven per cent, which ensured that provincial cuts would be echoed in most city halls. It was exactly what Klein had ordered—everybody suffered, some more than others, and everyone, he promised, would ultimately benefit.

In education, however, the cuts splattered enough blood to stain the government. The education minister, Halvar Jonson, a mild-mannered former school principal and former president of the Alberta Teachers' Association, seized control over all education taxation. He consolidated more than half the school boards in the province, and reserved the authority to appoint school superintendents for himself. The cabinet's axe-wielding surged further than anyone had envisioned when he slashed the classroom hours of kindergarten the government would fund in half. Tory backbenchers were particularly astounded because this move hadn't been supported at the education roundtables, nor had it passed through the usual committee channels. Kindergarten cuts simply emerged as a done deal, conceived and delivered by Jonson behind cabinet walls.

Defending his cuts, the education minister cited "thousands" of studies questioning the value of early childhood services. Most of them were academic papers that barely addressed the topic, including some bogus references completely unrelated to the issue. It was the government's first major misstep and it created the perception that Klein was either eliminating the deficit on the backs of four-year-olds or imposing tuition fees on toddlers. It didn't matter how you looked at it, the image was negative and it caused his government grief for years.

Many have speculated about the inspiration for the Klein cuts. David Osborne and Ted Gaebler's *Reinventing Government: How the Entrepreneurial Spirit Is Transforming the Public Sector* was promoted throughout the government by Jim Dinning, but Klein never bothered to finish reading it. Sir Roger Douglas, the former New Zealand finance minister, wrote a book entitled *Unfinished Business* that was passed around by MLAs, but it never turned up on Klein's reading list. In Toronto in 1994, someone asked Klein if he was following F.A. Hayek's *The Road to Serfdom*. The premier furrowed his brow, never having heard of the writer or the book. "Do I look like the kind of guy who would read those books?" he asked rhetorically.

In the end, Klein's model was partly all of the above and mostly none of it. The trendy books reflected an appetite in the general public for sanity and prudence in government spending, and nowhere was that hunger more ravenous than in Klein's kingdom. The complicating factor was the average Albertan's almost allergic reaction to any and all tax increases, especially the introduction of a sales tax. As a result, balancing the province's books had to come solely from spending reductions.

Klein was ideally positioned to conduct the experiment. His was a government successfully divorced from its duplicitous past, but not yet tainted by the negative consequences of its future. He was a leader generally trusted by the public to put the good of the people ahead of party loyalties while implementing the cuts. The gloomy assessment of the province's finances by the independent financial review commission had braced Albertans to accept government-inflicted miseries that few would have imagined possible in another era. The cabinet sensed a paradigm shift and seized on the possibilities it offered—politics was no longer the art of walking on eggshells.

Everything was put up for negotiation or sale. Nothing was too sacred to remain untouched and no action was too far right to be considered. "There was a lot of testosterone and a certain amount of ideology around the table," Dinning admits. With barely any study, the Tories spun off land titles, motor vehicle registration and driver testing to private operators; they turned provincial park operations over to fee-charging entrepreneurs and contracted out road paving and maintenance. All this was done in the firm belief that the private sector would always deliver better service for less money than government. They explored the privatization of prisons and, in a move that threatened to turn Alberta into Alabama North, Klein mused about bringing back chain gangs and using inmates to labor on public works projects. Only when it was pointed out to Klein that putting inmates, the majority of whom were native, on public display with picks and shovels would attract major, and controversial, coverage on North American television did he relent.

Klein, the former environment minister, introduced a "Special Places" program to set aside twelve per cent of Crown land for preservation, but he refused to veto oil exploration on the reserved land lest, in the words of his own environment minister, it be "sterilized." Companies were permitted to self-monitor their pollution. Mosquito abatement spraying was curtailed as a cost-saving measure. Klein mused about selling unused hospitals to private investors, who would turn rural treatment centers near the U.S. border into stomach-stapling centers of medical excellence for visiting Americans. His government introduced "charter schools" that offered varied programming under enhanced parental control, although, when pressed to define the concept in the legislature, Klein wasn't sure what specifically the charter schools did. More and more of the burden for government services was shifted directly onto the user, as the province introduced or raised 250 different fees, including a leap in health care insurance premiums. In one of the few legislative moves to receive widespread applause, the former journalist introduced freedom of information legislation that, while criticized for being full of loopholes, was better than nothing at all.

Still, when you hammer it all together, Ralph Klein's government should have faced lynch mobs of protest and single-digit popularity ratings. Instead it experienced a phenomenon that would ultimately attract global attention and accolades—the deeper they cut spending, the higher they rose in the polls. It was an inexplicable paradox.

Gleefully celebrating their rising fortunes, Alberta Progressive Conservatives gathered at the Banff Springs Hotel in April 1994 for their two-day convention. It was still too early in their mandate to claim victory, most felt, but defeat was no longer an option. Jean Charest, then a Conservative leader whose federal party could have fit into the front seats of Klein's Volkswagen Beetle, showed up to marvel at the changed political mindset. He declared that Alberta was setting the "national agenda for Canada."

The theme song for the convention video was the Rankin Family's "Rise Again," and it set the perfect musical mood as the faces of the "Class of '93" MLAs scrolled across a backdrop of Alberta landscapes. Half a dozen hard-right backbenchers, who called themselves the "Deep Six," hosted the wildest hospitality suite of the convention and handed out lapel pins featuring their signature teal-colored bowties. The pins instantly became the must-have souvenir of the gabfest. The six MLAs—Murray Smith, Lorne Taylor, Ed Stelmach, Jon Havelock, Lyle Oberg and Mark Hlady—considered themselves rebels doomed to a life on the back bench. Ultimately, all but Hlady would end up as senior cabinet ministers.

In his opening-night speech, Klein announced the Alberta Advantage: the pursuit of a targeted number of jobs to be created by deregulation and fiscal prudence, in a low-tax environment, with no government subsidies or loan guarantees. Earlier that day, the convention had braced for a nasty confrontation. Organized labor, opposition parties, teachers and health care workers had vowed to disrupt the convention, storm the mountainside and deliver a message Klein could not ignore. Security barricades were erected and a pair of RCMP cruisers waited expectantly for trouble. Reporters gathered to peer down the street for the incoming barrage of fury and disgust. Sure enough, placards appeared in the distance and chants could be heard, but when the marchers reached the hotel's signature statue of CP Rail builder Sir William Cornelius Van Horne, their numbers totaled only 150 of the usual left-wing, union leader, New Democrat types.

Watching in disbelief from the balconies of their hospitality suites, Tory MLAs guzzled Kleineken Beer ("beer with a full-bodied Conservative taste"), laughed uproariously at the sight of a protest molehill on their mountain, and savored their triumph. Their enemy had been exposed as small, weak, predictable and disorganized. You could feel it. They'd won. The heightened testosterone that Dinning noted in cabinet received an adrenaline surge at that convention. The rest of the convention buzzed with talk of going deeper, faster, even further than the cuts already outlined. Klein felt it too. He called it "scary."

In what seemed, at the time, an odd escape from the adoring throng gathered to sing his praises, Klein passed on the convention's Banff Springs main dinner and invited me to join a group of seven at a Greek restaurant in town. The precise details of the dinner have long since escaped my memory, but a supremely confident Klein confided that Dinning had just briefed him on the upcoming year-end financial situation. The deficit was already in its death throes, he grinned. Surpluses would be routine from now on. His revolution was already on the wane.

Twelve

The Pink Slips

B AD THINGS, THEY SAY, come in threes. And the first of three nasty personnel problems to confront the Klein government in 1994 was playing a video lottery terminal in the Banff Springs Hotel lounge, where I was having a drink with *Edmonton Journal* reporter Joan Crockatt to wind up a day of Tory convention coverage. Deputy Premier Ken Kowalski had fellow MLA Carol Haley drooped affectionately over his shoulder. Behind him, an MLA named Diane Mirosh, who had been romantically linked to Kowalski for several years and in the late 1990s moved into a condo near his home after his divorce, was staging a noisy protest as the jealous, jilted lover. Two machines further down, Colleen Klein was spinning the reels, as her husband looked on with a bemused smile.

Kowalski didn't pay either woman much attention as he poured money into the one-armed bandit, bent on maintaining what appeared to be a continuous losing streak. But watching Kowalski that night, so closely juxtaposed with Klein, you sensed something was amiss. The deputy premier exuded confident power, while the premier looked like the second-stringer. Kowalski obviously wasn't worried about the optics of the lotteries minister pumping hundreds of dollars into slot machines while a pair of reporters watched every move. He showed no concern about juggling the amorous attentions of not one, but two female MLAs in front of his boss, who knew he was a married man. His aura was stronger than Ralph Klein's that night, but if Klein was displeased in any way, he didn't show it—his wife had just hit a seven-hundred-dollar jackpot.

The full significance of the Ken Kowalski story to the subject of this book has its roots in an almost dysfunctional loyalty streak. Ralph Klein will support those around him with a stubbornness that can overshadow any and all practical considerations. He has shown he's capable of costing thousands of people their jobs by cabinet decree, but he'll cower in his car or scurry for home to avoid pink-slipping people directly, from the lowliest secretary to the most powerful cabinet minister.

Hiring has never been a problem for Klein, in any of his political capacities, but when a firing must be done, he shuffles the job to his chief of staff. This includes cabinet shuffles which, when they entail demotions or removals, he delays until the issue grows to critical importance. He's a sucker for a hard-luck story or a teary-eyed pitch, as his hiring of appointment assistant Sheryl Burns and the rest of his secretarial staff during his first tour of the legislature demonstrated. "Unless there's a compelling reason to fire someone—extreme incompetence or insubordination or people getting screwed up in their personal lives—why would you do it?" he asked me rhetorically. "Change for change's sake I don't think is good. I find it disruptive when things are going along smoothly. There's no need to change."

From his first entry into politics, Klein has refused to fire anything but blanks. When his first secretary didn't work out, Klein circled city hall in his car for an hour to avoid the trauma. Years later, as premier, it was decided that Burns had to go.

Sheryl's marriage to Tom Burns, one of Edmonton's top lobbyists at GPC Government Relations, created an on-going embarrassment for the government, particularly when she regularly booked Klein for events with GPC clients or hosted private dinners at her home. During Klein's first year as premier, word began to seep out that Rod Love wasn't the premier's real gatekeeper but that Burns was the power beside the throne. It was an intolerable slight to Love, doubly so because it was the truth. While her job performance was acceptable, the one black mark on Burns's record was having rejected a request from the Boeing aircraft company for Klein to open what would have been a major convention in Edmonton. Miffed at the slight, Boeing cancelled the event. Using this as ammunition, Love finally convinced Klein to move Burns out of the premier's office and insisted this was a transfer notice the premier would have to deliver. Love left the office one afternoon for cocktails with journalists, and confided gleefully to us that his nemesis was being gassed at that very moment. The next morning, to Love's furious amazement, Burns was still at her desk. A gusher of remorseful tears convinced Klein to change his mind and keep Burns employed in a slightly altered capacity. She ultimately outlasted Love. In the spring of 1998 it fell to Klein's next chief of staff, Peter Elzinga, to shuffle her off to a position arranging the province's 2005 centennial celebrations.

Dealing with Ken Kowalski, however, became a problem Klein could not avoid. Kowalski was a career bureaucrat with a master's degree in Chinese history, who, in 1979, left a position as deputy minister of transportation to become a career politician. He was strategically Machiavellian, ruthlessly arrogant, fiercely partisan—in short, everything Klein was not.

When the 1992 leadership race began, Kowalski did not appear on the campaign's internal list of MLAs supporting the Klein candidacy. He insists he was a cheerleader from day one, but apparently kept that a secret until ten days before the first ballot, when he cast his lot with the former Calgary mayor in a news release. Once on the team, Kowalski quickly elbowed his way into the inner circle in a brash, take-charge style that convinced Klein he'd found his rural kingpin. Kowalski promised to sell thousands of memberships for the deciding vote. Indeed, the votes for Klein in Kowalski's Barrhead riding almost tripled between the first and the second ballot. Kowalski's reward for such overt bravado was to be crowned Klein's right-hand minister.

In his multifaceted capacity as deputy premier, minister of economic development, house leader and minister of lotteries, Kowalski's meticulous and authoritative style flourished. Klein's staff were amazed, and mortified, by their deputy premier's thick, painstakingly crafted briefing books for every public appearance. These detailed the specific routes he would walk, the hot local issues and the biographies of those who would greet him at every hand-shaking opportunity. The level of organizational detail was in sharp, regal contrast to Klein's methods. The premier would habitually emerge from his car to wing it, knowing little, if anything, about the place or the people he would meet.

Stories circulated in the legislature of backbenchers cowed by threats from Kowalski about the fate of lottery grants in their ridings. One cabinet minister recalls digging in his heels against Kowalski, refusing to surrender a block of tickets for a visiting production of *Cats* he happened to hold. When he found his departmental grants suddenly tied up in Kowalski's bureaucracy, he capitulated and apologized to the deputy premier in person. The grants flowed immediately. Kowalski denies the incident.

It was a method of operating that Klein's friends held in contempt. In 1994, when Klein confidant Art Smith was struggling to establish an economic development authority similar to the one he had started in Calgary, he clashed with Kowalski over the authority's responsibilities. He complained to the premier that Kowalski was resisting any role for the private sector that might divert power away from the department of economic development. Sensing Kowalski's disconnect with his Calgary power base, Klein brought him to Calgary to try and warm up the frosty relationship with Calgary's business elite. The meeting seemed friendly enough, Klein recalls, but whispers about who was really in charge of the government persisted.

Despite the fractious relations between Kowalski and other members of Klein's government, it must be acknowledged that Kowalski was the brain behind some of their most successful policies. As lotteries minister, he was responsible for flooding Alberta's bars with more than six thousand video gambling machines, which ultimately led to an annual billion-dollar government revenue jackpot. He negotiated a series of widely acclaimed reforms to legislative procedures that stand to this day, and which paved the way for more free votes and gave MLAs every Friday off to spend in their constituency. When Stockwell Day jet-skied onto a Okanagan Lake beach the morning after claiming his federal seat as leader of the Canadian Alliance, the first parliamentary initiative he announced was a federal version of Kowalski's Friday constituency day.

It wasn't Kowalski's policies that galled his fellow MLAs, however. In 1993, at the precise moment a dozen acute care centers were being squeezed shut under the pressure of shrinking budgets, a monument to Kowalski was rising in his Barrhead-Westlock riding an hour's drive north of Edmonton. That the hospital was needed to replace a dilapidated facility was not the point. The galling optics of the project had some MLAs swearing to humble, heel and, if possible, oust their deputy leader. They didn't wait long.

In November 1993, Sir Roger Douglas was invited to deliver a pep talk to the caucus based on his experiences trying to salvage New Zealand from its mid-1980s debt and currency crisis with a program of rapid-fire budget cuts too severe for his own Labour government to stomach. Klein was away at the time and Kowalski happened to be in Calgary. Acting premier Dinning introduced Douglas to the caucus, who listened with rapt attention as he urged them to follow his model and cut deeply, quickly and on multiple fronts, the better to confuse the Opposition, bamboozle the media and divide the forces of protest. Douglas finished to a standing ovation and the caucus returned to its agenda, buzzing with ideology. So much so that an information item on their agenda about hospital construction ballooned into a motion to cease and desist all capital projects immediately, including the construction project in Westlock. It passed to thunderous desk pounding by the vast majority of MLAs.

A few minutes after the vote, the phone rang in the government's offices at the McDougall Centre in Calgary. An MLA friendly to the deputy premier proceeded to give Kowalski a precise rehash of the unexpected turn of events. Kowalski flew back to Edmonton in a rage, demanded an immediate meeting with Klein and threatened to resign on the spot if the decision wasn't reversed. "When he started to pack up his things, threatening to quit, I had to call caucus together. These are times when we have to make sacrifices," Klein sighs, the memory annoying even now. "But there always seemed to be something we'd have to do to accommodate Ken."

"Douglas had inordinately and perhaps unrealistically pumped us up and we probably miscued without the premier there," shrugs Dinning.

Klein called the caucus to a rare evening meeting and appealed to them to reverse the decision, "for a friend," he offered, so that Kowalski could keep his word to his constituents. The MLAs reluctantly agreed. Kowalski got his hospital, but he also won himself dozens of bitter enemies who felt he was standing in the way of the government's fiscal progress and impugning their political integrity. "The air came out of the balloon a bit that day," notes Dinning.

It took six months for Klein to realize that he had made a serious mistake by not letting Kowalski resign. When construction cranes went back to work pouring his hospital's foundations, Kowalski felt he was invincible in his suite of offices sealed off from his fellow MLAs. He acted with fearless arrogance. Kowalski shrugged off any culpability in obtaining a contentious loan guarantee for his constituency's Swan Hills waste treatment plant. His insistence that it was just an extension to a prior deal was later disputed by the province's auditor general. Kowalski became involved in the controversial renegotiation of the loan to the Ghermazian family for the West Edmonton Mall, when he opposed a buyout by Toronto-based Gentra Canada Investments Limited and raised the exposure of the government-owned Alberta Treasury Branch in the deal to $420 million from $75 million. His trip to Mexico to negotiate a four-lane trade expressway raised eyebrows, particularly as the highway hadn't been listed among the government's priorities. The itinerary also, inexplicably, included overnight visits to Tucson and Las Vegas. Both pit-stops were cancelled after news of them seeped out.

Kowalski finally met his Waterloo at a September 1994 retreat in Lethbridge. MLAs were horrified as he interrupted Klein's speeches in mid-sentence and repeatedly lectured the caucus with unsolicited advice. "He crossed the line," recalls Rod Love, who became so fed up, he packed his bags to return home early. "What's going on?" Klein asked when he spotted Love at the hotel checkout counter. When Love accused Kowalski of being the government's albatross, the premier pressed for specifics. "It's not one thing. It's a thousand things," Love told his boss. "Out-of-control unelected officials, we can handle. But out-of-control elected officials who jeopardize your whole agenda, we can't handle. He's turning off caucus, getting the membership mad, the public's picking up on it and the entire agenda is at risk here. This thing is not going to work as long as he's around."

Klein was astonished; he was skeptical and said so. "Don't take it from me, phone around," Love urged. Over the next few days, Klein did just that. He privately contacted MLAs and party executives and found deep animosity and a startling unanimity of opinion in every corner of his party. Kowalski was making their lives miserable.

The clincher came when party president Eric Young offered, without being asked, that Kowalski was the party's only political negative. Klein called Love the next day to deliver the death sentence in two words: "He's gone." The process began, however, with Kowalski being put on probation. The private notes of party executive director Peter Elzinga show Kowalski was repeatedly warned to mend his ways before being fired. On September 16, five weeks before he was pushed from cabinet, Klein met Kowalski to try and head off further problems. Elzinga followed up by phone and ended up listening to Kowalski complain bitterly about how Love had undercut his authority and had leaked details about the appointment of his lover, Diane Mirosh, to an economic development post. When Elzinga gently raised the possibility of Kowalski taking a lower profile role in the government, Kowalski rejected it with typical bravado: "The government would not survive without me."

It was a risk the government was willing to take. At 5:00 p.m. on October 20, 1994, Kowalski was returning to his office from the inaugural meeting of the Alberta Economic Development Authority. He was in an upbeat mood. The meeting had gone well and Kowalski sensed a new spirit of cooperation around the table. But Art Smith knew what awaited Kowalski and tried not to smile as Kowalski left the meeting. As he neared the legislature, Kowalski's car phone rang—the premier would like a word with him. Kowalski turned his car around and headed to Government House for what he was sure was merely a debriefing on the positive progress with the authority. He entered the second-floor premier's office and was met by a row of nervous frowns from Klein, Elzinga and the premier's deputy minister, Vance MacNichol.

Klein did not offer to shake hands. He told Kowalski there were serious difficulties with some aspects of his performance, but refused to elaborate. He said he was leaving for a meeting with the lieutenant governor to announce changes to his cabinet. Klein himself would become economic development minister and there was no other place at the table for Kowalski.

"You're firing me," Kowalski gasped.

Klein, typically escaping a confrontation, put on his coat and started to leave the room. "Ken, it's over," Klein recalls saying as he walked out the door. "You don't have the confidence of many members of caucus. It's come to the point where you perceive yourself as premier and there can be only one premier."

"He just fired me," a flabbergasted Kowalski repeated to no one in particular.

Elzinga suggested he might enjoy a posting with a foreign trade office, but Kowalski said he didn't want to leave Alberta, where his handicapped child lived. Vance MacNichol suggested he might take the chair of the Alberta Energy and Utilities Board, a high-profile regulatory body whose chairmanship came with a $120,000 salary and a car. Kowalski accepted with barely a moment's hesitation, and, as if on cue, Klein returned to the room. Kowalski pleaded to be allowed to save face, that no public backstabbing result from either side, and pledged his loyalty to the party and its leader. An hour later, the cabinet was informed and the new Alberta energy appointment announced. Treasurer Dinning phoned Rod Love immediately afterwards. "You're going to face a shitstorm in Calgary," he warned. The powerful energy industry wasn't going to take kindly to being regulated by someone without oil experience, who had been dumped on them in a convenient patronage appointment.

Such was the lofty status of Kowalski that his firing created a media sensation almost on par with the ousting of a premier. The story gained momentum seven days later when he was fired once again. Dinning's prediction had been correct. Calgary's oilpatch had never been a big fan of Kowalski, and it was in an uproar at the prospect of him lording over their regulatory body. Elzinga's notes put him in an office with Love, energy minister Pat Black and Kowalski to deliver the news. Black was typically direct: the appointment was being revoked due to concerns the province's regulatory independence would be tainted by a patronage appointment. Elzinga produced a letter offering Kowalski a three-month consulting contract with the Alberta PC party at ten thousand dollars a month, with the scope of his duties still to be negotiated. The memo referred to "numerous expressions of interest from private sector industries relative to hiring you on generally the same terms and conditions that would have been yours had you assumed the chair of the AEUB. My understanding is that such employment will be offered to you before the expiration of this consulting agreement."

The employment offer came within hours from a company that would gain notoriety one year later to the day. A deal was relayed to the government by Tory insider Thompson MacDonald. He was a director in a fledgling high-tech Calgary company named Multi-Corp, the software enterprise whose ribbon-cutting Klein had presided over during his Hong Kong stopover a year earlier and a company that would trigger two investigations by the provincial ethics commissioner into the conduct of the premier and his wife. Multi-Corp was willing to pay Kowalski two hundred thousand dollars a year to serve as point man for marketing the technology in China, MacDonald said. But Kowalski rejected it immediately. Love, MacDonald and Black went back to Love's office to phone Klein with the news. After telling Klein that Kowalski would be sticking around to haunt the government as a backbencher and apologizing for having given him bad advice, Love dashed onto the balcony outside his office, tears streaming down his face. "I let Ralph down," he told MacDonald.

Several days after Kowalski's downfall, Peter Trynchy, who had helped plot the execution, declared his support for his fallen comrade. "He's done a terrific job and I hope that I can follow in his footsteps," the transportation minister said. He would get his wish almost immediately as the second of three Klein ministers to fall from grace.

In 1994, Peter Trynchy was the longest-serving MLA in the legislature. He was elected with the first Peter Lougheed government in 1971, and he proved himself an old-school politician when he divvied up construction contracts for a Paddle River Dam project with Kowalski, ensuring their respective constituencies received guaranteed pieces of the action. The Alberta Liberals pinned another juicy scandal on the minister when a CBC television investigation discovered Trynchy's driveway had been paved by Sandstar Corporation, a company under contract to his ministry.

The ethics commissioner, who operated the disclosure confessional where MLAs declared their potential conflict of interest, was a fatherly former Social Credit MLA named Bob Clark. When he was called to investigate, he questioned the timing of Trynchy's payment for the paving and noted that the cancelled cheque was issued only after the potential conflict of interest was exposed. While he cleared Trynchy of breaching the Conflict of Interest Act in the end, he said the minister demonstrated "poor judgment" and "inappropriate behavior" when he hired the company to do the work at his Mayerthorpe home. A furious Trynchy blasted the investigation as McCarthyism and threatened to sue both the Liberal MLAs who had raised the issue and the ethics commissioner, a man beyond reproach. It was too much for Klein. While Trynchy had been among the first and most enthusiastic backers of Klein's leadership bid, the premier fired him without remorse or personal contact. It was a one-sentence pink slip and had the entire legislature abuzz. Klein, the habitual pushover, appeared to have found his spine.

In the spring of 1996, there was yet another firing to be done—the most distasteful, to Klein, of the trio. Mike Cardinal, the soft-spoken social services minister, was Klein's personal friend, regular fishing companion and, at Klein's insistence, the first Cree Indian to hold a major cabinet portfolio in Alberta's history. Assisted greatly by the shrewd instincts of his well-connected communications director, Bob Scott, Cardinal had performed well in the portfolio. He slashed welfare rolls and introduced self-help and work programs for recipients. By mid-1995, he'd managed to cut three hundred million dollars from departmental spending as caseload numbers plunged to 57,521 in the fall of 1994 from more than 94,000 cases just eighteen months earlier.

Cardinal had suffered a hiccup or two. His demand for deadbeat dads to own up to their child care responsibilities or lose their vehicle registration seemed hypocritical given his own history, having not supported an out-of-wedlock child for a time during his thirties. Cardinal's downfall really started, however, when his wife complained directly to the premier about her husband's romantic dalliances. As a rule, Klein turned a blind eye to MLAs fooling around in the capital. He jokingly referred to the legislature's Thursday afternoon departures as the time when MLAs "leave their loved ones behind to return to their wives." A few cabinet ministers were in torrid, adulterous relationships during his first term and in the second term, two senior ministers—Jon Havelock and Lyle Oberg—would leave their wives to move in with their ministerial assistants, with nary a raised eyebrow from Klein. In Havelock's case, his estranged wife and mother to his two children was so overcome with grief by the failed marriage, she committed suicide.

Cardinal's wife managed to schedule a fifteen-minute meeting with the premier that dragged on for almost an hour, as she poured out her heart to a sympathetic Klein. Coincidentally, a package arrived at Rod Love's office a few days later, containing a tape allegedly full of Cardinal's heavy-breathing conversations with another woman. A mortified Love reported the tape to the ethics commissioner and returned the parcel to the sender.

Klein was loath to do anything about Cardinal's personal behavior until, in May of 1996, government pilots reported Cardinal had ordered a bizarre detour in their flight plan to retrieve an unauthorized woman passenger. Cardinal offered no legitimate explanation for the passenger pickup, and Klein sensed that a misuse of government property had occurred. Reluctantly, he ordered staff to find a gentle exit from cabinet for his friend. It was easier said than done. Both Love and Stockwell Day, then the house leader, contacted Cardinal about resigning and were angrily and profanely drummed out of his office. Finally, clean-up hitter Peter Elzinga was assigned the deed. He summoned Cardinal to party headquarters, where he gently recommended the minister resign. Cardinal told him to "fuck off." Elzinga's friendly demeanor turned to ice and his hooded eyes narrowed as he patted his breast pocket. "I don't give a shit if you resign or not, but I've got two letters in my pocket. One is for you to sign, the other is for me to deliver to you if you don't sign the first one." Cardinal quit, citing personal reasons, on May 31, 1996, the third Klein minister in eighteen months forced from cabinet.

Thirteen

From Revolution to

Reinvestment

O N JANUARY 1, 1995, the world discovered the northwestern corner of North America where, in the Canadian province of Alberta, an unlikely alchemist was mixing together all sorts of policy poisons and discovering the elixir of political life. The *Financial Times* of London had already identified the strange phenomenon of a politician whose popularity increased as his spending decreased. In December 1994, *Barron's* magazine christened him Canada's Newt, after Republican house leader Newt Gingrich. Klein suggested, perhaps, that Gingrich was America's Klein.

It was the *New York Times* article on New Year's Day, however, that triggered an avalanche of interest in Klein's Alberta experiment. "Despite imposing some of the severest economic cutbacks in Canada since the Depression to eliminate a budget deficit, the government of Alberta enjoys more support today than when it was elected 18 months ago," the influential daily marveled. The *Wall Street Journal* quickly followed suit, running a three-part series on the Alberta phenomenon of promising misery and delivering popularity. "Mr Klein's record shows that voters are more prepared to accept spending cuts than the politicians realize." Two weeks later, when it christened him "Canada's Reagan," the *Journal* stated, "By articulating common sense solutions to problems, he's become a hero to many average voters. What astonishes Canadians is that Premier Klein's downsizing agenda is popular."

It wasn't merely the elimination of the deficit that was impressing the fiscal right. Premier Roy Romanow had, after all, balanced Saskatchewan's budget a few months ahead of Klein in that economically ravaged province. Unlike anywhere else, Alberta was doing it exclusively on the spending side of the ledger. The process of cutting budgets while freezing taxes, to unprecedented popularity, was a uniquely Albertan phenomenon. No one knew what to call it, so reporter Ashley Geddes, writing in the *Financial Post*, coined a phrase for it: Ralphonomics.

In his home country, Ralph's reviews weren't unanimously rapturous. *Maclean's* put him on the cover under the heading "Ralph's Way: Cutting to the Bone in Alberta." *Saturday Night* magazine called him "Ralph the Knife." In *Canadian Forum* magazine, Klein was crowned "King of the Jungle." *Globe and Mail* columnist Michael Valpy was vociferously unimpressed, warning Klein "one day will invoke the same faintly embarrassing memories for Albertans as Bible Bill Aberhart." Not surprisingly, the mid-term report card issued by the Fraser Institute, a right-wing think tank, was full of praise. "In an era when many politicians pretend to be conservative, Premier Klein appears to be a true role model," it gushed over his government's eleven per cent spending cut that was accomplished while maintaining the lowest taxes in the country. Klein's personal popularity with Albertans soared with his notoriety outside the province, reaching a seventy-three per cent approval rating in March 1995. Not even Peter Lougheed could have matched that during the reign of his blue-eyed sheiks, when he decided the people of Alberta were going to be the principal beneficiary of oil and gas development. In a *Calgary Herald–Edmonton Journal* poll, fully eighty-five per cent of the 813 people surveyed gave their approval to Klein's cuts in government department spending. Only when hospital closures began to enrage the public did his government's approval rating dip below fifty per cent. In 1994, the largest protest of his government took place when fifteen thousand people turned out in Edmonton to protest the conversion of the acute-care Grey Nuns hospital into a community care center.

Despite his popularity at home and his international prestige, the cutbacks were exacting a heavy personal toll on Ralph Klein by 1995. When his grand-daughter Chelsea came home from school to report that her teachers were saying Alberta was in trouble because of a mean, uncaring man leading the government, it bothered him terribly. He denounced the teacher in the media, but it had an impact that lasted for years. "One night the phone rang after midnight and it was Ralph," Dinning recalls. "He'd been in the cups a little and he said I'd been doing a good job, but added that 'This stuff really pains me. I know it is the right thing to do but it hurts personally.' You could tell he was lonely." He was also battle weary. Budget cutting is not second nature to Klein. He was, and is, a natural-born softie who adjusted to taking the hard line out of a sense of duty. Believing that the outcome was right helped him cope with the stress, but occasionally his kinder, gentler side would find its way out of his mouth.

This became obvious only three months into the spending reductions when Klein visited Newfoundland in December 1993. He returned traumatized by the sight of the mothballed cod fishery and the double-digit unemployment. After learning that Alberta held $261 million worth of high-interest debentures against Newfoundland, loaned from the Heritage Savings Trust Fund during the heady days of Peter Lougheed, Klein resolved to reduce the interest rate to help that province's struggling economy. "Newfoundland without cod," he confided to me during a long night on the town, "is Alberta without oil. We've got to try and help them."

Frankly, I thought it was the booze talking and ignored it. After all, the thought of helping another province out of monetary compassion while his home turf was in serious budget-cutting turmoil seemed preposterous, even in Klein's world. It wasn't until two weeks later, when he told *Financial Post* columnist Diane Francis the same thing and she published his comments, that I took his talk seriously. His treasurer, however, did not. Jim Dinning declared the notion dead on arrival, demonstrating Klein's weakness and Dinning's resolve for keeping the Alberta fiscal agenda on track. "I was in New York for a meeting with the credit rating agencies and someone came up to me and said, 'The word on the street [is] that your premier is going to write down the loan for Newfoundland'," Dinning recalled. "I as much as said the premier wouldn't be crazy enough to say something like that." Indeed, in a direct affront to Klein's leadership, Dinning phoned reporters to declare the suggestion out of order—and upon his return received a stern rebuke from party director Peter Elzinga. "Later, I talked to the minister of finance from Newfoundland," Dinning says, "and he told me, 'I know Ralphie means well, but he is not helping us with the credit rating boys, because if Alberta feels the need to subsidize or prop up the province of Newfoundland with a lower interest loan, they'll wonder, What's going on that you haven't told us?' So it was, in essence, 'Thanks for your generosity and it might be nice, but in the medium and long term, it ain't helping us'."

In February 1995, the province of Alberta posted its first balanced budget in ten years. Four months later, it announced the fiscal year had actually ended with a $958-million surplus, eliminating the threat of a deficit in the coming year and thus completing the balancing act a year ahead of schedule. The resulting publicity put Klein into high orbit internationally. He was invited to discuss the Alberta economy before 120 of the world's business elite at the annual Bilderberg convention, courtesy of Canadian newspaper magnate Conrad Black, who, as owner of the province's two largest newspapers, phoned Klein regularly. Seating at the conference was alphabetical, which placed Klein between American news anchor Peter Jennings and former secretary of state Henry Kissinger. Celebrity rarely impresses Klein and his only recollections of the all-star event are Kissinger's habit of nodding off and the oppressive security around the perimeter of the Zurich conference center. It was "interesting," he says, but there were few lessons to be learned from the globe's blue-chip executives.

Indeed, most of Canada was looking to Klein for inspiration. "Everyone is watching Klein to get some measure of how far they can go," University of Victoria political scientist Norman Ruff remarked at the time. "But the big question is whether this is an Alberta phenomenon, this ability to slash and burn and remain popular, or can it work elsewhere?"

The first to try to copy elements of the Klein revolution was rookie Ontario premier Mike Harris. While the Common Sense Revolutionaries went about their agenda differently—spending cuts were secondary to tax cuts—the shake-up-the-status-quo attitude toward delivering social services, health care and eduction was similar. In the months leading up to his policy launch, Harris MPPs were pounding on Klein's door for information. Rod Love delivered the keynote address at the Tory candidates' school in April 1995. In August 1995, a few months after he was first elected, Harris asked Klein to stop over en route to the annual premiers' conference in St. John's, Newfoundland. The pair met alone for the first time in a Royal York Hotel suite, and turned a scheduled fifteen-minute chat into an hour-long exchange of ideas.

Their friendship was obviously in full bloom a few nights later when I ran into Klein and his entourage in a George Street blues bar in St. John's, called Fat Cat's. The Kleins were sipping cocktails on the patio with their best friend, lawyer Jack Donahue, and they waved me over. Donahue, the organizational wizard behind some of the best Conservative conventions, was bouncing around the notion of holding the 1996 premiers' conference at the Jasper Park Lodge and using a train to carry the dignitaries from Edmonton to the scene—a concept he later carried to a spectacularly successful implementation—when four young men in suits, with cell phones glued to their ears, swarmed onto the patio.

They demanded a cloth from the waiter and started wiping down the seemingly clean chairs, counting the number of seats, pointing at me with quizzical looks and reconnecting via cellular to the mysterious sources on the other end. The fuss persisted for a few minutes until they assumed a hushed reverence and stepped back from the table. In walked Mike Harris with then-wife Janet. I soon found myself seated beside Colleen Klein, across the table from Harris, trying to avoid detection lest the discovery of a journalist in their midst ruin the relaxed social ambiance. After talking policy, fishing and golf with Klein for half an hour, Harris finally grinned at me and reached out for a handshake.

"Mike," he said.

"Don," I responded.

"So what do you do?" he asked.

"Media," I reluctantly confessed, figuring the ruse was up and the atmosphere poisoned.

Harris didn't miss a beat. "Just be thankful you don't have those bastards at the *Toronto Star* to deal with," he winced. Klein smirked at Harris's mistaken impression, but didn't correct it and returned to sharing the secrets of how to stage a revolution without suffering in the polls.

The Ralph Klein revolution clocked in at just two frantic years. It lasted until the end of 1995, when a gusher of oil, gas and lottery revenue replenished the treasury's reservoirs and lowered the anxiety felt by Albertans. The precise month of fiscal surrender was November 1995, and it happened in the basement laundromat of the Calgary hospital where Ralph Klein was born.

The new regional health authority had told 120 laundry workers that their $7.50-an-hour jobs were being replaced by a contract with K-Bro Linen Incorporated of Edmonton. The workers had taken a twenty-eight-per-cent pay cut a year earlier to stay competitive with the private sector, but that evidently wasn't enough. Their jobs were to be out-sourced. The next day, with nothing left to lose, they staged a wildcat strike.

The laundry workers' plight touched a chord with many of Alberta's public service unions. A bus driver spontaneously parked his vehicle to block the hospital entrance, nurses launched a work-to-rule campaign to show sympathy, other hospital workers hit the picket lines in solidarity. All told, twenty-seven hundred people walked the line to help 120 minimum wage earners stare down the mighty Klein machine. Less than a month after pledging "there's no surrender" to the federal government, which was withholding up to six hundred thousand dollars a month in transfer payments in a dispute over Alberta's decision to fund fee-for-service private health clinics, Ralph Klein looked into the angry eyes of Calgary laundry workers—and blinked.

Stockwell Day, labor minister at the time, had introduced legislation to encourage contracting-out initiatives. Day always believed government's role is limited to policy and regulation, with delivery of services best left at arms-length from the public sector. He drafted and introduced a bill to create delegated authorities to deliver government services. The Alberta Liberals, under the guidance of interim leader Bettie Hewes, whipped up considerable concern over the bill's privatization potential and Klein had ordered the bill abandoned. "The bill was getting all kinds of flak and Ralph didn't like it, so he said, 'Just do the strategy. You don't need the bill to do what is going to work anyway'," Day recalls.

The laundry workers, however, set Klein's antenna tingling. This, he decided, wasn't going to work. "It threatened our whole agenda," Day recalls. "Ralph phoned me and said something was going wrong. We wanted to allow people to contract out, out-source, right-size—anything but the word privatize—but he asked me to come back and have a look at this thing." Day returned to find Klein had already ordered a six-month moratorium against the laundry contract. Day met with the laundry workers to negotiate damage control. "The guys were upset that we'd given this contract to some huge company but hadn't asked if the guys in the sweatshop, literally in the sweatshop, if they could do it. We left them out of the loop. It did end up out-sourced, because they had a chance to put in a bid and saw they couldn't compete. We ensured every single one of them got retrained for different jobs in the hospital."

Once he started blinking, Klein couldn't stop. A week later, after settling down the laundry workers, he called off fifty-three million dollars in proposed hospital cuts, poured another forty million dollars into home and community care and cancelled a hundred-million-dollar cut in physician services. In year-end interviews, he acknowledged that his health care vision had been flawed and his cuts too deep. Doctors should have been consulted first, he admitted. "We hit the wall with health and we had to pull back," he concluded. "If there was one mistake it was not involving the doctors earlier." The sudden veer from restraint to reinvestment alarmed people close to Klein. Jim Dinning privately began to contemplate his retirement from politics and top aide Rod Love decided he'd seen enough. For Love, the revolution was over; the envelope was no longer being pushed; he was going to quit at year-end.

The government was settling down to run on autopilot. Klein was clearly getting comfortable, viewing his revolution like a completed home renovation project: the hard work was finished, it was time to enjoy the view.

Unfortunately for Klein, life was going to get very uncomfortable, very quickly.

Fourteen

The Near Death Experience

EVEN FIVE YEARS AFTER the final report that cleared them of ethical wrongdoing, Ralph and Colleen Klein can't bear to utter the name of the Calgary high-tech company that almost forced him to resign. They call it "the M word" if they talk about it at all. In a career remarkably clear of personal scandal, their involvement with Multi-Corp Incorporated caked the Teflon premier's record with enough mud, in late 1995 and for most of 1996, to badly tarnish his man-of-the-people image. It appeared that Klein had exercised political privilege to buy stock on special and favorable terms for considerable financial reward for him and his wife. The premier was investigated twice by Bob Clark, Alberta ethics commissioner, and Colleen was subjected to vigorous public scrutiny. For the first time, Klein's personal popularity tumbled below his party's approval rating.

On October 25, 1995, a tall, steely-eyed high school teacher, mid-way through his second term as a Liberal MLA, rose from his seat during Question Period, gave the premier an accusing glare and took a deep breath. He then proceeded to list a group of Tory insiders who had bought stock in a high-tech computer company Klein had promoted during a trade mission two years earlier. Reporters monitoring the action from the gallery above exchanged raised eyebrows: Interesting allegation, but did it have legs? Frank Bruseker saved his best ammunition for the post-Question Period scrum where he revealed that Colleen Klein had purchased ten thousand shares in Multi-Corp shortly after her husband cut the ribbon at the company's Hong Kong office.

The premier immediately denied any impropriety, but his sixth sense detected this was no ordinary shot in the dark. The Liberals clearly had a paper trail in their hands and the optics were all on their side. What was worse, a premier who prided himself on accurately anticipating every Official Opposition move was now being educated on the fly by Liberal revelations. News dribbled out daily of others very close to Klein who held Multi-Corp shares. His former television station boss, Thompson MacDonald, was a key investor. Rod Love, who calls Multi-Corp president Michael Lobsinger a close personal friend, had bought shares through his wife. So had Klein's top Calgary aide, Hugh Dunne. Longtime pal Ross Glen, who had booked Klein to help promote his furniture store opening the very next day, had put money into Multi-Corp too. Klein also remembered Multi-Corp's valiant offer in 1994 to take Ken Kowalski off the government's hands with a generous two-hundred-thousand-dollars-a-year employment package. The sheer number of Klein cronies in on the action had a bad odor about it. For a former journalist with a knack for turning a whiff into a scandal, Klein knew his situation was unlikely to pass the smell test.

From his regular perch in the observation deck, monitoring what was supposed to be a routine Opposition attack over health care or the auditor general's latest condemnation of the Swan Hills Waste Treatment Plant, Rod Love didn't need a mirror to see himself turning pale. "I knew there was trouble ahead three seconds after Frank Bruseker stood up in the house," he says. "The frustrating part is that I've never held the stock in my life and neither has Ralph Klein. But I knew what it would look like with the wives holding stock in this and my being friends with Lobsinger. Then we found he also cut a ribbon and I thought, 'Oh fuck, now I know how that's going to look.' It was never a feeling of 'We've been caught,' but I've been in the business long enough to know how the media is going to connect the dots."

The first dot had hit the map during Klein's inaugural overseas mission as Alberta's premier. On November 20, 1993, at the tail end of the tour, Klein cut a symbolic ribbon at the Hilton Hotel in front of twenty observers to open Multi-Corp's Hong Kong base. Company officials gave the premier a short demonstration of their technology, which held out the promising possibility of translating English into Chinese and back again over fax lines and the Internet. Until then, shares had traded as a highly speculative penny stock on the Alberta Stock Exchange. Fifteen cents was the close a month earlier. But three days after the ribbon-cutting, heavy trading drove the share price up to $1.45.

As far as Klein was concerned, the company opening was just another routine ceremonial chore that was throwing him off a very tight schedule. "I didn't know Multi-Corp from a hole in the ground. I didn't know Michael Lobsinger from a hole in the ground. There was this Multi-Corp reception where a demonstration was set up and it was very exciting, but that was it as far as I was concerned," Klein says.

Colleen Klein, however, showed more interest in the technology than her husband, and acted on her impulse as soon as she returned. She contacted her brother, Ted Hamilton, a prominent stockbroker in Calgary and a shareholder in the company. He wholeheartedly recommended the purchase and expedited the delivery of shares for one dollar apiece, a price below the current trading value, courtesy of the private holdings of Multi-Corp corporate secretary Larry Novak. As it happens, only a few weeks later, in a speech to the Hong Kong Business Association in Edmonton, Klein referred in passing to Multi-Corp as one of three promising home-grown business prospects for the Asian market.

What caused the ethics commissioner to squirm during his subsequent investigation was not just the below-market issue price offered to Colleen, but also the terms of payment. Colleen Klein would not have to settle the account for her shares until after they were sold, paying ten per cent interest over the interim. It was a sweetheart arrangement by any definition.

Klein remembers his discomfort when Colleen told him about the stock deal over the kitchen table at home. He cautioned his wife, a novice at playing the stock market, that if the shares were a gift, they would have to be returned. Colleen insisted they weren't a gift because she would ultimately have to pay for the shares with interest. Nonetheless, Klein insisted his wife register the investment with the ethics commissioner. "Why? It's none of his God-damned business," she fumed. A month later, she reluctantly filed the disclosure statement, but omitted the special payment terms. It was a mistake that tainted her husband's record and very nearly cost him his job.

Perhaps the reason the Multi-Corp affair did not strike Albertans as sufficiently sleazy to drive Ralph Klein from office, as it most certainly would have in most other provinces, is the unpretentious nature and selfless charity of the central figure in the scandal—Colleen Klein.

She was born Donna Evelyn Hamilton on November 26, 1940, in Victoria, B.C., the daughter of a single mother named Jessy and her air force boyfriend, Ted Hamilton. Only fourteen months later, after giving birth to a second girl, her mother succumbed to a debilitating bout of post-partum depression, and the search began for a branch of her family tree for Donna to live on. It was a journey not unlike the odyssey her future husband was enduring at the same time. She was given up for adoption to her paternal grandparents and renamed Colleen. At age four, her grandmother died and she moved on to live with her great-grandparents, who raised her on a ranch. She started her education in a Vancouver convent before being reclaimed at age six by her biological father, now serving in the air force, and a stepmother she came to treasure as her own mother until her death in 1995.

Born with a port-wine birthmark across part of her face and the side of her neck, which she now carefully disguises with makeup, Colleen found herself the subject of regular taunting and bullying by classmates. It was not a treatment Colleen endured without a fight. The scrappy, Scottish blood in her triggered regular bouts of angry shouting, shoving and vicious hair pulling when she was required to defend herself from the torment. Even though the shuffle between guardians in her early years and the regular transfers to follow her father's air force career made finding and keeping friends difficult, Colleen says she had a happy childhood, even if it meant having only her imagination for companionship.

After graduating from high school in Calgary, she worked menial jobs in gas stations and at the race track, where she timed stock cars, until she settled into a job at the Lakeview Calgary Co-op, the grocery store where she shops to this day. Her first marriage, at age sixteen to Fred Pinder, was an acrimonious thirteen-year relationship that ended in 1970 when she fled the family home at night, clutching their two pre-teen daughters. She turned to the courts for protection, citing allegations of physical and verbal abuse, and obtained a restraining order against Pinder until their divorce could be finalized. About a year later, fate came calling for Colleen at Calgary's Westgate Hotel bar, where she met her next husband, Ralph Klein, having a drink.

Despite the apparent old-fashioned sacrifice of her own job for her husband's career, and her fierce stand-by-your-man attitude, Colleen Klein is not the sort to putter around in the kitchen, cooking up home-made dinners for hubby's return from the office. Within weeks of Klein's surprise mayoralty victory in 1980, she started using her newfound fame and connections to raise what ultimately became millions of dollars for charities, with a consistent preference for children's causes. She was among the first to fundraise for Calgary's Ronald McDonald House and has provided unwavering support for the Kid's Kottage, an organization that gives parents a time-out from their children in moments of crisis or extreme stress. She helps choose the benefactors of her husband's charity golf tournaments, has been a fixture on the Canadian Liver Foundation's annual 100-hole golf classic and quietly gathers used books during her husband's political tours to ship to native centers in remote northern Alberta communities.

In the mid-1970s, a long-sought reunion with her birth mother confirmed what she had suspected for much of her life—a native ancestry. Her grandfather's relationship with a Cree woman had been denied by her father, who insisted right up to his death he was of pure Scottish blood when, in fact, he was half native. "I felt I'd been looking in the mirror all those years and only saw half a face. Part of me never existed. When I found out the truth, I was a whole person again," she says. Rather than continue the family secret, Colleen revealed it in an inspired move to boost a campaign against the epidemic of aboriginal youth suicide.

In Klein's second term as premier, Collen charged into political activism. In 1997, she was appointed to a committee that was planning projects to mark the province's centenary in 2005. In 1999, she chaired a Children's Forum, which brought together academics and experts in the field of social services to discuss the care of children in general, and the identification and protection of children at risk. It produced over a hundred vague recommendations in 1999 which Colleen resolves to still see implemented, even if it requires intensive pillow talk with the man who shares her bed.

Her influence is easy to see in other areas. In the fall of 1994 she arrived in a Calgary bar one night where I was having drinks with Calgary MLA Heather Forsyth and a pair of vice squad detectives. We had just toured Popcorn Alley to see first-hand the johns on the prowl for underage sex on the kiddy stroll. Colleen listened with rapt horror to the plight of these kids and the legal loopholes that prevented police from apprehending children or charging their pedophile clients. The subsequent elevation of Forsyth's private member's bill to being the next legislative session's flagship legislation was always attributed to Colleen Klein's influence. The bill became known as the Colleen Amendment.

A few months later, Aline Chretien took the seat next to her during a Team Canada tour to China, and Colleen did not miss the opportunity to educate Canada's first lady on an issue she felt strongly about. Hoping to find a powerful ally for Alberta's judicial crackdown on child prostitution, Colleen raised the subject of the controversial legislation with the prime minister's wife. Mrs. Chretien delivered all the politically correct lines, but there was little eye contact, and Colleen concluded that it was a sympathetic, but ultimately meaningless, encounter. Undeterred, she mailed Aline Chretien a copy of Alberta's new law. Two years later, she had yet to hear back from 24 Sussex Drive.

Colleen doesn't hesitate to use her exclusive access to influence her husband's cabinet picks. While Klein is generally sheltered from the gossip and scandal of his MLAs' private lives, Colleen keeps him up to speed on what's going on, and based on horror stories from their estranged spouses, she has, at times, taken an open and vocal dislike to certain ministers. In at least one case, a minister in her bad books suffered a sudden demotion in her husband's next cabinet shuffle. After the 2001 election, she lobbied hard to get the minister of community development, Shirley McClellan, appointed the first woman treasurer in Alberta's history. She didn't get her way entirely, but McClellan was elevated to the position of deputy premier, partly to accommodate Colleen's demand for a greater prominence by women in the government.

Colleen was a keynote speaker at the gathering of Conservative candidates prior to the 2001 election. In her speech, she stressed the importance of family and insisted, speaking from considerable personal experience, that a candidate's family should not be overlooked upon entering the political world. "When Ralph was elected, I took over the responsibilities of parenting," she says. "Unfortunately, Ralph missed many special moments in the children's lives. For the most part, I think most of them understood. The real danger in politics is that it can turn the family into strangers and strangers into the family."

The intermingling of politics and family spelled bad news for the Kleins. In early 1994, Colleen's Multi-Corp shares were rising in dream-like fashion, doubling in value by mid-January. They doubled again by the following October, the same month Thompson MacDonald, acting for the company, approached Love to offer Kowalski a job. When the details started to break almost a year later, the Liberals and media had a field day with the tangled web of strange coincidences, multiple insider connections, sudden windfalls and apparent conflicts. In November 1995, Ralph Klein vowed to resign if he was found guilty of a conflict of interest, and for two long days, the ethics commissioner, Bob Clark, held Klein's fate in his hands as he wrote up his report. In order to clearly prove a conflict, Clark would have had to link Multi-Corp's rising share value to Klein's ribbon-cutting or to his fleeting mentions of the company in speeches. It was a connection Clark couldn't prove. Thousands of firms had received the same kind of endorsement. Nor was Clark able to prove the premier had received inside information beyond the optimistic banter any company president would share with a trade mission leader over dinner. In the end, Clark ruled that a "technical breach" of the law had occurred, but he dismissed Colleen's undisclosed share purchase arrangement as "unintentionally incomplete." It was a verdict of considerable tolerance and was immediately branded a whitewash by the Liberals. The Kleins and the Loves announced plans to sell their shares and donate the proceeds to charity as an act of public contrition. While he may have been cleared on a technicality, this was the closest Ralph Klein ever came to getting caught with his hand in the cookie jar.

In April 1996, Liberal leader Grant Mitchell and Frank Bruseker opened the new session of the legislature by indignantly arguing that the ethics commissioner had not probed deeply enough into either Colleen's favorable payment terms or Klein's meetings with Multi-Corp's president, Michael Lobsinger. Klein, they discovered, had returned to Hong Kong in late 1994 as part of a Team Canada mission, and Lobsinger was seated at the Alberta table during one mission breakfast. Even more unsettling, Lobsinger joined the Kleins, Hugh Dunne and a handful of government officials that evening for a private dinner aboard a Chinese junk on an excursion to South Lamma Island.

The Liberals gloated at having the Alberta premier on the run, and Klein didn't help his situation any by losing his cool both in the legislature and at news conferences. "This is a smear campaign. It is vicious, it is reckless and it is hurtful. This is the political equivalent of a drive-by shooting. They don't care who they hit and they don't care who they hurt," Klein shouted in the legislature one day, his finger stabbing the air towards Bruseker. An hour later, he stormed out of a news conference, and refused to answer any more questions about Multi-Corp. The next day, he skipped Question Period because, as communications director Jim Dau so eloquently put it to a scrum of reporters, "He doesn't want to deal with the bullshit."

Hounded by the Liberals on oversights in his first report, Bob Clark reluctantly opened another investigation into the premier's 1994 dinner with Lobsinger and his visit to a Chinese province that later signed a deal with Multi-Corp. The second probe ultimately cleared the Kleins in December 1996, but the full year of dogged, withering public attention turned the personable, accessible premier, who was still the toast of the conservative world for his fiscal success, into a cranky, preoccupied shadow of his old self. Klein's legendary communications skills deserted him and his testiness grew as the saga unfurled, one new wrinkle at a time. The premier's relationship with the press gallery, civil at the worst of times, developed into an us-versus-them hostility. "It was hard to get the real story out. We'd deal with one allegation and something else would pop up," recalls former Klein communications director Fay Orr. "The premier was in a terrible frame of mind. You'd try to prep him for media and he'd get all angry. He was so frustrated because he wouldn't perceive he'd done anything wrong and it impinged on his integrity."

Around the cabinet table, Klein's ministers watched in alarm, not knowing what to say, as their leader sat slumped in his chair at the head of the table, lost somewhere between a sleepwalk and a stupor. "It hurt," Klein admits now. "I don't know how to describe it, but every day during that ordeal I had pains in my stomach, anxiety pains. It was that people simply wouldn't let go. Bruseker wouldn't let go, [*Edmonton Journal* reporter] Charles Rusnell wouldn't let go. He dogged my wife and my brother-in-law and me and everyone else associated with it."

The strategic brain of Rod Love was equally distracted by the public attention his wife's purchase of Multi-Corp shares was receiving. He no longer surfaced to monitor his boss during Question Period or at news conferences, but kept himself holed up in his office, fearful he would spread the taint to his boss. His self-imposed isolation, however, only made things appear worse.

Klein fired Dunne, his southern Alberta director, in early 1996 for reasons that were never clearly articulated, although Klein now allows that Dunne was "not entirely truthful" on some of the Multi-Corp information. Around the same time, Colleen Klein donated the fifty-one-thousand-dollar profit she made on her ten-thousand-dollar Multi-Corp investment to charities for aboriginal youth. A few months later, the premier publicly severed all ties with Thompson MacDonald. In an unprecedented act for Klein, he declared that his former newsroom boss was no longer a friend and instantly destroyed MacDonald's government relations business, a cold shoulder that took years to warm up again. Klein's final act of damage control was to appoint an ethics panel to review the Alberta government's conflict of interest guidelines. It recommended changes which would have given the province some of the toughest legislation in Canada, but, as the scandal faded from the front page, few of the far-reaching provisions were ever implemented, including a requirement to avoid perceived conflicts of interest that would have encompassed the Multi-Corp saga.

By the time Bob Clark's final all-clear report was issued in December 1996, Klein had bounced back in the polls and the Opposition's fixation with the saga was becoming tiresome to the media and public alike. "If I'd been on the other side, I would've been as aggressive as Bruseker was," Klein reflects. "But I didn't know the arrangements. That is what saved me. The arrangements were through Colleen's brother."

"It was the most traumatic thing that's ever happened to me," says Colleen Klein. "I can't even bear to hear the word. What hurt me more than anything was that I let Ralph down. But I've taken that chapter and put it aside. It's closed for good."

Flickers of doubt remain that the entire Multi-Corp story has been told. The job offer to Kowalski did not become public until 1998, and, despite the nightmares the Multi-Corp experience caused, Rod Love joined the the company as a director in 2001 after it had been renamed Zi Corp. The company's ties to the first-term Klein regime appear, even now, to have been inordinately friendly and pervasive, even by Alberta standards where coddling the Conservatives is the only game in town for corporations seeking favors.

To this day, though, it is hard to prove, or to believe seriously, that Multi-Corp was a scheme by the Kleins to flex their political muscle for easy money. The scandal was, however, a clear reflection of the very tight circle that binds Ralph's world. He socializes with few, listens to even fewer. Multi-Corp was a hot stock market tip passed through his closest aides and advisers to him and his wife. Forgetting their delicate circumstances, they accepted generous purchase arrangements and—just their luck—Klein's political value plunged as the stock's rose. Klein should consider himself fortunate; other premiers have been hounded from office for much less. As the following months would prove, Albertans can be patient enough to forgive Klein his mistakes.

In early 1997, feeling personally vindicated, Klein turned his attention to a pressing matter. He was preparing to call an election and his goal was never clearer: revenge. He wanted to wipe the Liberals off the Alberta landscape and he set his sights on one MLA in particular—Multi-Corp tormenter Frank Bruseker. The word went out from the Conservative election headquarters—money and manpower would not be an obstacle to getting Tory candidate Greg Melchin elected in Bruseker's Calgary Northwest constituency.

The deficit was a fading memory when retiring treasurer Jim Dinning posted the February 1997 budget, which boosted spending by $900 million and still recorded a $2.6-billion surplus. Minutes after the budget speech was read, Ralph Klein called his second election for March 11, 1997, with a firm promise to do nothing but defend his first-term achievements. His campaign slogan: Promises Made...Promises Kept. Klein deferred all questions of new spending, which he described as "reinvestment," to a Growth Summit that would call upon Albertans later that year to draw up a blueprint for their bold new post-deficit society.

If the first election was the revolution, the second was the vindication. Despite a twenty per cent slash in spending, which, if population growth and inflation are factored in, was actually closer to thirty per cent, Klein was coasting toward re-election. He had wisely struck a truce with his only true opposition—Alberta doctors—by lifting a cap on physician billings. Most nurses pocketed a deal with their regional health authorities before or during the campaign. Suspense at the electoral outcome was in short supply.

The leader of the Alberta Liberals, Grant Mitchell, faced an opponent supposedly tainted by personal scandal and vilified for harsh cost-cutting. Mitchell opened the campaign with a promise to ban video lottery terminals and raise spending for health and education. But Klein had him boxed in. When Mitchell attacked the cuts, Klein called him a fan of big deficits.

When Mitchell promised to keep the books balanced, Klein wondered how that was possible without more and difficult budget cuts. Besides, Mitchell was facing the same paradox as all Klein opponents. Whenever Alberta voters believe Klein has screwed up, they trust him more than anyone else to fix the problem. The election came down to Klein listing his kept promises, pointing to the hot economy and letting the Liberals quibble over his methodology.

Three weeks into the sleepy twenty-eight-day campaign, with the polls showing Klein had an electoral hammerlock on every region of the province, a new issue surfaced. The spectre of Alberta becoming New Brunswick West, and replicating former premier Frank McKenna's 1987 seizure of every provincial seat, had become a distinct possibility. Could he—and should he—win them all? Even in Edmonton the polls gave the Tories a twelve-point lead suggesting the virtual one-party state of Alberta would be confirmed in reality at the ballot box.

Grant Mitchell refused to accept a tactic that his own candidates had adopted late in the campaign, abandon any pretext of forming a government and sell voters on the merits of keeping some Liberal Opposition. Mitchell steadfastly believed he could still be premier. "The polls are wrong," he insisted. But the spectre of a complete wipeout of the Opposition was resonating with the public. Former high-profile Liberal MLA Michael Percy, who quit in 1997 to become dean at the University of Alberta business school, was sensing the shift. "Voters started coming back to the Liberals due to the fear of the sweep," he told the *Edmonton Journal*. "I would not, like Grant, dismiss the polls and say they were wrong. I think the polls were correct and people responded strategically. You could feel the electorate turn."

It would be too little, too late, however. Even the pro-Liberal *Edmonton Journal* could not deny the big picture as the campaign wound down. "Voters looking for a party to actually govern Alberta have only one choice," the paper's editorial board noted in an election eve lament that trashed Mitchell's performance. "It's a Ralpherendum. Ralph wins."

And so he did. The Alberta Conservatives' share of the popular vote rose from under forty-five per cent to more than fifty-one per cent as

Klein swept sixty-three of the eighty-three seats. With only two exceptions, a constituency in downtown Calgary and another in Lethbridge, they won every one of the fifty-nine ridings outside greater Edmonton and boosted their share of the vote inside the capital from thirty per cent to nearly thirty-eight per cent. The Liberals were reduced to eighteen seats and suffered a precipitous ten per cent decline in the popular vote inside their Edmonton stronghold. A year later, Mitchell would quit as leader. The New Democrats returned to the legislature with a pair of seats in the capital.

In Calgary, Klein's Multi-Corp nemesis, Frank Bruseker, had been beaten decisively by accountant Greg Melchin. Years later, Klein aides would call me up and cackle with glee at learning that Bruseker was back in the education business—working as a substitute teacher. Such was the high price he paid for incurring the wrath of Ralph.

At the Klein victory speech in an old Edmonton airport hangar, however, the smiles were noticeably tight on election night. The great expectations of total annihilation were so high, a mere landslide was considered a disappointment. The capital had again resisted Klein's charms.

Fifteen

The Sultans of Spin

RALPH KLEIN IS A communicator first, a politician second. Arguably, without the first trait, he'd be a second-rate politician. He can be an excruciatingly average public speaker, and he has a shy streak that sometimes makes one-on-one encounters with him awkward. What sets him apart from the pack of politicians is what you see at news conferences and in scrums. In those settings, the media become his Stradivarius. He is a natural in front of the lens, and the less his brain is filled with factual clutter, the better he performs. "The premier was tough to prep," recalls Fay Orr, his communications director during the second term. "You had to brief him very quickly, in five or ten minutes. You couldn't get into a lot of depth or take a long time. It was a challenge to brief him so quickly, with one sentence per issue. He'd want to know 'What's the issue?' and 'What's the line?' but he didn't want to be blind-sided either. We'd give him the top two or three things, highlight the key points and send him out the door."

His brain only superficially loaded, Klein still faces the press utterly relaxed. He gives a wink to his favorite writer, *Edmonton Sun* columnist Neil Waugh, as he enters the press room and opens the floor to questions with a groan or a grin and an "Okay, shoot." He never shows fear, apprehension or hesitation. He doesn't play to the cameras, he banters with the reporters, usually on a first-name basis in seemingly unguarded conversation. If he's hit with an unanticipated question and draws a blank for an answer, he'll admit bafflement and scan his briefing notes like he hasn't seen them before (and often he hasn't), searching for inspiration. He doesn't hold back anger, laughter or even tears during these exchanges. If he's enjoying himself, he'll brush off the aides trying to urge him off the podium and let the questions flow until the reporters run out of gas.

His news conferences are legendary for being like the proverbial box of chocolates—you just never know what you're going to get. Klein has a habit of scooping himself, and often enough, others as well. Minutes after Jean Charest telephoned Klein to confide his decision to leave the federal Conservative leadership for the Quebec Liberals, Klein faced reporters and let slip the news. He has been known to change policies even as the cameras are rolling. Midway through the loud and hostile news conference following his government's invocation of the Constitution's notwithstanding clause in a bill to limit court awards to the wrongfully sterilized, Klein signaled sudden discomfort with the bill. Minutes after leaving the press conference, he ordered the bill yanked off the order paper and killed. Covering Klein is considered a form of journalism unto itself. The press gallery has even given it a name: Ralph Says.

For someone who is a natural in the spotlight, Klein is surprisingly reticent about national exposure. The prospect of a Canada-wide television podium, which would drag most premiers out of bed into a studio long before sunrise for an interview on Newsworld or "Canada A.M.," holds no appeal for Klein. His staff doesn't even consult him on such requests; they automatically decline. "He isn't interested in national media, but he'd get excited over appearing in international publications like the *Wall Street Journal* or *Barron's*," Fay Orr recalls. At first ministers' conferences, Klein makes little effort to find the uni-mike. He'd much rather let publicity-seeking premiers hog the spotlight, and he pauses to chat to the assembled horde of scribes only if there's a clamor for his comments. If there are issues Klein wants to highlight, he'll summon the Alberta media to his hotel room for a private chat late in the afternoon.

For a politician, he displays a unique trust in the media. The lowliest of federal cabinet ministers would never enter a scrum or face an interview without a staff member present to record every word for immediate transcription back at the office. Klein's staff have never bothered recording or transcribing his comments. It's considered a waste of staff time and tape.

Klein's relationship with the media is amicable enough that he's even been able to negotiate reduced access at the most critical point in the political cycle. During the March 2001 election, when Klein found himself getting swarmed by boom mikes and cameras at every pit-stop, something he found personally irritating and felt interfered with campaigning, he approached journalists to suggest a compromise—a scrum at the beginning and conclusion of every campaign day with unfettered access during only one of two daily campaign stops. Surprisingly, they agreed. "It worked only because the leader had built up a trust with the media over the years, and reporters knew that if he said he would be in a certain place at a certain time, it would happen," Klein wrote in his field study of the campaign for a Mount Royal College correspondence course. "Had the trust been broken, the media would have gone back to the free-for-all that occurred earlier in the campaign." He is, however, cynical of the media's motives. "I'm getting tired of dealing with the media," Klein admits. "There's a multitude of ministers. If there are questions, ask them. The trick is not the action, but it is the reaction. Can we get the premier crosswired with one of his ministers? That's the game now."

Klein's stable of spin doctors meets daily when the house is in session to decide what news is released, how it's presented and where. They have the power to suppress, expedite, leak, shred or rewrite news from any minister in order to extract the maximum benefit from good news and minimize fallout from the bad. If positive news appears too blasé for the press gallery, they move the announcement to Calgary, hoping to generate buzz away from the Dome. If negative stories are piling up in multiple ministries, they dump them all at the same time on the same day, preferably late on a Friday, and, ideally, just before a holiday weekend. On the TV series "West Wing," this strategy for overwhelming the media's resources in order to minimize the depth of negative coverage is called "taking out the trash." In Alberta, where it was introduced most blatantly in 1993, it's called "bundling" the news or "carpetbombing" the press gallery. "It looked pretty obvious to me that if you had some bad news to wrap it up with other bad news," says Love of the process he implemented. "You don't just give them one stick and say, 'Go ahead and hit me'."

Much has been written of Ralph Klein's media manipulation tactics. They have been portrayed as a twisted attempt to impregnate reporters with government mind-think, somehow rendering their minds incapable of independent thought or action. Most of the criticism comes from those who have never covered Klein or witnessed the more aggressive media-handling tactics deployed in other provincial capitals or on Parliament Hill. An early Klein biographer, writer Frank Dabbs, insists "the price of access for journalists was to assent to his terms. As a tool for suppressing critical inquiry, this was unparalleled."

This theory falls apart, however, for a premier as unconditionally accessible as Klein. As mayor, he'd scrum on command. Early on in his tenure as premier, he was available to the media two or three times a day. Eventually reporters themselves complained of the endless, rolling scrums. It wasn't until Klein stakeouts reached the extreme of reporters pouncing on him outside the legislature fitness center that communications director Jim Dau instituted regular daily news conferences. For any reporter hoping to trade positive coverage, there is very little further access to negotiate. The only one-on-one interviews Klein gives are during his annual year-end parade, when journalists from any accredited outlet, friend and foe alike, get their own time slot to quiz him on any topic. The only time that process had even a hint of being manipulated was when *Herald* reporter Steve Chase ingeniously decided to bring along a bottle of Beaujolais to our year-end interview in 1997. He presented the red wine to the premier as a Christmas greeting. Klein walked over to his kitchen, popped the cork and started pouring. Our fifteen-minute interview was thus extended to the full happy hour it took to down the bottle, with the added benefit that the premier became more talkative as the wine level dropped.

If there is one lever Klein uses to extract positive coverage, it is his government's leak strategy. "Leaks are political currency," Klein observes. He understands the value of a leak as more than just a carrot to dangle in front of the media donkeys to keep them on track. He has a cagey understanding of how news exclusives work. Klein regularly laments good news getting buried under piles of negative reaction. A scoop, by its very nature, eliminates that problem and goes one better. It guarantees greater play for the story than it would otherwise receive and usually results in more favorable reporting, without the clutter of Opposition reaction.

"The essence of our leak strategy on any particular issue is what do we want to leak to whom to get maximum benefit to the organization," Love says. "It was a simple litmus test, to whom and when to leak to get maximum political benefit." If the story was national, it went to the *National Post*, starting on that newspaper's first day of publication when Klein's speech to a United Alternative convention was deemed sufficiently newsworthy for the paper's inaugural front page. If the story was provincial, it went to either the *Calgary Herald* or to one of the Alberta papers in the Sun newspaper chain. The *Edmonton Journal*, which was a harsh critic of Klein's budget cutting throughout the first term, was rarely blessed by the brown envelope. The *Herald*, also critical of his deficit elimination strategy, was only given inside information because it was the hometown paper for the premier and some of his top ministers. One thing was certain—the morning a major leak creased one paper's front page, the other major paper in that city would be quickly demanding a quid pro quo brown envelope. On rare occasions, leaks on unrelated issues were used to relieve pressure building on the government in other areas. Thus, when a cabinet minister was being fired, the phone had a habit of ringing with a voice on the other line whispering the latest budget surplus figure.

Unauthorized leaks did occur, despite the harsh consequences if the culprit was discovered. Witchhunts were rarely conducted, however. "You'll never find a leak," Love shrugs. "It's between the guy who leaked it and the reporter who received it and neither's going to squeal. But if there'd been a bad leak, we'd bring all the executive assistants into the room and have a long discussion and say, 'This is dumb because it did not get us the maximum political benefit. The journalist will turn on you faster than anybody else. If you think you did it to make a friend, you're wrong. If you think you did it to help this organization, you're wrong. If you think you did it because you're smart, you're wrong'."

Through the darkest days of the budget cuts, Klein needed a media outlet he could bash, the better to present himself as an underdog fighting the soft, left establishment. The so-called "Southamnistas"—the *Calgary Herald* and *Edmonton Journal*—served Klein well in this regard by offering up hostile commentary on his every budget-cutting move. Shortly after he became premier, Klein delivered a blistering blast at the *Herald* in a *Globe and Mail* interview. "I've never had the support of the left-wing *Calgary Herald*, a paper that appeals to the academic elite," he fumed, conveniently forgetting it was the same paper that had crowned him "Calgarian of the Decade" just three years earlier. "It is the most obnoxious, off-side, out of tune newspaper I've ever seen." In contrast, the consistently supportive Sun chain was hailed as a godsend at every opportunity. In a not-so-subtle dig at Southam reporters, Klein placed a copy of the *Edmonton Sun* prominently on the dashboard of his car whenever it was parked at the legislature.

The major dailies in both chains became less confrontational and selectively supportive as the cutbacks eased and the good economic times returned, but one media enemy remains to this day—the Canadian Broadcasting Corporation. Radio or television, local or national, French language or English, if they're sporting the exploding CBC logo, Klein hates them and makes no effort to hide it. "It goes back to the day when I was on the beat and I'd hold up two microphones, one for radio and one for television," Klein recalls. "Because of their union structure, we did three times the work of three reporters at the CBC. It used to offend me when I'd see a sound person and a producer and a cameraman and a reporter, and the same for French and English radio."

As a firm policy, Klein refuses all but a few extraordinary requests from the CBC for interviews, and he behaves badly when he does appear. Jim Dau recalls a rare CBC interview Klein accepted during the Conservative leadership race. He roused his irritable candidate at

5:30 a.m. to make it to the studio on time, only for Klein to be surprised by the sight of his chief rival, bright-eyed morning person Nancy Betkowski, seated in another interview chair. "I hate mornings and I hate the God-damned CBC," a furious Klein thundered to no one in particular.

During one aggressive interview on CBC Television's "The Journal" in the early 1990s, Klein got so fed up with the host's interruptions that he unhooked his microphone and stormed off the set. He soon returned and demanded that she listen to his full answer before asking her next question. The one exception to his anti-CBC bias was the late Peter Gzowski, host of the radio network's "Morningside" show. Gzowski, in Klein's eyes, was a rumpled reflection of what he had been like as a reporter. "I am looking forward in early January to going to Vancouver at CBC expense to appear on 'Front Page Challenge,'" Klein grinned in a soft dig at the public broadcaster at the start of a December 1994 interview.

"Oh, you're not supposed to say that," Gzowski whispered back.

"Why not?" Klein retorted, unaware "Front Page Challenge" was a guess-the-guest show.

"You just gave it away," Gzowski replied.

"You can cut that out if you want," Klein suggested, not realizing he was on a live broadcast.

Even today, with his overwhelming majority government facing no significant political opposition, he can't resist a poke at his favorite electronic scapegoat. In an academic paper he wrote on the 2001 provincial election, Klein quoted long extracts from the report of a CBC panel that slammed the corporation's own television coverage of the Klein campaign, specifically on the issue of electrical power deregulation—a move which triggered wild price spikes to Albertans shortly after it was implemented in late 2000. In one incident, described by the panel as "a badly staged pantomime," someone wearing a disguise was introduced on a local CBC newscast as an authority on the negatives of electrical deregulation. Even the person's voice was electronically altered. No counterbalancing viewpoint was presented, thus violating CBC's statement of journalistic fairness principles. One panel member also noted an anti-Klein bias in the CBC's interviews with the party leaders. "With few exceptions the questions directed to Klein were colored with severe criticisms and by contrast the Liberal and NDP leaders were introduced with fairly positive spins," the panel member noted.

Klein has sought retaliation at every opportunity. His "Ask Ralph" television production and his radio call-in shows were carried on the independent networks now owned by CanWest. When his annual state-of-the-province address is televised, he refuses CBC's offer to carry it at no charge, and opts instead to pay private broadcasters for the same service. "There are some good people at CBC and I've worked with a lot of those producers, switchers and reporters. It's not a problem with the individuals, it's with the corporate philosophy," he says.

In the spring of 1997, a letter to the editor appeared in the *Calgary Herald* in response to a column of mine. The column had welcomed the rookie MLAs in the successfully re-elected Conservative government to a meaningless life of back-bench drudgery. Issued above the name Marisa Etmanski, the popular communications coordinator for the premier's office who, in fact, had nothing to do with its creation, the sardonic letter is instructive in how Klein's spin doctors viewed the Alberta press:

Now that *Herald* columnist Don Martin has made you oh-so-clever about the way the legislature works, we thought it might be helpful to tell you about how the legislative press gallery works. The gallery, incidentally, is otherwise known as the ratpack, the beast, the mob, and other adjectives normally found only in adult magazines.

- The media will tell you that they are your friend. That is not true. This will become painfully obvious to you the minute you get into trouble. Count your friends in the media then.
- The media will tell you they need the story immediately because of their deadline. There is no deadline. They want to file their stories so they can go to the bar.
- As you agonize over whether or not to leak a story to a reporter, the reporter's final argument will be to lower his or her voice and solemnly inform you that "the public has a right to know." Actually, the reporter's assignment editor has made it clear that getting this

story is a career-defining moment. The public is not part of the equation.

- A reporter will tell you that you might as well confirm a story because "two or three MLAs" have already done so. Don't buy it. If you confirm a rumor, you will be the first.
- There is no such thing as "off the record." But, having shot your mouth off, the best you can negotiate for is "reliable source."
- Reporters will always tell you that you are doing a great job. This compliment will be swiftly followed by a request for information on the budget. Just to help the readers understand, of course.

A final word.

If war was declared tomorrow, and you went on a talk show, you will get a question about "distinct society". Don't answer it. More people have talked their way out of the legislature than into it.

You're welcome.

Marisa Etmanski
Ministry of Truth

Alberta's current Minister of Truth is both a creature and a creation of the mass media. Ralph Klein both understands it and uses it to his benefit. He'll rein the message in and harness the messengers to drive home a difficult agenda. He instinctively knows journalism's enormous capacity for support if properly stroked, and its dangerous potential for opposition if ignored. He has perfected the black market currency of the strategic leak. He knows that any friendly gesture, be it calling reporters by their first name, eliminating a petty obstacle to their ability to do their job, golfing in the annual press gallery tournament or taking reporters out for the occasional private nightcap, reaps subtle, long-term rewards.

He approaches strategic communications through the colorful prism of his own experiences. As a former reporter himself, Klein has been there, done that—whether buying the government line or slanting its message, depending on who presented what and how. He instinctively knows that a journalist shunned is more dangerous than one given straight answers. He knows that answering a question with a "maybe" means "yes," and a "no" answer means "maybe." He dodges government protests because, he says, their news value is diminished if he ignores them. Despite a notoriously thin skin, he respects critical comment on policy. He will nurse a bitter grudge from a cheap personal shot for a long time, though.

Above all else, he is a skilled reporter in charge of a communications empire with millions of dollars at its disposal. It is an empire dedicated to telling only one story—the facts according to Ralph Klein. And as the minister in charge, all Klein aims to sell is the truth, the selective truth and nothing but his truth—so help him Ralph.

Sixteen

The Changing of the Guard

O N DECEMBER 8, 1997, almost five years to the day after Klein was elected to the premier's chair, the Siamese twins of Alberta politics separated. Barely two years into the Tories' first term, Rod Love was already worn out, impatient with the pace of change and bored. On a business trip to England in mid-1995, he sat down on a park bench in London with his wife, Charlene, and promised the mother of his three young children that the first term of Klein's government would be his last. Love kept his promise, and after his boss's successful re-election, he submitted his tearful resignation.

Despite his image as the dark force behind the premier, the entire legislature staff showed up at a caucus meeting to lament his departure. Warnings circulated ominously—and accurately—among the MLAs of serious problems ahead without Love in the legislature. The perception that Klein was lost without Love's cerebral genius to guide him has been the only real source of aggravation between this intensely close pair of friends.

"They might have Ralph Klein, but we have Ralph's brain," quipped the CBC television producer responsible for booking analysts for the 1992 Calgary civic election. Calgary's independent station had landed Klein for their commentary, the CBC had booked Love. Or so they thought— within an hour of the producer's quote hitting the headlines, Love cancelled, slamming his phone down in a huff. "I know a lot of people thought Ralph couldn't take a bio break without Rod, but they didn't know Ralph," argues Colleen Klein. "He may ask you for advice, but it doesn't mean he'll take it. He just enjoys getting a different perspective."

The truth is, it's doubtful either could have reached his current pinnacle without the other. Love needed Klein to sell difficult policies to the public; Klein needed Love's attention to strategic detail. While Love has fought other federal, provincial and civic election battles, most of them have been unsuccessful and nowhere has he been able to replicate the magic of his Klein connection. There was an almost telepathic link between the two. In the mid-1990s, I sat in on one of their Question Period prep sessions for a feature article. I was astounded to see them finishing each other's sentences and feeding off each other's energy as they devised deadly, clipworthy comebacks to every expected Opposition attack. "He's almost too brilliant sometimes," the premier says ruefully of Love.

Love picked the right time to leave. His aura as the invincible evil genius guiding the Klein administration never completely recovered from the Multi-Corp scandal. During his time in provincial politics his circle of wealthy friends had given him expensive tastes that dramatically exceeded his five-figure income, even with help from his five-figure expense account. On his exit from the legislature, he bought himself a couple of expensive suits and hung out his shingle as a one-man strategic consulting company to a Rolodex full of blue-chip clients, including the Progressive Conservative Party of Alberta. The Liberals were barely able to contain their relief at his departure, convinced that Klein would quickly fall apart.

In the spring of 1998, soon after striking out on his own, Love was briefly intrigued by Jean Charest's move from federal Conservative leader to leader of the Quebec Liberals. Love crafted an insightful analysis of the federal Reform and Tory feud that included a warning that Bay Street bucks would dry up if the right wing remained fragmented without a fresh face and fresh policies to unite behind. The obvious catalyst for such a reunion was one Ralph Klein, with his perennial sidekick as the mastermind. Love founded the "24 Club" (a reference to 24 Sussex Drive) whose "members" wore buttons featuring the number twenty-four underneath their lapels. They flashed these at each other with a conspiratorial grin. It was a gag with the potential to grow into something serious if Klein was interested. The premier toyed with the notion briefly, but then ordered Love to stand down; he wasn't going anywhere. Even so, Love's analysis was eerily prophetic of the developments that ultimately drove Preston Manning to create the United Alternative (the precursor to the Canadian Alliance party) two years later. It was the right idea, but the wrong leader. Love did end up briefly serving as chief of staff to Stockwell Day when he won the leadership of the Alliance, but left the problem-plagued leader of the new federal party soon thereafter.

Rod Love Consulting was created to sell only one product—Klein's thoughts, if not his actual brain. The former chief of staff commanded hefty retainers and expensive hourly billings from companies like Imperial Oil and TransAlta Utilities for communications advice, political intelligence and the odd whisper in the right cabinet ear. In very short order, his one-man operation was billing clients in excess of three hundred thousand dollars per year. He counted arms-length government agencies such as the Calgary Regional Health Authority and Mount Royal College as clients. He was appointed to the board of governors for the University of Calgary, a delicious irony for a dropout from that university, and in 2000 he joined the board of directors of Zi Corp, the renamed Multi-Corp. The lucrative earnings enabled Love to embrace the upscale lifestyle he always wanted. His posh Mount Royal home is within walking distance of his modest corner office in Highwood Communications, the ad agency of choice for the Klein Conservatives, and his sports club and golf course are just a few minutes' drive away in his cherry-red Mustang convertible.

Love and Klein regularly golf and gamble together. While some insiders say their relationship has been cool since Love's modest contributions to the 2001 election, if this is true, then Love is now back in the thick of things with his former boss. Klein says Love has an important external advisory role. "Rod will always be a friend and a confidant," Klein says. "We see each other constantly. If there's a political problem, we discuss politics and we discuss approaches to various situations I face. He's close because we're close. We're like brothers."

After Rod Love's departure, finding a replacement was no contest. Ralph Klein's shortlist had only one name.

Peter Elzinga was a very reluctant recruit. When Klein called on the longtime ally and fishing buddy, he was pulling down six figures at the Conservative party headquarters, where he happily worked as the executive director with his wife, Pat, and collected federal and provincial pensions worth $25,000 a year. The party was coming off a successful election, with Edmonton slowly warming to Klein's Tories, and fundraising was a cinch. Elzinga sat on the board of an Edmonton power company, served as honorary consul to Brazil and had been elected president of Edmonton's Northlands park. Life was good. Responding to Klein's call forced Elzinga to ditch his outside interests, quit the party post and put his pension payments on hold. As compensation, Klein upped Love's old salary by almost fifty per cent, and offered Elzinga about $120,000 per year.

If you wanted to find the antithesis of the impatient, temperamental, unelectable, strategic mercenary who is Rod Love, then Elzinga is it. This former MP and MLA is described by fan Colleen Klein as a "gentle giant." He is a towering six-foot-three, with big farm hands and an easy smile that bursts across his well-creased face. He calls everyone "my friend," refers to most males as "brother," and never misses a chance to pump his listener's ego with sycophantic praise, which makes him impossible to dislike, yet difficult to trust wholeheartedly.

Elzinga's public demeanor was beautifully captured in a photograph taken just a few seconds after an equally defining snapshot of Ralph Klein. In the Don Getty government of 1991, the two cabinet ministers attended a news conference to announce the green light for the controversial, billion-dollar Al-Pac pulp and paper mill. A protester rushed the stage and passed down the line of dignitaries, giving them each a furious middle finger, one after the other. Klein didn't hesitate when his turn came—he flipped the bird right back, an act immortalized by the click of an alert photographer's shutter. Elzinga, on the other hand, was captured on film with a broad "glad ta know ya" grin on his face, eagerly reaching out in an attempt to shake the protester's hand, the same hand with the single finger salute still raised. That's the man in a sixtieth of a second: Peter Elzinga is the good ol' boy who never stops trying to make new friends. But taken as the whole story, it's a dangerous illusion.

Elzinga went straight to work proving his cuddly exterior masked a heart of cold steel. He secured Klein's permission to clean house and bring in a team he could call his own, a particularly difficult go-ahead to get from the notoriously loyal premier. Elzinga ousted virtually every member of the premier's office staff with strong links to Love, burying them in distant bureaucratic outposts. He even managed to re-deploy Sheryl Burns, the premier's long-time appointments secretary who had outlasted Love, despite their frequent clashes. Love loyalists were mortified and beseeched their former guardian to call on Klein to stop the carnage. Once Klein assigns a person specific responsibilities, though, he invariably gives them free rein to do their job and rarely intervenes without extreme provocation. Love knew better than to attempt any rescue missions for his former staff.

In the latter half of the government's second mandate, Elzinga faced an uprising of MLAs who felt ignored and unappreciated by their premier. They were frustrated at being overlooked for cabinet posts and were becoming bored by a steady stream of consultation summits, which they viewed as nothing more than make-work projects. Elzinga attempted to boost morale by opening the doors for MLAs to access Klein. He spent hours giving them his sympathetic ear to bend, albeit with little to offer in the way of concrete change. It did little to stop the hand-wringing of MLAs. They felt he was a simple hayseed planted in very shallow soil, accused him of favoring Edmonton MLAs, blamed him for questionable cabinet picks and slagged him privately for not being the intellectual equal of Love.

To his credit, Elzinga did not take the griping personally. At a Jasper policy conference breakfast in 1999, I was seated with three MLAs in a restaurant as they eagerly and mercilessly dissected many of Elzinga's faults. A few days later, Elzinga called me up to recite their complaints verbatim. His wife had been eavesdropping from a table just around the corner. He laughed it off. "I know what they're saying about me," he said.

"No worries. You need a thick skin in this business." That year Elzinga's Christmas present for his friends was a book on the inspired political genius of Machiavelli.

Born in Edmonton on April 6, 1944, Peter Elzinga spent twenty years as a Conservative MP and MLA, representing voters bordering the northeastern edge and surrounding districts of his hometown. He first met Ralph Klein shortly after the 1989 provincial election when the rookie environment minister, the star recruit who leapfrogged straight into cabinet without paying his party dues, was getting a cool reception from other MLAs. Elzinga could empathize. When he retired from federal politics in 1986, his reward for running as a provincial Tory was the agriculture portfolio in Don Getty's first government. Many fellow MLAs resented his instant elevation to the executive council. Elzinga slipped a note of encouragement to Klein during their first cabinet meeting and invited him to pop by the office for a drink later. "I didn't feel I was part of the family," Klein recalls. "I was a suspected Liberal. A lot of cabinet ministers and backbenchers felt it was unfair of me to go directly from the city into a cabinet post. I could sense around the cabinet table an uneasy feeling. I had a hard time getting anything through. Whenever I had a tough time, Peter would always send me a note urging me to 'hang in there, brother'."

The pair hit it off, politically and socially. Elzinga was given the economic development portfolio in his second term, which should have put him on a collision course with Klein, who was the cabinet guardian of trees and rivers. Instead Klein and Elzinga worked together to attract recycling industries to the province, and Elzinga stepped in as peacekeeper between Klein and the forestry minister, Leroy Fjordbotten, in their standoff over tougher pulp mill pollution controls and clearcutting. Economic development was becoming a handful of a ministry as the 1990s dawned. "The worst three years of my political life," is how Elzinga describes it. During that time, billions of dollars were draining into boondoggled moneypits, watched over by a government with little political will to stem the losses. Elzinga encountered strong resistance when he tried to stop the flow of public funds and succeeded only in cutting off loans and loan guarantees to a handful of lesser government investments. Throughout it all, he always had time for after-hours drinks with his little rookie buddy. These meetings usually lasted until Elzinga headed home and Klein hit the bars with Steve West.

Despite all the schemes that drained big money out of his ministry, Elzinga kept a surprisingly low profile during his term as Getty's economic development minister. The only flare-up came when it was discovered he was pocketing a $10,300 out-of-town living subsidy as a resident of Sherwood Park, a hamlet barely a twenty-minute drive from the legislature. "If I could go back in my political career and make one change, that is the change I would make," Elzinga says. "There was nothing illegal or immoral in what we did, but I can understand why people would be irritated with me, and they were."

In the summer of 1992, Elzinga served notice that he would not seek re-election, but Getty's departure pushed him back into the political fray as the loudest, proudest cheerleader for Klein's leadership bid. He was the first senior cabinet minister to publicly commit to Klein, and Klein gave him responsibility for bringing in Edmonton support. After the leadership race, his reward was to be named deputy premier, a role he shared with Ken Kowalski during Klein's inaugural government, with the specific task of shaking up the government's organizational charts. When Elzinga restated his decision to quit provincial politics in 1993, Klein appointed him the party's executive director, a staff position with the seemingly innocuous responsibilities of fundraising, memberships sales and trying to woo Edmonton voters back to the Conservative party.

Unexpectedly, however, Elzinga found himself the party's political executioner. For reasons that to this day he doesn't fully comprehend, he was assigned the task of dismissing three problem ministers from cabinet. "He's not to be underestimated," Klein cautions. "Peter is much more of a people person, very smooth, polite and good with people, but very tough when he needs to be." Kowalski was the first body Elzinga was assigned to bury in the backbench, followed weeks later by Peter Trynchy, who was driven out of cabinet on a paving scandal. After Love and Stockwell Day both failed to secure Mike Cardinal's resignation for the inappropriate use of a government aircraft, it fell to Elzinga to give him the choice: quit or be fired. "You have to exercise great decency but you have to have hardness and strength or you don't survive in this business," he shrugs by way of explanation.

As the party's executive director Elzinga in 1994 was almost implicated in a contentious deal between the Klein government and the Ghermazian family, owners of the West Edmonton Mall. The Ghermazians were seeking a massive government refinancing package for the mall after having defaulted on their second mortgage. There was a push from within the party, particularly from Kowalski, to keep the city's major tourist attraction under local ownership, and Elzinga attended a meeting with the Alberta Treasury Branches and the mall's ownership to sign a $420-million bailout. The deal was so sweet that the government-owned bank suggested bribery might have been used to obtain such favorable terms and launched years of court action to try and prove it. To date, Elzinga has not been implicated in any wrongdoing.

It wasn't until 2001 that Elzinga really stepped out from behind Love's shadow, when he engineered Klein's third-term victory. The party's deep electoral penetration of Edmonton, in a campaign that insiders describe as the smoothest of the three election victories under Klein's leadership, removed any lingering doubts about Klein's ability to survive without his first political aide. As the architect of the new cabinet, Elzinga earned the loyalty of Klein's ministers. As chair of the government's weekly strategy committee he is responsible for troubleshooting and it's now an accepted reality that the gateway to the premier is Elzinga's office.

It is never seen in public, but an intense rivalry persists between Love and Elzinga. Forces loyal to the former chief of staff gleefully blame Elzinga for the surge of spending that began during Klein's third term in government. The same voices have delighted in every policy flip-flop that accompanied the release of a devastatingly amateurish budget in the spring of 2002. While personal acrimony may exaggerate its significance, Klein's notoriously heavy reliance on his chiefs of staff suggests that his performance is closely linked to the competence of those in the pivotal top position.

Seventeen

The Revolution Adrift

I N 2 0 0 1, ALBERTA VOTERS were passing judgment on a government marked by runaway spending, accelerated debt repayment,
revolutionary tax reform, a non-stop series of consultation summits, a
power deregulation plan and a private health care bill that attracted the
most furious public backlash of Ralph Klein's tenure. Despite all the busy
sounds that emanated from the legislature, it had been an empty term, the
work of a government with a drifting, lazy eye and no fiscal or policy com-
pass to follow. Klein wanted only to sit back, enjoy the view and wrap up
what he had called his Alberta home renovation project. He promised
reporters a boring second term and aimed to deliver it by simply shovel-
ing energy price windfalls into the craters left by his budgetary bombing.

Klein's MLAs had a different view. The status quo, simply enhanced by
spending escalations, was intolerable and they weren't about to suffer in
silence. The social conservative ideologies of Stockwell Day and others
faithful to the Bible Belt beliefs of central Alberta had been suppressed
during the first term by the sheer weight of the fiscal agenda. Now, with
the deficit-elimination pressure off, abortion, gay rights and activism on
the judicial bench were among the emerging targets.

The class of 1993 MLAs had also graduated members with no allegiance
to social conservative dogma into their second term with the 1997

election. They, too, were brimming with ideological zeal and burned to alter the delivery of government beyond merely balancing the books. They were addicted to the exhilarating pace of change—and desperately searched for a new policy fix. Gary Mar, a Calgary lawyer who swept into cabinet as a rookie in 1993 and began a steady climb up the ladder that culminated in his appointment as health minister in 1999, was concerned about the policy vacuum. "After 1997, when the deficit was looked after, if you asked caucus or cabinet to identify the goal, many might have said to reinvest in government priorities. But then if you asked them 'What are those priorities?', you'd get very different answers," he says. "We were a group of very committed people looking for a cause to commit ourselves to."

As Ralph Klein surveyed Alberta at the five-year point of his reign on December 5, 1997, he could easily see the markers that delineated the rocky path of his cost-cutting revolution. The 33,683 employees on the government payroll the day of his leadership victory had been culled to 24,628, for a half billion dollars in payroll savings. Program spending was down eighteen per cent, and while the core areas of health, education and social services had suffered steep reductions, those departments had been cut the least; in fact, damage control had already necessitated a billion-dollar bump in spending in those areas. The province's $8.3-billion net debt, the amount owing beyond the value of government assets, was set to be wiped from the books a year ahead of schedule. The amount of money the government invested in bad industry loans and diversification boondoggles had been cut in half. Revenue had unexpectedly surged by three billion dollars, or almost twenty per cent, spurred on by royalties from higher-than-forecast energy prices and a bonanza of income tax from the buoyant economy. Alberta had also hit the jackpot with its fling with video gambling, which was pumping another five hundred million dollars into government coffers, putting gambling proceeds ahead of oil royalties as a source of government revenue for the first time.

Seeing its government flush with so much money, the Alberta public began to sour on their province boasting the lowest per capita program spending in Canada. Albertans had made their sacrifice and debt repayment wasn't a sexy enough repayment for tattered school textbooks, large class sizes and long surgery waiting lists. As well, the province's population had soared by five per cent, nudging the three-million mark, with a proportionately soaring demand on government services. Klein had always promised Albertans a reward for their pain. With a two-billion-dollar surplus on the books at the end of 1997, both the money and the motivation to spend it existed and Alberta's King Midas was prepared to fling open the vault.

In early 1997, Klein convened a Growth Summit policy convention in order to prepare for the March 1997 election campaign. Unfortunately, it didn't provide much of a roadmap. One hundred and twenty delegates set out their wishlists of priorities that were wrapped up at the end of the convention into warm and fuzzy "overarching issues." The result was a hodge-podge of 243 motherhood ideas and conflicting concepts. Frustrated delegate Pat Seale spotted the problem immediately when delegates in her workshop argued for a hardline approach to reduce smoking one minute, but insisted with equal vigor that the government not discriminate against smokers the next. "So now the government can say whatever it wants," Seale complained to reporters. "It consulted the people and yes, they say we should have smoking sections for people in every facility or no, we shouldn't have anybody ever smoke again." She recalls expressing her concern to the workshop facilitator. "He told me that we are doing a shotgun approach to make sure that we generate all the ideas possible and I said: 'How many shotguns do you need?'"

The policy drift of the cabinet and caucus was all too apparent to Rod Love, and he was equally dismayed by the government's loss of fiscal resolve. In December 1997, he left the only political gig he'd ever known. It may have been coincidence, but immediately after Love's departure Klein stumbled into a series of political gaffes which should have been caught with proper supervision.

Klein's first mistake was to take pen in hand on a Friday afternoon and write to the St. Stephen's Ukrainian Catholic Church in his own Calgary constituency. He invited the church, if it didn't like the source of the money, to return an eighty-thousand-dollar grant it had received from provincial gambling revenue. Church opposition to video lottery terminals had become a regular theme for Sunday sermons, so when Calgary's Bishop Frederick Henry waded into the dispute, saying he too favored removing VLTs from bars and hotels, Klein let his tongue do the tripping. "Maybe this is a strong word to use, but there is a question of hypocrisy," Klein said. "The largest percentage of money that goes back to communities is from VLTs." The churches were outraged and demanded a retraction, but Klein refused to deliver anything more than a token clarification.

Barely had that ruckus died down, when the Institutional Confinement and Sexual Sterilization Compensation Act, the Everest of monumental policy mistakes, landed with a thud in the Alberta legislature. Facing seven hundred claims from mentally impaired Albertans who were institutionalized and wrongfully sterilized under the province's 1928 eugenics law (the first legislation repealed by the rookie Conservative government in 1971), the justice minister, Jon Havelock, had successfully lobbied cabinet to limit the amount of compensation that could be claimed as legal redress by the victims. His March 1998 legislation gave them settlements of up to $150,000 and invoked the notwithstanding clause of the Charter of Rights and Freedoms to block any legal challenges that would hinder an expeditious end to the proceedings.

The bill was not as mean-spirited as many suggested. Havelock, a former corporate lawyer in Calgary, knew that the vast majority of claimants were represented by lawyers on contingency. The thought of the compensation process plodding along and racking up huge legal bills for settlements that might not reach the victims before they died appalled his professional and personal sensibilities. But politics is often a process of commendable logic subject to an emotional override. In the bill's five double-spaced pages, Havelock sealed his political fate and crafted a legacy that would haunt him until his retirement in 2001.

In the fifteen minutes between the bill's introduction and her opening shot in the Question Period that immediately followed, New Democrat leader Pam Barrett, a petite firecracker of a socialist and a media darling, read the legislation, detected its fatal flaw, alerted her office to call in the attack dogs and returned to the assembly in a fury. She screeched her outrage at victims, already disfigured by a violation of their human rights, losing their legal rights as well. She tore the bill in half in disgust, and blasted it as "the most gutless and arrogant bit of legislation I have ever seen."After Question Period, she stormed into Klein's daily news conference with a victim of wrongful sterilization in tow.

Havelock, armed with only his briefing notes, stoically defended the bill, while Klein watched the unfolding spectacle in the press room with befuddled alarm. He'd seen backlashes before, but Barrett was a personal friend and occasional cocktail companion, not prone to acrimonious grandstanding at his expense. Her unrestrained anger seemed genuine and the incredulous questions from reporters in the room triggered a twitch in Klein's political antennae. As the premier left the press room with communications director Fay Orr, he quietly whispered to her that he might have to yank the bill.

The next morning, Havelock called me at home, mildly concerned by the firestorm of media coverage across the front pages of the country. He was convinced, however, that it would all die down as the inherent logic of curbing lawyers' contingency fees registered with the public. "I hear they're going to pull the bill," I told him. He snorted. "That's ridiculous."

Behind the scenes, Klein was in full and fast retreat, cutting his justice minister out of the damage control strategy. The next day, his communications staff were told to leak news that the bill would be retracted immediately after the caucus meeting. The word spread through the press gallery: Jon Havelock was being hung out to dry. "Watch and learn," a grim Klein told me as he entered the legislature. Inside, his shaken justice minister stood in the house, eyes locked on the text he'd been ordered to read: an unqualified apology and withdrawal of the bill. "I was stupid on that one," Klein muses. "I listened to Havelock, who was a lawyer and made the case in my mind. I didn't take into account the human rights issue. I thought the average settlement would be a fair settlement given the amount of time that had taken place since they'd been sterilized. I thought it was the right thing to do until Pam raised the human rights issue and the alarm bells went off and I thought, 'Uh-oh, she's picked up a point out there that I didn't think would be as severe as it was.' The bad thing was that we did introduce the legislation, but we had the courage to stand up and pull back within twenty-four hours." Still, it was a classic Klein scenario. If he's keenly interested in an issue, little escapes his attention, but if it's a matter that hasn't reached the public's radar screen and is not easily summed up in a paragraph or two, the premier can easily overlook a budding controversy.

The backlash over the Sterilization Compensation Act spooked Klein into deciding not to use the notwithstanding clause again without first putting it to a public referendum. Later that month, he was under pressure from the Stockwell Day-led faction of caucus to opt out of an expected Supreme Court gay rights ruling. Delwin Vriend, an instructor at an Edmonton religious college who had been fired for his open homosexuality, had taken the government to court. In his case, he argued that his rights were violated because Alberta's human rights legislation did not extend to wrongful firings, evictions or union memberships based on sexual orientation. When the Supreme Court ruling came down, reading gay rights protection into the legislation, the memory of the wrongfully sterilized debacle was still fresh in Klein's mind. Even though the premier's office was swamped with more phone calls on this issue than any other of his reign, most of them urging him to contest the ruling, Klein appeared before his caucus in a combative mood and minced no words in his rejection of any tactics designed to thwart the court's judgment. "I think it's morally wrong to discriminate on the basis of sexual orientation," he told the caucus. "This is where I have to take a leadership role, like it or not, and this is my stand." Caucus voted two to one to accept the court ruling over Day's loud objection. As the minister of social services in the previous first term, the right-wing, tax-fighting social conservative from Red Deer had captured headlines in a transparent breach of the firewall between his personal convictions and legislative responsibilities. He arbitrarily denied lesbians the right to become foster moms. To pacify Day, Klein allowed him to study "fencing" in the human rights legislation so that it denied same-sex couples the right to formal marriages or adoption. Day hit the phones immediately. He called church leaders and religious organizations late into the night to mobilize evangelical support for his assignment, but Klein gently smothered the idea a year later, refusing to put gay rights back on the agenda.

On the eve of the 1997 election, the finance minister, Jim Dinning, announced his retirement and stepped out of politics. After the Tories returned to power for their second term, Ralph Klein made a curious selection for a treasurer he knew would be presiding over a vigorous spending surge. He handed the assignment to Stockwell Day. Klein's new caucus did not have much political strength among its rural MLAs, so Day stood out from the lightweights as a logical choice for the top cabinet job. He had a youthful exuberance that contradicted his forty-seven-year-old birth certificate, and the charismatic former lay preacher presented well before the cameras. Klein had an inkling he was asking for trouble, putting an MLA known to be the unofficial whip for social conservatives into the unofficial role of deputy premier, but he decided Day was a gamble worth taking. "All I wanted was someone who would carry on what Jim Dinning had done and not back down," Klein shrugs now. "The portfolio was pretty well settled. Stockwell had done a pretty good job in social services and there wasn't a hell of a lot he could screw up as long as he stayed the course."

When Day strolled to the podium to announce his first of four budgets, he held up a sparkling loonie coin, declared that it was soaked with the sweat of taxpayers and resolved to keep it safe from the spendthrifts who would squander it carelessly. He was immediately dubbed the loonie treasurer. The real dilemma confronting Day, however, was the lack of any clear course to follow. Despite having given the thumbs-up to any and all spending initiatives, there was one policy direction delegates at the Growth Summit didn't support—Day's pet crusade of tax reform and reductions finished near the bottom of a very long and wide priority list. While the broad cross-section of Tory representatives generated a fruit basket full of education, health care and social-service spending initiatives, from which Klein could pick almost any preference and point to the summit for his justification, tax cuts were only endorsed by five per cent of the delegates.

Day's preferred approach was to eliminate some of the temporary surtaxes that the Getty regime had imposed to curb the deficit, or to introduce a flat tax on income. The last thing he wanted to see happen under his watch was exactly what the summit demanded—a massive catch-up in budgets for so-called "People Development" programs, particularly education. Undeterred by the summit's cold shoulder to tax cuts, Day's first budget delivered one. Spending reductions were also reversed across the board. Nonetheless, in a bid to correct what he attributed to oversight by the Growth Summit, Day ordered up another round of public consultations six months later to ask Albertans what tax cuts and reforms they wanted in their future. The government was clearly determined to keep asking questions until voters coughed up the answers it wanted.

During his term as finance minister, Day was swamped with spending requests, some of them encouraged personally by the premier, to bump up education, health and road construction. He lacked Dinning's cabinet influence to stop the flood of new spending that the treasury board was approving. In the four years before he left (in the spring of 2000) to seek the Canadian Alliance leadership, Day presided over a $3.6-billion spending surge on a $17-billion budget. Per capita spending increased by $926 in just three years, including the largest one-year spending escalation since the heady Peter Lougheed era. "I agonized more in the post-97 years than I did 93–97," Day confesses. The first term "was literally a delight because you could hold up a banner and say, 'Here's why we're reducing the role of government, we've got a deficit and a debt'." Soaring energy prices triggered a revenue supernova in 1999. Two billion dollars more than Klein budgeted showed up in the books, and Day recalls how tough it was to watch enormous surpluses pile up in his treasury. "A surplus means somewhere we're taking too much money from people, so somebody's paying a price they shouldn't have to," he argued.

Day scored a personal victory in March 1999, when he secured cabinet approval for an eleven per cent single rate of tax, which, in order to preserve Alberta's status as Canada's tax haven, had to be quickly reduced by half a point to match Ontario's tax reductions. By this time, his social conservative roots were showing, which did little to impress the premier or his senior cabinet ministers, and his influence began to wane.

In May 1996, Day had attended the Winds of Change conference in Calgary, a meeting of neo-conservatives where the notion of expanding the Reform Party into the Canadian Alliance was first proposed. Failing to spot the reporter in the audience, Day suggested to the conference that serial killer Clifford Olson should be placed in the general prison population where "the moral prisoners will deal with it in a way which we don't have the nerve to do." It was front page news for days and turned Day into a hard-line right-wing figurehead. It also kickstarted the exposure that would lead to his eventual entry into national politics. A few years later, in 1999, Day's published outburst at Red Deer lawyer Lorne Goddard, a school trustee who had defended a convicted pedophile, triggered a protracted lawsuit that resulted in taxpayers picking up the tab for a settlement and legal fees that cost almost eight hundred thousand dollars. As punishment, Day was quietly removed as chair of the powerful agenda and priorities committee, a signal to insiders of his rapidly waning influence. When he resigned to seek the Alliance leadership in the spring of 2000, behind his back most of Klein's office staff were relieved to see him go.

While Stockwell Day would ultimately become the leader of the new Canadian Alliance, in early 1998 it was Ralph Klein who was being wooed to make the jump to federal politics. Following Jean Charest's departure from the Federal Conservative leadership for Quebec provincial politics, Klein was thought to be a leading candidate to replace Charest. He considered it briefly, sensing it might be the best way to re-unite the Tory and Reform parties under one banner. However, friends warned Klein that, being a high school dropout with a legendary drinking record and an occasionally rocky private life, he would likely not endure the microscopic examination typical of the national press gallery, who would not be as tolerant of his foibles as the Alberta media were. Colleen worried about the change too. There would be enormous demands on his time and she worried how Klein, who had never served outside government, would perform in Opposition. On March 27, 1998, at what was an otherwise sleepy Tory policy conference in Red Deer, national television networks went live from a Klein news conference where he ruled out a bid for federal office forever. "The strength of this country lies in the strength of the provinces," Klein said. Besides, Colleen joked, Klein would be "very lonely" if he went to Ottawa. She wasn't leaving her Calgary home, even for 24 Sussex Drive. "If we were twenty years younger and had that energy, it might be a consideration. But we've got to finish here and I know the energy it takes to look after Alberta. Imagine the energy it takes to be a good prime minister and look after Canada?"

After he made his decision, Klein went back to running a provincial government more lost and adrift than ever before. The growing surplus in 1999 was a mere teaser for the six-billion-dollar royalty gusher in 2000, double the previous record high set in 1985. Even gaming profits nudged the billion-dollar mark, double the jackpot of only six years earlier. Alberta was showing signs of economic maturity as its GDP moved to within striking distance of British Columbia's. Despite oil price crashes in 1997, which drove the price down to almost ten dollars a barrel, neither the industry nor the government panicked by handing out boxes of pink slips. A new sense of invincibility had taken hold in Alberta, a confidence that the province's low taxes, deregulated business climate and bustling technology and research sectors were achieving the diversification dream first promoted by Peter Lougheed in the roaring 1970s. The provincial economy had turned platinum.

Klein budgets continued the trend of posting laughably pessimistic forecasts that were quickly rendered obsolete by wildly lucrative energy windfalls. Klein's spending kept pace with the revenue rise, most noticeably in 1999, when he forgave a billion dollars' worth of debt and deficits run up by the regional health authorities and school boards. He boosted road construction, health and education by $1.5 billion and created a five-hundred-million-dollar endowment for scientific research. He eliminated the province's net debt a year ahead of schedule, and he accelerated a series of surtax reductions.

When he wasn't throwing money at problems, he was ordering up summits, task forces and forums to decipher the public mood and help voters feel involved in his directional confusion. Faced with rumblings of a revolt against video lottery terminals led by Calgary oilman and long-time Tory bagman Jim Gray, Klein called a Gaming Summit to see how far Albertans were willing to go toward becoming Las Vegas North. Justice Minister Havelock was equally unfocused, still reeling in the aftermath of the sterilization fiasco. He established task forces on aboriginal justice, the Young Offenders' Act, child prostitution and judicial compensation, and afterwards, topped it all off with a full Justice Summit to re-examine all of the above. Iris Evans, the children's services minister, called a Children's Forum and named Klein's wife, Colleen, as a co-chair.

Ralph Klein didn't want to preside over an unfocused fat-cat legacy though. He wanted to create a legacy to call his own. He decided that the issue to get his belly burning again was health care.

Eighteen

The Third Victory

O N THE NIGHT OF MARCH 12, 2001, they gathered in a
south-side Calgary hotel that had seen better days to watch
Ralph Klein's greatest victory. On one side of the penthouse
suite at the Carriage House Inn, a small-screen television was tuned in to
CFCN television; Klein's 1970s employer was carrying election coverage
hosted by Darrel Janz, the same anchor who had introduced Klein's news
stories three decades earlier. Colleen Klein sat with her husband in front
of the television, holding his hand as the early returns trickled in. Surrounding them were their five children and several grandchildren. The far
side of the suite featured a well-stocked bar surrounded by a dozen friends
and advisers, who were drinking hard and smoking heavily.

Seated in a corner by himself was Peter Elzinga, the premier's chief of
staff and top election strategist. Elzinga was nervous. The polls had been
good—too good. Apathy and complacency are unpredictable opponents in
the dying days of any run-away campaign. Every opinion poll proclaimed
that a third Klein majority was in the bag, but Elzinga had specific goals. He
desperately wanted a huge Edmonton breakthrough to compensate for the
capital's rejections of the Tories at the polls in 1993 and 1997, and he
wanted to prove that Rod Love's campaign prowess was not without equal.

Klein had a different goal in mind. He wanted to dispatch to the footnotes of Alberta political history his third Liberal leader in as many elections. And if this one suffered special pain and humiliation, it would be the sweetest victory of all. Nancy MacBeth, his twelve-year provincial nemesis, had returned to the legislature as leader of the Alberta Liberals during Klein's second term. Twenty-eight days before the election, when Klein had set forth on the campaign trail, he'd confided a dark mission to his closest friends: "I want to see her cry."

On November 16, 1998, Nancy MacBeth, the remarried and renamed Nancy Betkowski, returned to the legislature as the third Alberta Liberal leader to face the premier. She had been wooed by Liberal MLAs in 1994 after Klein's first victory drove Laurence Decore from the Liberal leadership, but she didn't like the thought of continuing what was a family feud. "I was hurt, sad, angry and all those things and I thought, 'This is really sick and I don't want to do those things.' It would've been motivated not by principles, but by personalities," she recalls.

When Klein's second victim, Grant Mitchell, retired from politics in the spring of 1998, the Grits went back on bended knee to MacBeth. She was a reluctant recruit. Even though it disturbed her to see her twin passions of health care and education, the departments she'd run as a member of Don Getty's cabinet, ravaged by the drive to eliminate the deficit, it wasn't until her teenage son and her husband, Hilliard, both urged her into the race that MacBeth let her name stand. Photogenic, trilingual and undeniably smart, MacBeth returned to politics with a decisive first-ballot victory in the leadership race. With a two-thousand-vote victory over the Tories, she reclaimed Mitchell's Edmonton McClung constituency as her seat in a by-election on June 17, 1998.

If Klein's office was worried about the rival they called Lady MacBeth, they didn't show it. Gleefully they plundered the archives for newspaper clippings and cabinet documents they could use to embarrass the new Liberal leader when her public positions conflicted with her old views as a Conservative cabinet minister. They had a field day. They filled half a dozen binders with statements and policies from MacBeth's past, tabbed and indexed by issue, ready for return fire when a minister or the premier came under attack in Question Period. MacBeth promised fireworks upon her return to the legislature as Klein's official opposition, but despite the emotional antagonism, for the most part her opposition fizzled.

MacBeth was surprised how easy it was to get under Klein's thin skin. She baited him with claims that he was creating a two-tiered American-style health care system. She knew that if she irritated him enough, he might stray from his carefully scripted message. "He'd always avoid answering questions. He'd have his little sheets and stay on message, but in terms of reacting to the questions rather than responding, he was much more a reactor than a responder," she says. Klein didn't get through his first Question Period with MacBeth before their political debate turned into a personal feud. He dragged MacBeth's brother, a Calgary radiologist, into the debate as proof that private health care ran in her veins.

For the most part, Klein's strategy was to coldly refuse to acknowledge MacBeth was in the legislature. "I would never look at her, but I could hear this shrill voice and it was wonderful," Klein muses almost nostalgically. "Shirley McClellan kept looking at her, and I'd whisper out of the side of my mouth, 'Is she crying yet?' Of all the Liberal Opposition leaders, she was the meanest. It was personal from day one, and it goes right back to the leadership."

Just how summit-addicted Klein's government had became was evident in late 1998, when Klein shocked Health Minister Halvar Jonson. On a live talk-radio show, he spontaneously announced plans for a Health Summit. Only a day earlier Jonson had declared consultation on health legislation unnecessary. But Klein had heard the Liberals were about to call for an all-party health care committee, and he decided to "pre-empt" them. Thrown together hastily in three months, the Health Summit attracted two hundred participants, who called for equality of access to a publicly and adequately funded system under the five principles of the Canada Health Act. They offered traditional and non-traditional choices, some in the public system, some not. The government delivered its usual response and accepted the broad principles, but behind the scenes it was getting ready to push off in its own direction—allowing contracts with private surgical clinics.

Klein had attempted health reforms repeatedly in his first six years as premier, but he kept running into the most formidable enemy of them all—doctors. He admits not consulting doctors early in his reign was a grievous error. He also acknowledges that he fell short crafting a vision for health care redesign. The structure of health care in Alberta had been changed to create regional health authorities, but creating a fiscal crisis to force efficiency into the system had not produced the desired result. Doctors were still paid fees. Attempts to track patients through smart cards were shelved. Rural hospitals had resisted being turned into centers of surgical specialization. Everything Klein tried, failed.

What was needed, he figured, was competition from private health care providers who would deliver public health services through profit-driven frugality. Klein used the example of hospitals always buying brand-new hospital gurneys for $1,500 while medical surplus retailers were flogging perfectly good used merchandise for $90. The difference would be profit, and profit would motivate the search for other efficiencies. This was the root of Klein's much-ballyhooed health care agenda. There was no secret pact with American health care companies to create a private, parallel two-tiered system. Nor was there a desire to delist treatments or surgeries. From his days covering hospital boards as a reporter, Klein had seen waste in health care. He was also motivated by the suspicion that his government's rapidly increased health care funding was being thrown into a black hole of salary increases, from which neither greater economy nor efficiency results. Ask Klein to define his health care philosophy, and he doesn't hesitate for a second. "My ideology is the money. Period."

At the mid-point of his second term, Klein decided to act on health reform and damn the consequences. "What's the point of having a majority if I don't use it," he told his colleagues. Just one month after his Health Summit recommended little by way of private sector health care, Klein's government introduced Bill 37. It opened the door to overnight stays in private clinics or, as Klein called them, "non-hospital surgical facilities." Klein sold it as a government veto over for-profit private hospitals, but the public wasn't buying any of it. The reaction was fast and furious. Medicare defenders blasted it as the welcome mat for entrepreneurial hospitals. There were waves of petitions and protests.

Confused by the strong backlash to a bill he viewed as innocuous, Klein put the plan on hold until the fall of 1998. He wanted to figure out a less contentious approach. His next suggestion, that overnight stays should be allowed to proceed under tightly controlled circumstances, unleashed another round of angry public reaction. It frustrated Klein no end. He told his spin doctors to solve a problem he viewed as a simple communications failure. "He felt if we could communicate it and get ahead of it, we could succeed," says former communications director Fay Orr. "But we gave the Friends of Medicare too much time to prepare and they got a counter campaign out ahead of us."

Bill 11, the Health Care Protection Act, was introduced in March 2000. Copies of the bill were mailed to every household in Alberta with detailed explanations of the act. There was a newspaper and radio campaign. Klein took to the air in a province-wide television address, insisting his bill was a benign attempt to protect public health care by swearing allegiance to the Canada Health Act, banning private hospitals and prohibiting payment for government-insured procedures. He dispatched Orwellian-sounding "truth squads" of MLAs to speak in the bill's defence. But for the first time, the public seemed to doubt Klein's believability. Opponents' television commercials featured the demolition of the Calgary General Hospital as the defining image of Klein's health care policies. Klein always knew it was a bad idea to blow up his birthplace.

On Groundhog Day 2000, Pam Barrett stunned Albertans by quitting as leader of the Alberta New Democrats. She was the one party leader Klein called a friend. She could denounce the premier in Question Period and walk into his office two hours later for a glass of wine or join the Kleins for dinner. Barrett gave Klein a heads-up about her resignation the night before it was announced. She told him before she told her own party executive.

Her official explanation was a near-death reaction to anesthesia in an Edmonton dentist's chair. Her dentist corroborated the story. Many people say it was the catalyst for a decision triggered by problems with drinking, her health, the death of her mother and an abusive common-law relationship. Her battle with the bottle was not unlike Klein's. A television reporter who had detected booze on her breath at a breakfast show was preparing a story on her problem. Shaken by her experience at the dentist's office, Barrett decided it was a good time to leave.

Klein respected and held a great deal of affection for Barrett. They performed their assigned roles as lead characters in the theater of political drama, but neither took their stark policy differences personally. They enjoyed each other's company socially. Barrett recalls one dinner where she invited the Kleins home for a nightcap only to find the place a filthy mess and her roommate already well into his nightcaps and eager to lecture the premier on various policy shortcomings. Klein took the abuse for almost an hour with a tolerant grin on his face while Colleen fidgeted, anxious to get back to their condo.

After Barrett quit, Klein offered her several jobs. She briefly accepted a position on the Alberta Arts Foundation, then moved to Vancouver to write about her stormy life and near death. She returned to Edmonton in early 2002. Her departure was good news for Klein's government, coming as it did on the eve of a crucial legislative sitting to pass Bill 11. The most stormy session of his eight-year-old government was set to begin without Klein's most charismatic and media-friendly opponent in her seat.

A year to the day before the 2001 election, with Bill 11 in a final debate, thousands of people gathered for nightly vigils on the legislature grounds. During one particularly boisterous protest, dozens of folks stormed into the legislature through a press gallery window, inadvertently left open by Broadcast News reporter Jim Macdonald. They assaulted a security guard and leaned over an observation gallery, trying to climb onto the floor of the legislative assembly. Nervous MLAs fled their seats, and the house was forced to adjourn. The nation was transfixed by the ruckus and people wondered what was going on in King Ralph's wealthy kingdom to trigger such an unholy fuss. The government used closure to push the bill through and adjourned for the summer, hoping the outcry would dissipate. The regional health authorities, all appointed by the Klein government, knew better than to inflame emotions by inking surgical contracts with private clinics. They put the contracting-out provisions of the act on ice. Another election would pass before the theoretical intent of Bill 11 would be tested in medical practice.

By September 10, 2000, the constant griping over health care funding had become a deafening howl. That night the premiers sat down to dinner with Prime Minister Jean Chretien at 24 Sussex Drive. Soaring health care costs were bleeding their budgets into the red, and it was barely possible to detect a federal pulse in the spending stream. Massive surpluses were piling up in Ottawa. The premiers wanted their mid-1990s transfer payment cuts restored with a hefty slice of the economic prosperity dividend tacked on as compensation.

There were other agendas at play, of course. Elections were looming in British Columbia and Newfoundland. In the coming months, four premiers, including Quebec's Lucien Bouchard and Saskatchewan's Roy Romanow, would resign. But the two seniors at the table faced the most pressing election timetables: Jean Chretien and Ralph Klein.

With the headlines full of jammed hospital emergency wards turning away patients in ambulances, Chretien badly needed health care damage control before he dropped the writ to seek a third majority government. Klein had the nasty Bill 11 backlash to calm down before he could face the voters. A good-news deal would go a long way to smoothing out the road to re-election. Which brings us to the dinner in question.

Conversation was cordial until after-dinner coffees, at which point Chretien began sounding out the room on the prospects for a new funding arrangement. Klein's voice barrelled from the far end of the table. "How much money you got?" The prime minister grins when he recalls the pragmatic Klein brushing aside the traditional posturing to get right to the point. "He was very clear. I said, 'I don't have much money.' He said, 'Have you got serious money?' I told him what I had and he said, 'Let's sign an agreement'." That's the way former Saskatchewan premier Roy Romanow recalls it, as well. "Ralph had already decided that we should sign the draft documentation that was before us. He quite clearly communicated forcefully his view that we ought to sign it." The next day, ten smiling premiers and three territorial leaders joined Chretien to announce a five-year, twenty-one-billion-dollar health care peace treaty. Six weeks later, Chretien called an election.

Jean Chretien and Ralph Klein differ only in party affiliation. Klein's a liberal Conservative; Chretien's a conservative Liberal. Theirs is a uniquely pragmatic pairing, one of political equals and worthy adversaries. They enjoy the longest unbroken relationship of first ministers since Louis St. Laurent and Ernest C. Manning. When they have differences, they write them off to political posturing. When they have similarities, they try to keep them quiet. It is, after all, bad politics for Alberta and Ottawa to appear too cozy.

They met when Klein was struggling with an epidemic of Calgary street prostitution. Chretien was the justice minister he turned to for help in combatting the problem. The mayor was instantly taken with the senior cabinet minister, who seemed to understand the street and the practical limitations of government intervention. Klein was very impressed. In fact, his career path would have changed dramatically had Chretien won the Liberal leadership one convention earlier. Shortly after winning a second mayoralty, Klein was approached by the Liberals to contest a seat in East Calgary. "I declined, but had Jean Chretien been the prime minister in 1984 instead of John Turner, I might have had a different attitude," Klein says.

Today they share a guarded personal warmth, but Klein is not inclined to go out of his way to appease the prime minister. "One time I went to Ottawa and I had made arrangements for dinner that night. It was nothing that serious. The prime minister took me aside and said, 'Come over for dinner,' but I said I was busy," Klein says. "I've never seen a man so upset. He said, 'You won't have dinner with the prime minister?' I said, 'Of course I'd have dinner with the prime minister, but I'm tied up. We're going out to a bistro'."

Chretien and Klein come from working class backgrounds. Neither has the physical properties to suggest poster boy leadership qualities. But they share a remarkably similar track record as leaders. Each led three majority governments, starting in 1993, each greater than the one before, a winning streak which has doomed a parade of dismayed official opposition leaders. They both inherited huge deficits and eliminated them with spending cuts first, tax cuts later. Each is wily, cagey, charismatic and ruthlessly protective of his party. They admire each other from a cordial distance and talk frankly in person.

The Klein government looks at Chretien as their final court of appeal if Alberta is not being shown the courtesy of common sense from federal ministers. "Despite his politics he is a likeable individual," a cautious Klein says of Chretien. "When he comes here, there's not a problem." The best example of this was the day federal health minister Allan Rock flew into Calgary to blast Bill 11 as the "green light" to private hospitals. Klein returned fire. He called the visit a "drive-by smearing" and fired off a one-sentence protest to the prime minister. He called Rock "a disgrace to you and your government." Chretien visited Calgary two months later to calm his irritated friend. "I saw your letter in the *Ottawa Citizen*, Ralphie," Chretien ribbed Klein in private. "You could've saved a few words just saying 'Fuck you'."

After the meeting, Chretien brought his health department pitbulls to heel. What Klein was proposing wasn't as villainous as it had been portrayed. "Everybody predicted this bill would do this or that, but he was telling me the contrary," Chretien said. "I told my officials, let's see what he will do. He said he would not break the five conditions of Medicare. I wasn't going to conclude anything before I saw what they were doing." As it turned out, the Bill 11 backlash was short-lived. Its transformation of treatments was negligible, and it was never in violation of the Canada Health Act.

Chretien says he always looked to Klein as the country's bellwether premier. "Mike [Harris] was more doctrinaire. Ralph and I are not doctrinaire, and we're very skeptical about those who are, because when you're doctrinaire, you try to justify your doctrine. Political life is not all that mathematical. He has no problem with me. He knows what I will tell him and I know what he will tell me. He is very predictable. If I come to the conclusion that something makes sense, probably Ralph will come to the same conclusion."

What made sense to Klein was to follow Chretien's lead and call an election shortly after the health care deal was announced. Klein circled March 12 as the date for his provincial election. But the flip side of soaring energy revenue flowing in and out of Alberta's coffers was the rising cost for voters to drive their cars and heat their homes. That rising cost was awakening a sleeper issue in the electorate. The issue would cost the Alberta treasury more money to resolve than all the health care increases combined.

The Electrical Utilities Act, an amendment to deregulate electrical generation and sales, passed unnoticed in 1995. Even cabinet ministers failed to understand the concept. The industry warned about the shock it would generate. Ron Southern, chairman of ATCO Limited and subsidiary Alberta Power, was one of the warners. The Klein government dismissed the concerns. They said the company was preserving a self-interest. Even after power generators cautioned that they were shelving expansion plans until the rules of the game were clarified, the government was unmoved.

Progress was slow until Steve West, the government's privatization guru, inherited the task from longtime Klein loyalist Pat Black. West pushed ahead unilaterally, unfazed by a lack of consensus. He figured the power grid was the natural next step after telephone deregulation and privatized liquor retailing, automotive licensing and highway maintenance. He ordered power generation segregated from the distribution network. Electricity would be sold at auction. West held the auction at the worst possible time. Power rates were at rock bottom levels, and the province required bidding to buy up twenty-year blocks of power from each generator. West confidently predicted forty utility company bidders would bring cash to the table. Only five showed up—and they were nervous about buying power two decades into an uncertain future. The bids were so low, the government pocketed $1.1 billion from the sale, billions shy of the expected taxpayers' return.

Most observers were betting the cabinet would immediately void the auction because it fell far short of any common sense reserve price. West and new Energy Minister Mike Cardinal blocked the government's retreat. The province was doing the right thing, the ministers ruled. They accepted the ridiculously low bids from the very same companies which had dominated the regulated market. For Klein, who always saw policy through a prism of common sense and simplistic assumptions, it was a free market theory ruined by unforeseen complications. Power plants take five years to build. They produce a commodity that cannot be stored. In Alberta, they operate in a market too small for big players to unleash the free enterprise forces of cut-throat competition. In the months to follow, chaos hit Alberta's power grid. There was the failed power auction. New generating capacity was slow to come on line. The North American market was hit by the meltdown of California's electricity supply.

Klein watched in alarm as his deregulation experiment was destabilized. He admitted he did not grasp the mechanics of electricity deregulation. "I have no idea what this means," he told the *Edmonton Journal* editorial board as he studied a sheaf of briefing notes. What he did understand was the need to deal with waves of panic hitting his office from major industrial power users. The energy minister was on the receiving end of outrage from industries watching their rates rise in triple-digit percentages. Klein decided there was only one way to fix the deregulation mistake: mega-money.

He introduced a modest twenty-dollar monthly rebate, followed by a power rate price cap he immediately raised by forty per cent after one power company president publicly denounced the intervention as "Ralph's own National Energy Program."

Klein doubled the homeowners' rebate and introduced a credit scheme for small business. He topped these off with a generous six-hundred-dollar dividend that gave every two-person Alberta household a total package of power and natural gas price protection worth seventeen hundred dollars. The schemes would cost the Alberta treasury four billion dollars, almost a quarter of its spending in the pre-election year. The public, overlooking the cavalier use of their own money as a bribe, marvelled at the small balances and credits on their power bills. Klein labeled opposition protests as "anti free-enterprise" rants, and ignored his government's aggressive intervention in the market to facilitate open competition featuring few new players.

Power deregulation was the triumph of ideology over Klein's

traditional practicality, a dogma-driven attack on a system that delivered dependable supplies of low-cost power to Albertans. "It has taken a well-functioning oligopoly and turned it into a dysfunctional oligopoly," concluded Calgary writer Andrew Nikiforuk. In 2002, the Klein-friendly C.D. Howe Institute lamented the sorry state of the botched Alberta initiative: After the rebates, deregulation had "given the province the dubious distinction of jumping from one of the lowest to the highest electricity rates in the country."

"Look, a whole bunch of things went wrong," Klein ruefully admits. He remains unapologetic about the outcome. "The price of natural gas went up to astronomical levels, three or four Alberta generators broke down, almost as though someone threw wrenches into the God-damn fans, California was screwing up and the economy was at an all-time super-heated level, generating huge demand for electricity. Competition is occurring."

By late 2000, money was pouring in at a rate Klein knew wouldn't last. Thanks to a $2.2-billion, four-year boost in health care spending, there was less anxiety about Bill 11. He had smothered the deregulation mess with costly rebates. He was riding on the strongest economic tailwind anyone had seen since his days as a rookie mayor of boomtown Calgary. After a relaxing Christmas holiday, Klein decided the time wasn't going to get any better for an election. Minutes after the Throne Speech, on February 12, 2001, he invited Albertans to join his government for a Future Summit, another move to deflect campaign demands for new spending, then he dropped the writ for what was expected to be his last election fight. He urged Albertans to vote Tory "for a positive future."

Everything about the campaign followed the government's script, including the weather. March in Alberta can be an ugly, unpredictable month. Statistically, that's when the province gets its greatest snowfall, and temperatures can plunge to minus thirty for weeks on end as Arctic highs and Pacific lows fight for supremacy on the weather map. But March 2001 defied *Farmers' Almanac* predictions when wave after wave of chinooks rolled over the Rockies. There was a bright blue arch in the western sky.

It was the warmest winter since 1988, when Klein hosted the tropical Winter Games as Calgary's mayor, an Olympics when snow had to be scraped off the higher mountain elevations and hauled to Calgary for ski-jumping events witnessed by spectators in tee-shirts and tanktops.

Nancy MacBeth found the campaign hard. She was a Liberal leader fighting a Conservative premier who was spending the motherlode of budgetary surpluses like a New Democrat. She entered the campaign with less than half the government's support in the polls. Mount Ralph loomed large with sixty per cent of the voters in pre-election opinion polls. Still, MacBeth was confident the lingering backlash against Bill 11 and power deregulation would be enough to unseat the incumbent. But from the sound of the writ dropping, glitches plagued her Liberal campaign. MacBeth had a thirty-year-old Buick hauled to the front steps of the legislature. She said it was a "gas-guzzling rustbucket" symbolic of an Alberta Conservative party seeking its ninth consecutive mandate. Klein harrumphed in indignation. "Some people in this province still drive thirty-year-old vehicles," he said and told them they should be offended by the analogy.

MacBeth introduced a ten-point fiscal policy—but only listed nine points to an unimpressed Chamber of Commerce. She called media to a French fry plant in Lethbridge. The plant had served notice it was delaying a factory expansion partly due to rising power bills. She was denied access to the property by its owners. She paid twelve hundred dollars for an airline ticket for Klein to fly to Ottawa to collect money from Canadian Alliance leader Stockwell Day to repay the eight-hundred-thousand-dollar legal fees and settlement cost for a defamation action launched against the former treasurer. Klein had taken pains to distance himself from Day by calling the costs "obscene." He announced he would donate the ticket to a children's charity. This put MacBeth in a bad light when she asked for the ticket back.

MacBeth campaigned hard and non-stop. She woke up at 5:00 a.m. for a pre-dawn walk to prepare for eighteen-hour days of hectic campaign appearances. Klein's eight-hour days on the hustings began at noon, and he promised little beyond status-quo stability. Public opinion refused to budge in MacBeth's favor. In desperation, with ten days to go before voting day, MacBeth unleashed television ads showing bejewelled hands exchanging money with liquor glasses as a backdrop. The anouncer hinted darkly at power companies benefitting mightily from donations to the Conservative party (conveniently overlooking the fact that Liberal MLAs received more in power company support than Tory MLAs). Klein mocked her tactic as the last gasp of a faltering campaign. As if to ice the majority re-election cake, he made costly peace with his old enemies in health care by giving nurses and doctors a twenty-two-per-cent escalation in their salaries and fees, making them the highest-paid professionals in the nation. It was the cement of certain victory. Nancy MacBeth could only watch and weep as Klein bought himself the election.

Late on the afternoon of March 12, Ralph and Colleen Klein boarded their campaign plane with Peter Elzinga for the forty-five-minute flight to Calgary. Klein was surly. That afternoon, he'd been challenged by Broadcast News reporter Jim Macdonald about the propriety of holding a news conference in the premier's office on an election day. He felt the media had ignored the real issues on the public's mind by focusing on Stockwell Day's legal bill and on power deregulation. He poured himself a glass of red wine from a portable bar and watched the Prairie scroll beneath the plane. Then he poured himself another. Then another. He started to relax, confident in the polling and in the optimistic reports from the field. He was guaranteed another term as premier. Klein figured he had sixty-five of the eight-three seats. Colleen pegged it closer to seventy.

Peter Elzinga couldn't bear to look as the early results flashed on the small screen. There were only two points of serious suspense. The first was Calgary Buffalo, the seat Klein had helped friend Sheldon Chumir win for the Liberals in 1986 when he was mayor. It quickly fell into Tory hands. Then came early Edmonton results. Klein and Elzinga exchanged wide-eyed looks. Some of the strongest Liberals on the Opposition bench were falling to defeat. Gone were Howard Sapers, Karen Leibovici, Colleen Soetaert and Lance White. It took ninety minutes and a lot of pinching before Klein could believe he'd inflicted the ultimate humiliation. Nancy MacBeth had been defeated in the Edmonton seat she'd easily carried three years earlier.

Two hours after the polls closed, the Conservatives owned every seat outside Edmonton except for a lone holdout in Lethbridge, retained by the next Alberta Liberal leader, mild-mannered Ken Nicol. Strictly by the numbers, Klein matched Peter Lougheed's most lopsided electoral landslide with sixty-two per cent of the vote. He claimed more ballots cast for the party than any election in the province's history. The Opposition Liberals were swept back thirteen years, to finish one seat below their 1989 standing. The final count: Conservatives seventy-four, Liberals seven, New Democrats two. MacBeth conceded defeat graciously with dry eyes, robbing Klein of his campaign's sought-after satisfaction. "The people have spoken and I accept that result without question," MacBeth told somber supporters attending a victory party turned into a wake. She deferred questions on her political future for another day. "It would've been nice to make her cry," Klein smirked several months later. "Maybe bawl just a little bit."

Ironically, Klein struggled to hold back tears. His acceptance speech flowed from his heart and a blood-alcohol reading even he admitted would have rendered driving a criminal offense. Klein opened his victory speech with a welcome many people thought was arrogant. It was derived from an unscripted encounter in his riding with Liberal challenger Harold Swanson, a retired radiologist. Swanson had lamented that the province had deteriorated under Klein's reign. The premier had responded with a savage attack on "Harold's world, a world of $3.4-billion deficits, high debt loads, and an oversized public service." His eyes glistening and bloodshot, Klein took to a stage on the Calgary Stampede grounds with Peter Elzinga behind him and Colleen by his side.

"Welcome," he roared to the euphoric hometown crowd, "to Ralph's World."

Nineteen

Sober Second Thoughts

RALPH KLEIN REMEMBERS welcoming in the year 2002. It was a new experience for the traditionally hearty partier. For the first time in his adult life, Klein spent New Year's Eve at home with wife Colleen, a pot of coffee and a lot of cold medication. He was spiking a fever of 102 degrees Fahrenheit, and his wife worried he was fighting pneumonia. But it was a blessing, as it kept him away from the traditional temptation of his thirsty circle of friends with well-stocked liquor cabinets. For more than thirty years, Klein had celebrated New Year's Eve with friends, family and more than a few drinks. This was a good year to stay sober. Because this was the watershed, the year Klein recognized his drinking problem.

Three weeks earlier, Klein had visited the Herb Jamieson Centre, a 249-bed homeless shelter in downtown Edmonton. His curiosity about the plight of those of no fixed address had been piqued by a newspaper series on poverty in the *Edmonton Journal*. He asked his security escort, Tom Dombrosky, to pull over so he could investigate. He entered a cold outer hallway where five men, denied a bed because they had been drinking, were dozing on the floor. There was small talk, then an argument broke out. Klein wasn't doing enough to help the homeless, one man yelled. Klein suggested he get a job instead of relying on the government.

The suggestion was not well received. Some of the shelter's inmates gruffly told Klein they had jobs, but couldn't afford housing. Still argumentative, the premier was hustled out by his security guard. He tossed money at the homeless men as he left.

He woke up the next morning unconcerned, looking forward to the Conservative Christmas party that evening. He was scheduled to try harness racing as a jockey. He told a reporter he had visited the shelter during a year-end interview with the *Edmonton Journal*. Two days later, when he received a call from his communications staff, the incident started to take on a hard-to-sell recollection. A reporter named Chris Purdy had been tipped that the premier had verbally berated some down-on-their-luck types before throwing some money and storming to his car. One of the transients worked at a Domo gas station, and Purdy spent the day roaming the gas chain for the eye witness and found him. When CBC Television's "The Journal" called for reaction, worried staff in Klein's office talked to Dombrosky, who confirmed the essential elements of the story. Klein furrowed his brow. It sounded familiar, but his mind could not put everything into clear focus. Klein issued a statement of apology to the shelter and the transients he'd encountered and retreated inside his Lakeview home to recover from a back injury suffered during the horse race.

At some point over the weekend, under intense pressure from Colleen, who was furious at being kept out of the loop as the controversy unfurled, Klein looked in the mirror and made a life-altering call. He had spent twenty-one years in the adoring eye of voters who felt drinking defined his character, but enough was enough. "It's something I wanted to do for a long time and it wouldn't go away. 'The Journal' was going to run its account because it's far more dramatic than my account. I thought I had to do it publicly and be committed to it," he says.

Klein had been noticeably drunk at his third election night victory party. Even close friends seethed at those responsible for letting the premier drink to excess. That November, he'd introduced former U.S. President Bill Clinton, a hero of his, to a Calgary fundraiser in much the same advanced state of inebriation. When Klein walked into a memorial for local sportscasting legend Ed Whalen on December 17, 2001, he decided to let the waiting scrum serve as an ad-hoc confessional. Booze was more than a hobby, he said, it was a habit. "It's time," he told startled reporters. "I'm fifty-nine years old and I've got quite a ways to go in my mandate, so I'm just going to curb and control what I see as a problem."

Later that night, chief of staff Peter Elzinga told his friend and boss the worst of the controversy was over, that the issue didn't have legs and the public was solidly behind his pledge to reduce his drinking. Elzinger cautioned the premier to be careful how far he went in his comments. Klein insisted he had to tell the whole story. "If I hold back, it's going to weaken my resolve," he told Elzinga. He was opting for full disclosure. He was a borderline alcoholic performing an act of atonement for an incident he couldn't clearly remember. It was a cry for help.

The next day, Tuesday, December 18, Klein called a news conference. He didn't specify a topic. He didn't need to. National television networks went live the minute Klein walked to the podium. He didn't engage in his usual gregarious banter with reporters. He kept his eyes glued to a text he'd dictated an hour earlier. When he reached the point of thanking family, friends and the 160 strangers who'd called in support and encouragement that morning, he sniffled. Tears started rolling down his cheeks.

When the script stopped and the questions began, Klein went further than anyone expected. He delivered a public vow of temperance backed by an invitation for the media to keep an eye on him. His lifelong friend, the bottle, was a "devil," an "awful beast." His composure returned, and he smiled wryly at some questions, turned stone cold serious at others. "I do things I wouldn't otherwise do," he admitted when asked about alcohol's effect. Was he an alcoholic? "I don't know. Alcoholic is a subjective word. I do know I have a problem and I'm going to have to deal with it."

He was fed up with the incapacitating hangovers that triggered his staff's coded "Black Elvis" warnings of his foul moods. He was tired of the suffering that made morning-after meetings a hit-or-miss proposition and sometimes kept him in bed the entire day. Klein longed for a change in lifestyle.

Hundreds of e-mails arrived followed by two hundred letters of support. There were poignant confessions from journalists and politicians who had battled alcoholism. Klein had what he wanted—a wagon he could not jump off without unleashing a frenzy of media and public speculation. He had backed himself into a very tight corner—resist drink or resign politics.

His first drunk was on homemade chokecherry wine in the basement of the neighboring Shaben household. Young Ralph Klein, not yet ten, slipped away from his friends. It was an hour before anyone noticed he was gone. In the small, war-time house, it didn't take his friend long to find him holed up in a storage room, bombed out of his pre-adolescent mind on the sour, heavily fortified berry juice.

A year or two passed before his next brush with booze, a rum-chugging session on a toboggan hill. Pre-teen Ralph was hit the hardest by the unfamiliar effects of hard liquor. He tumbled down the snowy slope, eagerly chasing a runaway bottle.

Booze and Klein spent most of a lifetime together, a potent mixology of social politics and a playful personality. For thirty years he drank daily, enjoyed it, acknowledged it, slept late and missed work because of it. He used booze to simplify fiscal policy for the average voter, explaining Calgary's $978-million tax-supported debt in the 1980s as "the price of one Bloody Caesar per day per taxpayer for six years." He is probably the first premier to have a table in a seedy tavern dedicated to his drinking exploits. He is likely the first premier to have seriously considered opening his own bar. And he is almost certainly the first premier to have had a beer named after him—Kleineken, an ale labeled by Big Rock Brewery especially for the 1994 Tory party convention in Banff.

The St. Louis Tavern is Calgary's shrine to Klein's drinking notoriety. It is a tattered but intensely friendly basement saloon on the shabby side of the Light Rail Transit tracks, across from city hall. Civic employees used to sneak into the back alley door at lunch hour to wash down its famed chicken-and-chips with cheap draft beer. The practice was frowned on by the city mandarins until the bar's patron saint was elected mayor. Klein transformed the Looey into a trendy noon getaway. On Friday lunch hours, a burly barrel of fun named George Stephenson seizes the sound system to broadcast live horse races he makes up in his head as he goes along. Patrons wager loonies on photocopied race sheets and cheer on their favorite. The favorite rarely wins, and whatever horse is ahead at the final turn is invariably tripped up by bad luck, losing to a come-from-behind longshot.

As CFCN television's city hall reporter, Klein could be found here on many lunch hours and most weeknights. He downed trays of draft in eight-ounce glasses with a ragtag assortment of cronies who gave him the working-class pulse of his city's heart. He drank the best stories out of his sources. He also bonded to their thinking. When the east end was threatened with bulldozing by the commercial redevelopment expected from a proposed city hall complex, Klein promoted the plight of the evicted and displaced with biased passion. He bemoaned the loss of used furniture joints, pawn shops and, most important, the old-timer bars where hotel residents sang pathetic renditions of Stompin' Tom classics and rubbies with pickled noses and rotten teeth were beloved characters of a passing era.

The Calgary bar district was Klein's second home throughout his mid-thirties. He drank too much, too often in those smoky rooms, and he didn't always depend on cabs or designated drivers at closing time. One night in 1977, he was hauled over by police on Elbow Drive, a few kilometres from his house. The officer recognized the inebriated television talent slumped behind the wheel and let Klein off with orders to find an alternative method of transportation home. After the cruiser drove off, Klein stood for a few swaying minutes contemplating his choices. It was in an era before police attached tire clamps to drunk drivers' automobiles. Klein's car was left parked at the curb. With the keys still in his pocket, the temptation was too strong for his clouded judgment. Klein jumped into the car and drove straight into the arms of the police officer waiting around the corner. This time, there was no leniency. He was charged and fined three hundred dollars for impaired driving.

Klein had another alcohol-fueled run-in with the law in 1978. His hot-tempered bender ended with him in a vile, threatening mood. His wife called the cops to come and haul him off to the hoosegow. It was clearly a very ugly spat and fueled decades of rumors about the state of his marriage.

As rookie mayor, Klein hit the sauce with gleeful gusto. The drink was usually free, always plentiful. There was never a shortage of people anxious to join the new Calgary mayor for an all-nighter. The police chief offered to make a driver available to the mayor's office, but Klein declined. He believed it was too elitist a perk for a common man's mayor to accept. He soon came to regret the decision. A few months after his 1980 election, Klein attended an Italian wine-tasting with assistant Bruce Planche. After much tasting and too much wine swallowing, an inebriated Klein decided he would call the cops for a lift. "A sergeant answered the phone and he made some obnoxious comment about not being there to give Ralph a ride. I kicked up a fuss and a constable gave me a ride home, but the story was leaked," Klein recalls. Subsequent coverage kickstarted the legend of the carousing Klein, a mayor whose work day started at 11:00 a.m.—if he made it into the office at all—and ended after last call.

Word of his notorious thirst reached Parliament Hill circles. When Justice Minister Jean Chretien granted Klein an audience to talk about the city's prostitution problem, the two shook hands. Chretien gave Klein an apprehensive fatherly look. "I know your reputation," he said. "I can give you a beer, but no 'ard stuff, okay?" In the Ottawa airport later that week, a ticket agent asked the mayor, "What do you usually fly on?" "Rum and Coke mostly," Klein smirked. Former mayor Rod Sykes says, "Faults that would've destroyed almost every politician are tolerated with Ralph. He's looked on as a fat little drunk and as a great guy."

Klein's boozing, however, was no laughing matter. The hard drinking and the morning-after tardiness were taking a toll on his office. Midway through his second term, his staff members were in frequent turmoil over Klein's inability to meet his scheduled commitments. Assistants Rod Love and Wilf Morgan wrote a memo warning Klein he was teetering on the edge of an alcoholic abyss. They were barely able to contain their disgust at Klein's latest two-day binge. He had missed a University of Calgary business day, Hug Day at an elementary school, a political science class and the Easter Seal kick-off. They warned Klein his community relations were suffering severe damage.

"We are putting these thoughts on paper because we feel we are rapidly approaching a crisis affecting your career and your credibility as mayor," the two-page memo warned. "Twice in the last three weeks you have been unable to make your appointments and, while this happens to all of us occasionally, the last two times have been lengthy and dangerous because of the public nature of the incidents. We have been both good and lucky in covering for you, but quite frankly one of these days we are going to get caught and the ramifications of that can speak for themselves. There is a very real growing perception in the community that you have a serious drinking problem. The rumours are beginning to spread very rapidly with many people being able to verify the rumours. This is a political problem of the utmost risk. If it continues, you will have no family life, no career and very little credibility in the community. We write this as friends, not employees, but we are also questioning how much longer we will be able to help you survive or to survive ourselves in your office." The note hit Klein squarely between his bloodshot eyes. He grabbed a pen and scrawled a promise on the bottom. "Thank you for your comments. They are true and I will give a commitment to my friends to stay a good mayor." Almost fifteen years later, his aides are reluctant to talk about the memo. "It wasn't for us to say he shouldn't be drinking, but that's not to say there wasn't a time where it was getting in the way of the agenda," Rod Love allows.

Klein became careful about where, when and with whom he would let loose for a "toot," as he calls a major drinking bout. He started eating and drinking at the discreet Caesar's Steakhouse or huddled in the back room of a small upstairs pub opened by close friend Andy Gibson, across the street from the St. Louis. Klein accepted a tighter leash held by his wife, Colleen, and his staff. During the 1988 Winter Olympics, his promise to deliver the wildest party of the century was kept without any mayoralty incidents or missed commitments.

The self-control lessened when Klein left for provincial politics. He was no longer in a city where his arrival in any lounge created a public stir, and he was terribly unhappy being away from his family. Klein found a friend in Stephen West, a tall, tough, imposing MLA with a notoriously wild drinking streak. When he was confronted about his drinking at the announcement of his bid for the premier's chair, Klein didn't attempt to fudge the truth. "I've shared with some of my colleagues that I enjoy a drink or two. But I can change," he said, and paused. "That's not to say I'm going to totally quit."

When he was premier, the drinking continued at a pace Klein estimated at the "equivalent" to a bottle of wine per day, never specifying if that was a liquid volume comparison or alcoholic intake. Reporters noted traces of antacid on the rookie premier's mouth and viewed the giant bowl of white mints at the premier's door as less a hospitality gesture than a reminder for the premier to grab a couple to mask the booze on his breath as he left the office.

Even when he was genuinely ill or if his bleary-eyed appearance was the sign of an early wake-up call, boozing got the blame. During an annual premiers' summit in Toronto in September 1994, Klein was doing his usual post-meeting interview with local media. He welcomed former legislature scribe Jeff Harder of the *Toronto Sun* into the small gaggle of journalists. As the interview wrapped up, Harder noted room service wheeling in several pitchers of tomato juice. A few hours later, Harder joined Klein, his aides and several reporters for drinks. He left when dinner was served. The group carried on for several hours. Klein was the first to call it a night. He left the group before midnight to prepare for an early-morning meeting. That early rising was reflected in Klein's puffy eyes, constant yawning and general lack of enthusiastic attention for then-premier Bob Rae's long and rambling analysis at the wrap-up news conference. The next morning the *Sun*'s front page contained a devastating series of photos featuring Klein in a full-blown yawn and appearing to doze off. Harder's story, headlined "Toasted Western," was on the next page. It detailed the "buckets of Caesar mix" sent to Klein's room and the late-night carousing at the Royal York Hotel. It was a severely torqued story, and Rod Love was screaming for a full retraction within minutes of the paper hitting the streets. Harder stuck to his story and found himself forever on the outs in Klein's office. Staff with long memories recited the incident as the reason the premier apparently did not send his customary personal regrets to the family when Harder succumbed to cancer in 2001.

Klein found his lifelong habit of being late or missing meetings hard to conceal when he was premier. He missed a meeting with the Young Presidents' organization. He missed a chat with treaty Indian chiefs after a session-ending all-nighter in 1994. He was an "exhausted" no-show at the first cabinet meeting of his 1993 government. The last absence triggered a news story, and there were plenty of nudges and knowing winks around the table.

In 1995, he was asked by CBC reporter Elaine Chatigny if he ever missed work because of drinking. Yes, of course, a bemused Klein responded with a gentle smile. "Haven't you?" A few weeks after that admission ran in the *Edmonton Journal*, Klein's staff exacted a small measure of revenge. Rod Love went out for dinner with Joan Crockatt, the paper's legislature bureau chief. The night didn't end until Martini's bar closed in the early-morning hours. Love phoned me about eight hours later, nonchalantly asking if Crockatt had reported for duty. I yelled the question down the press gallery hallway and was told she had just called in with a severe bout of the flu. "Perrrrrfect," Love cooed. When told Klein's office reacted with apparent glee to her sudden night-before-related illness, a ghostly pale Crockatt dragged herself into work long enough to be seen by Klein's communications director before bolting for home.

Heavy drinking by Canadian politicians dates back to Sir John A. Macdonald. What's unique about Klein was his willingness to discuss his notorious thirst with unapologetic openness and to deal so directly with his problem. "I still enjoy red wine and a beer and I still enjoy going on a toot once in a while," he told me a month before his visit to the homeless shelter. "It's in my blood and I guess that's part of my nature." He has never received medical treatment for alcoholism. But he says, "I've had problems from time to time. I just say, 'Today's the first day of the rest of my life so let's start living it.' You know I find it's so good to wake up without a hangover. I say, 'Why do I do that to myself?' When I don't go on a toot and I haven't been on one for a while, I feel real good and I'm up and ready to go at it."

There have been no medical complications from his exuberant imbibing, but a friend says the doctor who treated Klein for broken ribs in May 1997 cautioned the premier about irregularities in his liver function. The allegation is denied by the Kleins. Interestingly, the premier eased off beer and hard liquor around that time, switching to red wine as his drink of choice.

Colleen Klein was increasingly concerned about her husband's drinking before 2001. When he lurched beyond tipsy, Colleen used a private signal. Her squeeze on his arm is a non-negotiable last call, a five-minute warning that it's time to depart for his own good. This was particularly evident in October 2000 at the celebration to mark Klein's twentieth year in politics. Members of his first election team, closest advisers and a few journalists gathered in a Palliser Hotel conference room to tell lies, share drinks, pose for a group photo and marvel at the mighty pinnacle climbed by their former carousing buddy. Klein spoke straight from the heart. He tearfully thanked his friends and settled into a steady drinking rhythm. By 11:00 p.m. his arm had been squeezed and he dutifully moved toward the exit. Colleen explained her dog Jessy was in the car and needed a walk. Yes, she insisted to incredulous looks from the group, Ralph Klein was leaving his own anniversary party before midnight so their pooch could take a piss.

All who have drunk and been drunk with Ralph Klein can testify to his enormous capacity to handle large amounts of drink with apparent immunity from intoxication's physical consequences. He may get maudlin and shed a few tears at a poignant memory, but he's the last to slur his words. With the exception of the homeless shelter visit, he usually retains the most vivid memory of events. This, as reporters will tell you, is a skill few in the media can replicate. Klein loves to boast he's given me more scoops than any other journalist during our soggy sessions. He'll look around, lean forward, lower his voice and confide some secret tidbit worth pursuing. "Just don't say you got it from me." He'll grin as you digest the data and imagine the thrill of lording an exclusive over the rest of the press gallery. But he always waits for the right time to share the information, the precise moment when he knows you'll forget the whole thing by morning. "I've given Donnie more scoops than any other journalist," he gleefully said at a roast to raise funds for, appropriately enough, the Canadian Liver Foundation. "But he just can't remember them."

As a premier in his late fifties, Klein was not the heavy drinker he had been as a mayor not yet turned forty. Although his coffee mug has been known to clink with rattling ice cubes, he rarely poured a stiff belt until the day's work was almost finished. Booze before a round of golf was a definite no-no, and he was loath to down a beer on the course; he insisted it affected his game for the worse. Klein used to take regular trips to his B.C. fishing lodge, with Peter Elzinga, who says the first night was good for a bottle of wine, but very little alcohol was consumed once the pair hit the water.

Klein's drinking habit was an integral part of his public appeal. Thousands of Calgarians will tell you they've personally had a drink with the premier. Many people talk about Klein's tendency to challenge fellow drinkers to an arm wrestle once he's loaded. "When you talk to people, invariably they'll say they talked to Ralph Klein or had a beer with Ralph Klein," shrugs health minister Gary Mar. "It may have been in the St. Louis in a group of thirty tables, but they'll insist they had a beer with him. He may have passed them on the way to the washroom and said, 'Hey, how are ya?', but they'll say they talked to him. It's striking to see how many people purport to have a relationship with Ralph Klein when it's tenuous at best."

Separating the mythical drinker from the new, sober reality is going to be Klein's most difficult political metamorphosis. There is a unique bond between Klein's personality and his home province. Three million Albertans have a vested interest in preventing his return to booze. An entire press gallery has an interest in exposing news of his return to the bottle.

At this book's deadline, he was still not drinking. He looked more energetic and thinner than he had in years. "You still have the yearning [to drink] when you're out amongst people," Klein says. He consoles himself with the knowledge that "it's much better to gamble sober. You actually make some money by knowing when to go away."

There is an ironic precedent for believing Ralph Klein will keep his devil inside a corked bottle. His mother, Florence Gray, was an alcoholic for decades. She went through three marriages where booze was her constant companion. It was a homeless shelter that forced her to confront the awful beast. She was a resident, not a visitor. In the mid-1980s, after hitting bottom on skid row, Florence quit drinking and hasn't touched a drop since. If it was her genes that gave Klein his thirst, perhaps her genes can give him the resolve to resist it, as well.

Twenty

Does the Belly Still Burn?

S O W H A T N O W ? T H E question was starting to nag at Ralph Klein as his third mandate unfurled. There were speculative whispers about the length of his political lifeline. Several obvious heirs apparents were salivating for a shot—Gary Mar in health, Lyle Oberg in learning and perhaps Ron Stevens in gaming. Former treasurer Jim Dinning coveted the premier's job from his position as executive vice-president of TransAlta Utilities.

But why quit? Klein's popularity with Albertans was only abating slightly. The roaring economy had slowed to a more manageable pace, and his government needed only a modest sustained uptick in world energy prices to eliminate the last traces of the thirty-billion-dollar debt Klein had inherited in 1992.

Then again, why stay? Klein has survived an era of brutal cuts and thrived during periods of budgetary largess. He reinvented Ralph the Knife as a shorter, friendlier, wealthier version of the original blue-eyed sheik, Peter Lougheed. He provided the citizens of Canada's tax haven with upgraded roads, hospitals, schools and cultural facilities.

The health care cuts had made Klein reluctant to enter hospital to have several broken ribs treated in 1997. After substantial infusions of cash, hospitals had become his fan club. In the summer of 2001, Klein stopped at the Foothills Hospital en route to a golf game to visit his ailing mother, Florence. He left me with his security guard in the car and walked through the front door alone. Half an hour later, we went searching for the premier to remind him of our imminent tee time and discovered him posing for group photos with the ward's nursing staff. It would have been a very different picture five years earlier.

Klein turns sixty on November 1, 2002. He has known nothing but public office since quitting journalism as a thirty-seven-year-old reporter. He has outlasted every premier in office on his arrival as a first minister. The scenario was graphically illustrated in a farewell salute to his Conservative understudy, Mike Harris of Ontario. In a March 2002 video, the producer took a photo of the 1996 premiers' conference in Jasper and deleted the people who had left or been forced from office. The segment ended with only Klein and Harris in the picture. Now Klein stands alone as elder statesman among premiers.

In some ways, it is a dubious claim to fame. Klein's got enough of a keen ear for water cooler conversation to know that most of what goes on between Canadian premiers is a skipping record of stale issues the public chooses not to fathom. The fabled communiqués at premiers' conferences, most of them sketched out by assistants long before the call to order, have become so similar in content as to be interchangeable. The clashes with Ottawa over health care, the internal obstacles to interprovincial trade, the social union and the incessant, inevitable, insatiable demands for more federal money are perennial fixtures. The rookie premiers may find them very exciting, but to Klein these gabfests have become the monotonous equal of mayoralty greetings to visiting business conventions. They contain a wearisome blur of high-minded rhetoric. Only the faces around the table change, with one notable exception—his.

Klein has, by almost any measure, lived an idyllic public life. His personal popularity has not yet dipped below fifty per cent in the polls through seven terms. His pluralities as mayor and premier have only increased. Klein went straight to city hall's top spot. He never logged time on obscure civic committees or mind-numbing task forces as an alderman. He has never warmed a seat on a government backbench or sat in opposition to tilt at government windmills. With one unnerving exception—the three-year stint as a junior minister of the environment in the ailing Don Getty government—every position has been his to control, every election his to win, every vote a Ralpherendum.

And yet there are signals Klein is entering the twilight of his career. The moment will arrive when there's nothing left to accomplish. As corny as it sounds, and he says it often enough to make corny an understatement, Klein needs a "burning in the belly" to stay in the game. Without a daunting challenge—his post-Olympic letdown, his lonely term as environment minister and most of his second mandate being obvious examples—Klein is an irritable, inattentive, less-effective politician.

Nudging aside the Peter Lougheed longevity record in the spring of 2007 to become Alberta's second-longest-serving premier, runner-up only to the twenty-five-year reign of the venerable Ernest C. Manning, is too much hubris and not enough historical significance to lure him into a fourth election. Nor is sticking around to preside over the Alberta Centennial on September 1, 2005. The celebration has been hit hard by budget cuts. He could, theoretically, host the bash and immediately quit, but he would be leaving his successor with a scant eight months left in a five-year mandate. Besides, with his third term under way, there's little to suggest there's a fight on the horizon worthy of another five years in office. The intestinal fire is flickering.

Klein faces retirement pressure on the personal front, too. Colleen is wearying of the onerous demands on their marriage and their expanding family, which now includes two great-grandchildren. She yearns for more time with her husband. Klein's newfound passion for golf has reduced their time together. He heads for the course many summer mornings at dawn. "It has, in the truest sense, made me a golfing widow," she laments. When Klein feels guilty about being away from home, he'll vacuum the television room or take her car out for a wash on the odd Saturday morning. She smiles ruefully. It hardly makes up for the long stretches on her own.

While his public pitch to curb his drinking was a godsend for Colleen, the decision haunts him at every restaurant or reception when a dozen curious sets of eyes sneak a peak at the contents of his glass. Friends who relished the late nights with Klein, when bottomless carafes of red wine crowded the table, miss their famous carousing buddy and feel uncomfortable imbibing in his presence. He's different, they say. They struggle to put a finger on precisely how, beyond the weight loss and clearer eyes.

The enhanced MLA severance package, which effectively reinstated the pension abolished in 1993, has given Klein a level of financial security he would never have dreamed possible as a journalist. By the summer of 2004, Klein is aiming to fill a gaping hole in his personal resume when he is awarded a bachelor's degree in communications through a correspondence program from Athabasca University.

The stars, sun and moon are lining up for a departure in 2004, but Klein relishes the role of being unpredictable. His views on retirement fluctuate, and there's every reason to suspect that, as this book goes to print, he has not completely made up his mind. "I'm sitting here in my office and it's a nice office and I look at what I'm getting paid and I see others moving on," he says, pensively sucking on a cigarette. "I look at the challenges and I think, 'This isn't so bad after all'. But other days I wonder, 'Why am I doing it?'"

What he would do is another question he's struggling to answer. "People say you can go on boards as a director. I don't know if I'm a board kind of person," he notes in obvious understatement. "I'd like to teach journalism. That's why I'm working on my degree. But I'd like to make sure the province is in really, really good shape before I go." It's obvious the fear factor that drives most veteran politicians to retire—the spectre of being handed an electoral pink slip—does not apply to Klein. He'll depart of his own accord, on his own terms.

With retirement on the horizon, the unspoken, unofficial mission to kick-start Klein's third term was to find a legacy to call his own. He salivated at the possibility of leaving the province without the burden of debt, which gobbles up billions of interest dollars in other provinces. He was tantalizingly close to becoming debt-free in the spring of 2001 until a bizarre form of fiscal hedonism engulfed his government. Nurses were given a two-year contract and became the envy of their peers across Canada. The government hoped the bait would lure thousands to the province from have-not regions. Alberta doctors were blessed with the nation's highest fee schedule, and Klein hinted teachers and civil servants were next in line to profit from the burgeoning bottom line. In the months after the election there was money to burn.

Finance Minister Pat Nelson's first budget propelled spending by $2.5 billion. The one-year surge matched the entire deficit Klein had set out to eliminate eight years earlier. The lean and mean public service was put on a growth spurt. Twelve hundred staff members were added to the payroll, most of them in children's services. A beaming Klein stood before reporters in the spring of 2001 to muse about the possibility of a ten-billion-dollar surplus to end Alberta's fiscal year. The unprecedented bonanza dangled the possibility of eliminating the remaining debt in just one more year.

But as any Albertan knows, once an energy boom is taken for granted and factored into wishlists or budget projections, it's doomed to bust. The twelve-billion-dollar rainy-day Heritage Savings Trust Fund is an apt symbol for Alberta. It was founded on the belief that good times are unsustainable and bad times inevitable. Like Don Getty, who found himself sandwiched uncomfortably between a Lougheed-driven spending surge and his mid-1980s inheritance of crashing energy revenue, Klein was suddenly squeezed between the windfalls he had budgeted for in three-year business plans and a real-time drop in natural gas and oil prices. In a matter of weeks, $1.5 billion in revenue was wiped off the books by free-falling royalties. Just four months after posting a $7.3-billion surplus, already a slight downer from Klein's earlier exuberant prediction, Nelson projected the surplus would suffer a precipitous meltdown to $12 million, a razor-thin line of budgetary black ink that would cover eighteen hours of health care spending. Nelson unleashed the attack dogs, demanding budget cuts across the board to keep the province from tipping into a deficit outlawed by its own flagship legislation.

Watching with detached interest from the sidelines, former Liberal leader Nancy MacBeth couldn't resist a satisfied taunt as she watched her old nemesis suffer the hangover of his spending binge. "He's had three back-to-back budgets that grew by close to forty per cent and now we're short of money," she said. "The problem is that he can't blame the last ten years on Don Getty. He's got his own record to deal with." Klein is unrepentant about his fluctuating fiscal resolve. "I'm a realist and I face reality. If we have a huge surplus and are able to do one-time spending and address some problems that need to be addressed, then we do it. If there's a serious decline in revenues and we don't have the money to do the kind of things people expect, then we bite the bullet and say no." It's ideology, Klein-style.

In the fading election afterglow, Klein's ministers and staff noticed that their leader appeared listless and detached. His drinking increased early in the third term and culminated with his embarrassingly intoxicated introduction of former U.S. President Bill Clinton at a Calgary fundraiser in November 2001, a month before he visited the Edmonton homeless shelter. There were rumors that the former president had requested greater separation between himself and the rambling premier as the evening wore on. During interviews, after he admitted his drinking problem, Klein acknowledged the Clinton incident as an example of booze adversely affecting his conduct.

He appeared bored by the flaccid forces of opposition. Seven Liberals and two New Democrats couldn't put up much of a fight against a premier with a Santa streak and a Midas touch. Klein found some of his ministers unimaginative. His government rolled out one-time spending announcements with promises of much more to come. He missed the revolutionary spunk of his first-term gang, and felt his cabinet had been taken over by "overly cautious" types who spent their days "nitpicking" over policy details without showing true spunk or spine. He wanted signs of the bold, unilateral, zealous confidence of his retired former drinking buddy Steve West, who had privatized liquor retailing and motor vehicle registries with nary a second thought or public consultation. "They take everything through the standing policy committee, through agenda and priorities and caucus and cabinet and then they wonder why their projects get shut down," Klein laments. "They're too structured. From time to time, I say to my ministers, 'Just do it. I'm getting no cards or letters on this particular issue, so do it!'" Klein was learning that triumph wasn't nearly as much fun as the struggle.

His cabinet ministers advance a different and more plausible interpretation. "The way Peter Elzinga's got the political system structured, we couldn't do the things we did in 1993 now," confided one minister in the spring of 2002. "If you decide to fart on a Tuesday, you've got to go through the agenda and priorities committee first. Everything's got to go through different committees and by the time it gets through the bureaucracy, it's months down the road." They'll tell you, almost without prompting, that Klein's disconnect from the day-to-day business of government is becoming a problem, particularly as he has left uninspired Deputy Premier Shirley McClellan and glitch-plagued finance minister Pat Nelson in charge during his absences.

If there was a shred of doubt that the Klein revolution had been deep-sixed, it was put to rest the day after the long August weekend of 2001. Unbeknownst to the premier's communications staff, a members' services committee of eight Tories, a Liberal and a New Democrat convened in a legislature conference room to approve a sweetheart substitute for the MLA pension plan. The original pension scheme had triggered such a backlash that Klein scuttled it during his first six months in office. He credited the dramatic move as the victory-clinching act of the 1993 election. On August 7, 2001, with the premier and most journalists on holidays, with only New Democrat Brian Mason voicing dissent, MLAs took ten minutes to approve a new RRSP savings arrangement which added $6,750 directly to their paycheques and sweetened the severance deal for all MLAs into a de facto pension plan.

Klein was surprisingly unapologetic about the decision to give retiring MLAs three months of their highest earnings for every year of elected service upon quitting or being fired by the voters. He compared his

position to that of a blue-chip corporate president and declared the retirement package "fair" and "reasonable." Such was the buoyant mood of
Albertans that hot, dry summer, the public barely objected, despite howls
of protest from the same Canadian Taxpayers' Federation which had
humiliated MLAs into axing their pension plan in the first place. Klein
could retire in 2005 with a five-hundred-thousand-dollar golden handshake. Life as a retiree was no longer a financial concern.

Klein focused his post-election energy on reforming health care. He has
been frustrated by the snail's pace of change throughout his reign as premier. He's seen federal studies, provincial task forces and countless
committee papers. All harped on the need to shake up the status quo, with
little follow-up progress. When I asked him to detail the substantial
changes in health care delivery during his three mandates, Klein could list
only one—the creation of regional health authorities. They are now standard in every province but Ontario.

He is acutely aware that the seventeen health authorities have consolidated the thick bureaucracies of individual hospital boards into sprawling
administration empires with little by way of substantial cost savings. Bill
11, vilified for allowing private clinics to deliver publicly funded treatments, is legislation he considers "benign," a mere baby step that redirects
existing health care dollars into different pockets. To stave off the rising
cost of health care for aging baby boomers, Klein asked former deputy
prime minister Don Mazankowski to probe the health care system for
inefficiencies with a very specific instruction—return with a revolution.

The initial draft of the Mazankowski report delighted Klein so much
that he leaked it. He was enthralled by the suggestion of a panel to dein-
sure services deemed extraneous to essential treatment. He was fascinated
by the concept of creating medical savings accounts to induce people to
spend their own health dollars more efficiently. He was resigned to the
need for Alberta, the only province except British Columbia to charge residents for health insurance, to raise premiums to cover a greater share of
the cost spiral.

The final report toned down the wording of the initial draft, and Klein released it on the eve of a Vancouver health summit in January 2002. He hoped it would inspire other premiers to follow his lead. But the national hype generated by Mazankowski's far-reaching recommendations triggered high anxiety among the premiers. Most of them marched to the conference uni-mike to insist that their province's solutions were far superior to any made-in-Alberta ideas. The first item of conference business was to smother all provincial reports and wait for the final report from the Romanow Commission on Health Care. Premiers voted to receive the various reports for information—and file them on a dusty shelf. Each province would go its own way on reforming the delivery of health care.

Undeterred, Klein returned to Edmonton and immediately ordered that the Mazankowski recommendations be studied for future implementation. "By 2005, if we undertake to implement some of these reforms being recommended, health care will look a lot different from a management point of view," Klein promises. "We'll certainly be able to slow down the cost spiral. We will go ahead and do what we can do, even if it involves some challenges to the interpretation of the Canada Health Act." The battle is opening on many fronts with no obvious resolution in sight.

Klein was also increasingly vexed by the Kyoto Accord, the 1997 international agreement that required Canada to crank down greenhouse gas emissions by six per cent from its 1990 discharge. Alberta generates thirty per cent of Canada's carbon emissions. Klein raised his concerns about the effect on his province at every opportunity, but received only bland assurances from the prime minister that the climate control protocol would not unfairly burden Alberta with clean-up costs. Klein ordered an analysis from his environment department. They crunched out worst-case scenarios that pegged the damage to Alberta's economy as much as five billion dollars per year. Yet still there was silence from Ottawa, where officials were quietly adding up the damage to produce their own estimate of Kyoto's economic impact.

In a calculated move designed to put Jean Chretien on the spot, Klein brazenly stepped to the podium during a trade mission news conference in Moscow in January 2002. He nudged aside the prime minister to read aloud a draft letter from premiers expressing their reservations about the Kyoto Protocol. Chretien was dismayed at having his news conference hijacked. Three premiers later distanced themselves from the content of the letter, but Klein accomplished his mission. He made Kyoto a front-page story that lingered for weeks as manufacturers, petroleum producers and the national Chamber of Commerce rolled out their own fearful forecasts of the economic mayhem that would hit the economy. For months after Moscow, Klein's staff noticed an unfamiliar icy chill in their communications with senior federal officials.

As the deadline for this book approaches, Klein is fluctuating between keen interest in matters of health care policy and the Kyoto Accord and lethargy about almost everything else on the government agenda. When he announced the country's first provincial tax on visiting National Hockey League players, Klein appeared utterly disconnected from the decision. "Don't ask me about the mechanics. I only have briefing notes I was handed an hour ago," he told reporters. He was lashed by Calgary mayor David Bronconnier for reneging on a commitment to share fuel taxes with the cities in his March 2002 budget and abruptly changed his mind. Minor items have flared into major headaches. Community lottery boards, which were going to hand out a modest fifty-million-dollar slice of the $1.2 billion in gaming money pouring into provincial coffers, were eliminated. Cities and towns and even Tory MLAs were in an uproar.

Klein was forced, by inter-cabinet turf wars between the ministers of labor and learning, to wade into a bitter showdown with teachers. Their contract expectations had been raised by Klein's giddy promises of payoffs to come. Thousands of teachers walked out of their classrooms to back their demand for more than the six per cent pay raise offered by the province. The cabinet, adrift while Klein was out of the country, reversed a two-day-old decision not to intervene in the dispute and ordered teachers back to work, saying there was a public emergency. For Calgary public teachers, whose strike was barely twenty-four hours old, that hardly constituted a public emergency. The decision was immediately overturned in the courts. Klein returned to find effigies dangling outside the legislature and downtown Calgary government offices. He began to feel the old wounds of his last run-in with teachers. The memory of his grand-daughter coming home from school in tears, wondering why her teacher was badmouthing her grandfather as a nasty man for cutting education budgets, had a lasting and very negative impact on Klein's view of the teaching profession. He introduced legislation to impose arbitration on Alberta teachers, and cut off their right to strike for the duration of the contract. He wasn't entirely displeased by the furious union outcry.

When the 2002 budget rolled off the presses in mid-March, it underlined Klein's commitment to fiscal pragmatism over ideology by abandoning a seven-year tax freeze. It imposed $722 million worth of new taxes, the first in seven years, on tobacco, alcohol and car registrations. It delivered a walloping thirty per cent increase in health insurance premiums and lifted the ceiling on school property taxes. It delivered inflation-beating boosts to health care and education to cover population growth, but the increases fell short of what had been projected in the three-year business plans. Still, the government forecasted an enviable surplus. Before the budgetary ink was dry, oil and gas prices were bouncing back and the Canadian recovery was on the upswing. It didn't take keen hearing to catch the sounds of Alberta's economic engine sputtering back to life. The province was getting ready to roar once again. Spending would undoubtedly keep pace.

Ralph Klein lacks a seminal moment. There's nothing in his background akin to the legend of the young Peter Lougheed, who peered from behind the stairwell of a Calgary mansion to watch eastern bankers foreclose on the family property (which, legend has it, instilled in him the passion to shift Canada's economic axis west to Alberta). Klein never craved public service for intrinsic purposes. His was not a calculated entry into politics—it was a fluke, a happenstance, a serendipitous case of being an anti-establishment candidate in elections when voters were in the mood to gamble on unproven abilities.

But to suggest Klein was a creation of blind luck or fortuitous timing would undermine the accomplishment. Sure, he became mayor just in time to land the 1988 Winter Olympic Games, but Klein suffered through five years of the worst economic strife to strike Calgary in a generation before he could serve as the Games host. True, he was flushed with enough oilpatch money to pay down debt, cut taxes and buy the last election, but he had to survive the electoral pitfalls of deep cuts to sacred services, daring privatizations and extreme deregulation. It has not been the easy ride it appears.

Klein's hold over Alberta is often in inexplicable conflict with his behavior. He was the hardest-drinking premier in a generation, yet there was no safer seat under his government than in the dry Mormon districts around Cardston. He was adamantly pro-choice yet adored in the Bible Belt, where pro-life sentiment is strong. He's always been a loud and proud Albertan, yet his reign has seen only minor flirtations with western separatism. His is a flexible ideology that senses the sway in Albertan thought almost before the pendulum moves. He is a communicator with the survival skills of a chameleon. The communicator in him will always make sure people have the chance to speak, but he promises nothing more than to listen. The chameleon in him will change stripes instantly if he detects a threat to his political environment.

His success cannot be credited to balanced budgets, lower taxes or debt elimination, because those were not Klein originals. The flimsy blueprints hammered into government policy by Klein were a hodge-podge cobbled from other jurisdictions, bureaucrats, cabinet ministers and assistants, guided from above in loose fashion by the premier's intuitive reading of the public drift. Being able to deliver harsh budget cuts without appearing mean-spirited, self-serving or a slave to muscle-flexing ideology is what set Klein apart from other premiers. He is almost inexplicably trusted by his electorate to make difficult decisions for the general well-being of the province. He is devoid of crass partisan purposes. His constituents accept that he's shrewd, but they don't see him as calculating. His self-interest is their self-interest because Ralph Klein is, after all, just an ordinary guy. How ordinary? Well, it doesn't get any more ordinary than the guy who sat down in the middle of a wedding reception for health minister Gary Mar, rolled up his sleeves and challenged one and all to arm-wrestling competitions. Or the mayor who was returning from a Calgary Flames hockey game on a freezing 1980 New Year's Eve to see a newlywed couple posing in front of city hall for pictures. He stopped the car and invited them inside his office for a celebratory nightcap to thaw out. Or the Olympic organizing committee director who personally delivered piles of leftover food from a lavish board function to the single men's hostel. He's a guy thousands of Calgarians will lay claim to having had a beer with, overlooking the fact they were sharing the room with a hundred people at the time.

His father, Phil, says he passed down only three bits of advice to his eldest son—never lie, defend what you believe in and admit your mistakes quickly. Those lessons, perhaps taught, perhaps intuitive, have prevailed in Klein's conduct. He has never been caught stammering a bald-faced lie. He may selectively highlight the truth and use staff to manipulate its presentation, but in an era when politicians are accused of fibbing as a regular ritual, he is uniquely forthright. He admits to error quickly, but not so easily as to appear specious. When he admits a wrong, it's usually about something that needed correcting.

At this writing, I've spent twenty-two years as a journalist, covering Ralph Klein almost without interruption. This book has a single-minded purpose to take that exposure: roll it up with input from his cronies, his opponents and insights from the Kleins to define the phenomenon known simply as Ralph. I imagined crafting a *Ralph's Politics for Dummies*, a how-to instruction manual for budding politicians on the secrets to getting elected and enjoying growth in popularity through good times and bad. On that count, I have failed. There is no road map to Ralph's World that anyone could follow to a successful electoral destination. It's not a learned behavior. You either instinctively know how to get there—or you never will.

I suspect the secret to much of Ralph Klein's success is what doesn't show up in the headlines or on television. It's what happens when the guy is out of the public eye, bonding with people one on one. This is precisely the skill he used so successfully as a journalist when he was looking for a newscast-topping human interest story.

The best example I can recall was at Yorkton, Saskatchewan's non-descript airport, where a boy of perhaps eight or nine, armed with an idiot-proof camera, was waiting for Klein. He was patient, much more so than the reporters and bureaucrats pacing the terminal floor with cell phones glued to their ears.

We had arrived to catch the Air Ralph flight to Edmonton which, we noted grumpily, was stopping in Calgary to drop off only one passenger—the premier—before chugging on to Edmonton. Half an hour after the scheduled departure, Klein was still missing. It was said he was keeping a rendezvous with the hotel treadmill. Finally, his car arrived and there was a rush for the plane to prepare for takeoff. "Come on, Martin, wheels up in five minutes," hollered Rod Love.

I hung back to see how Klein, running very late and anxious to get home, would handle the kid. The boy struggled to his feet. His dad applied encouraging pressure on the back of his snowsuit. The boy timidly intercepted the premier as he rushed toward the departure gate. Klein stopped in his tracks and extended his hand for a shake. The kid shook his head and raised his camera. "You want a picture?" Klein asked. "Sure thing." The nervous father aimed the camera at the grinning premier with his arm around the youngster's shoulder and clicked. "Flash didn't go off," Klein said. "Try it again." Again, no flash. The father apologized, thanked the premier for his time and started to steer the child away. "No, no. Let's go outside. There's still enough light," Klein urged. The mortified father, eyeing the Dash 8's right prop starting to turn, insisted it wasn't necessary. Klein insisted it was. So outside they went—the father, the son and the premier from the working-class subdivision of Tuxedo Park, searching for the right angle, the right background and the right light to make sure a Saskatchewan kid had a photo with an Alberta premier.

The premier was under intense stress at the peak of the Multi-Corp scandal at the time. He didn't have the slightest clue I was watching the effort he was making to accommodate a future Saskatchewan voter. I doubt he has the faintest memory of this encounter. But that's what gave it magic. That was the real Ralph.

If I have failed to unlock the secret to Ralph Klein's success in politics, I have lots of company. His wife shakes her head. "I just don't know how to describe it." His closest aide, Rod Love, shrugs his shoulders. "I guess that's why they invented the word charisma." His nemesis, Nancy MacBeth, won't even try to answer.

A borderline senior citizen in his third decade of undefeated rule, Ralph Philip Klein doesn't get it. He's a problem drinker who became the most popular politician of an Alberta generation, the high school dropout who put a friendly face on harsh fiscal policy, the poor kid from a broken, battered home who matured into the headline act of Canadian political theater. He is, for want of a better word, a one-man Ralphenomenon.

"Nah," he says with an embarrassed grin, when asked to explain his success. "It's about listening to people, reading the mail, monitoring the phone messages and correcting your screwups without delay. And mistakes will always happen," he cautions. "After all, I'm only human."

Perhaps his explanation is the phenomenon. Ralph Klein, for all his faults and because of all his faults, is one of us.

Index